SACRED SECRETS

To John

With Best Wishes

Mike

15.10.12

SACRED SECRETS

FREEMASONRY, THE BIBLE AND THE CHRISTIAN FAITH

MIKE NEVILLE

ABOUT THE AUTHOR

Mike Neville has been a Freemason since 1995. He is a member of Craft lodges in Surrey and London. He is also a member of the Holy Royal Arch, Mark, Royal Ark Mariner, Royal & Select Masters, Allied Masonic Degrees and Red Cross of Constantine.

Performing the rituals, including Tracing Boards and lectures in several degrees, began his research. From this he started to give illustrated presentations on his research across the UK. He has climbed Mount Sinai and visited various Biblical locations featured in Masonic ritual, including Jerusalem, the Dead Sea and Ephesus.

He is active in Masonic charity and was the chairman for the 'Big Event' in Surrey, which raised £100,000 for the RMTGB 2007 Festival. Mike is the lodge historian and has researched several members who served in the conflicts of the nineteenth and twentieth centuries. This has included Masonic battlefield tours and ceremonies to celebrate the bravery of members who were killed in action.

Mike is a Lieutenant-Colonel in the Army Cadet Force and holds the post of National Training Officer, Cadet Force Music, organising camps for bands and Corps of Drums from all over the UK. He has organised several ACF Outreach programmes to work with young offenders, particularly from inner-city areas. He is a trustee of the League of Mercy, a charity that rewards volunteers.

First published 2012

The History Press
The Mill, Brimscombe Port
Stroud, Gloucestershire, GL5 2QG
www.thehistorypress.co.uk

British Library Cataloguing in Publication Data.
A catalogue record for this book is available from the British Library.

ISBN 978 0 7524 8051 0

Typesetting and origination by The History Press
Manufacturing Managed by Jellyfish Print Solutions Ltd

Printed in Malta by Gutenberg Press.

CONTENTS

FOREWORD

BY THE REVD N. B. CRYER, M.A. PAST GRAND CHAPLAIN

The value of this book will soon be obvious to anyone, man or woman, who joins the Freemasons or who is interested in knowing about their ceremonies. In the 17th and 18th centuries when these ceremonies were being formed, there were renewed interest in, and knowledge about, the Bible that had now been translated into English. Those ceremonies were made up of constant references to names, places and events which a member of the Society still has to memorise and repeat as he or she progresses in membership. As this book will reveal, there is an astonishing amount of Bible information that is shared.

In an age such as the present when familiarity with the contents of the Bible is nothing like as common as it was once, the newcomer to our ceremonies and their stories needs help to understand just what it is that is being referred to. To know about the background to the people and places that are mentioned helps the member to learn more easily the facts he or she has to repeat. I can well understand the benefit that the contents of this book can offer. It may also surprise the interested outsider to know how much of the Bible is still used and required by Freemasons. I have the greatest delight in wishing both this book's author and its readers well.

The Revd N. B. Cryer, M.A. Past Grand Chaplain

1

THE BIBLE AND THE LODGE

INTRODUCTION

When Freemasons join a lodge, an 'Ancient Charge' is recited to them, giving the basic rules of the Order and advice on how to serve God, their country and their fellow men. The new Mason is directed to a 'serious contemplation of the Volume of the Sacred Law'. Whilst this could be the Koran or other holy book, in Western Europe, North America and Australasia, this will invariably be a King James Version of the Bible, open and in full view of all lodge members.

After the Third Degree, some lodges present a Bible to the candidate and so the Mason has no excuse for not following the instruction to 'contemplate' its contents. The Bible, however, is not the easiest book to contemplate or study. The language of the King James' version is beautiful, but archaic. It is too easy to give up attempting to understand the contents after a few verses. One Freemason said to the author, 'I know Aholiab and Bezaleel from the Holy Royal Arch ritual are in the Bible, but I had no idea where to start looking for them.'

This book seeks to explain the relationship between Freemasonnry and the Bible to the interested reader and at the same time help Freemasons to make the 'daily advancement in Masonic knowledge' that they are charged to do at their initiation and to understand what many consider to be the 'word of God'.

Too many Masons have just heard the 'bare bones' of the story or simply learned the ritual parrot-fashion and not understood its contents. For example, all Freemasons are told that the holy vessels used at King Solomon's Temple were cast in the 'clay ground between Succoth and Zeredathah' – now they can learn why this area was used for this purpose and where these places are located. The murderers of Hiram Abif, as told in the Masonic legend during the Third Degree, are said to flee towards Joppa – there is a very simple explanation as to why they decided on this escape route. Where a person, place or thing has a Biblical origin or is based on Christian doctrine or writings, this is explained. Older Freemasons should be aware that younger members of the lodge may not have had scripture lessons at school or attended Sunday School. Hence, many of the Biblical characters and stories will be unknown to them. The contents will also aid clergy, theologians and any other person interested in Freemasonry to see the clear links between ritual and scripture and will name the chapters of the Bible which have the most influence on the ceremonies.

The link between the Bible and Masons has of course been explored in popular fiction – *The Lost Symbol* by best selling author Dan Brown being the most recent example. It is, however, recognised that many have genuine concerns about the secret Masonic ceremonies and their blood-curdling oaths. The viewpoint is considered in the section on the Church and Freemasonry, where alleged comments of the current Archbishop of Canterbury are discussed. Some have claimed that the ritual is 'Satanically inspired'. Some have questioned the compatibility of the 'Craft' with Christianity. These issues will be addressed and the conclusions will surprise many of the critics of Freemasons. First, we must consider the Bible itself.

THE BIBLE IN THE LODGE

The Bible and Freemasonry have been inextricably linked for over 400 years, with the English version of the scriptures used in lodges since the sixteenth century. The Latin version may have been used much earlier, but owing to the incomplete history of Freemasonry, no one can be sure. The 'Volume of the Sacred Law', as Freemasons refer to the Bible, is a vital part of the lodge and the name itself may be derived from the Book of Psalms, which refers to the 'volume of the book' a phase later quoted by St Paul (see sections on Psalms and St Paul).

In lodges recognised by the United Grand Lodge of England it must be present and open when the lodge is at work. In fact, with one notable exception (see Noah below), the Bible is also opened in all Masonic ceremonies. According to Craft ritual, the Bible, together with the square and compasses, are the 'furniture' of the lodge and candidates must take their solemn obligations with their hands on it. In some degrees there is more than one copy of the Bible opened in the degree. In the Knights Templar Priest ceremony, there is a Bible placed on each of the seven pillars situated in the 'tabernacle' or lodge room.

In most ceremonies the Bible can be opened at any page, although there may be general guidance, such as displaying the Book of Kings or Chronicles, where King Solomon's Temple is described. Lodge tradition may also dictate a certain section to display. Some degrees, however, are more prescriptive. For example, the Royal and Select Master ritual book states exactly which chapter the Bible must be opened at in each of its degrees.

The mass-produced English translations of the Bible, which started to appear in the sixteenth century (following the invention of the printing press), and then the King James Authorised Version (published in 1611), have had an enormous influence on Masonic ritual, signs, lodge furniture and regalia. As we will see, many of the 'secret' words used by Freemasons are taken from the Holy Book. Additionally the hand signals or 'signs' such as those used in the Royal Ark Mariner degree are directly related to the Biblical account and the stories of Joshua's battles to secure the Promised Land are also a rich source of 'secret' signs.

In some degrees, officers of the lodge play the part of Biblical characters – some famous, such as Noah and Ezra, some more obscure, such as Zabud and Ahishar (see section on Officers of King Solomon). The colours and styles of the aprons and regalia worn in lodges appear to have their origins in scripture. The reader will see that nearly every major character and story in the Old Testament (and some from the New) feature in Masonic ritual. Many of these prophets also appear in the Koran, but the ritual has, no doubt, been derived from the Bible.

The first Bibles, published with black and white illustrations, immediately influenced the appearance of a lodge. These pictures depicted the interior of the Tabernacle and King Solomon's Temple with a chequered or 'Mosaic' pavement. This is now used in all lodges and features on the 'Tracing Boards' (see section on Masonic Terms Explained).

THE HISTORY OF THE BIBLE

It would be easy to assume that when Jesus died, the Old and New Testaments were combined and handed over to the new faith. Nothing could be further from the truth. It was not until nearly

400 years after the death of Christ that Pope Damasus assembled the first list of books of the Bible at the Roman Council in 382. He commissioned St Jerome to translate the Greek and Hebrew texts into Latin, which became known as the Latin Vulgate Bible. In 1546 the Roman Catholic Church declared that the Vulgate was the only authentic version – 1500 years after the crucifixion. Furthermore, Christian theology has continually evolved.

The word 'Bible' is probably derived from the word '*Byblos*', a type of papyrus and a booklet or roll came to be known in Greek as '*biblia*' or 'the writings'. The papyrus was exported to Greece via the port of Gebal, which became known as 'Byblos' (see section on Hiram, King of Tyre). In Latin, the scriptures were known as *biblia sacra* or 'sacred writings'. In time, the book became known as 'The Bible' and was referred to as one book, rather than a library of many. The current Authorised Version consists of 66 books, 39 in the Old Testament and 27 in the New. Some versions contain more and have variations. The Roman Catholic Douay-Rheims Bible (the Vulgate translated into English) contains several more books and the Psalms are numbered differently, with Psalms 10 to 146 differing by one.

The various denominations of Christianity have different versions of the 'canon' of the scripture. This word is derived from the Greek for 'measuring rod'. Books outside the canon are called 'apocryphal', which originally meant 'hidden' but now means 'not accepted.' The explanation of the Royal Ark Mariner Tracing Board quotes from what it refers to as 'the apocryphal Book of Enoch' and, as we shall see, there are several references in Masonic ritual from books not included in the Church of England canon. There are also several versions of each. Much of the Masonic ritual is drawn from the King James Version, but words and phrases from other editions appear in the ritual. For example, the introduction to The Christian's New and Complete Family Bible notes that it will guide the reader 'through the paths of happiness'. This phrase occurs in the Craft Installation ceremony prayer and as this version of the Bible appeared in 1803, it fits in with the period that the ritual was being written.

In all versions, the story of the Israelites is not seamless and the various books are not in chronological order. For example, the story of Job is the eighteenth book in the Old Testament, but the story is set at the time of Abraham, who features in Genesis. Some parts are repeated several times in different books, particularly in the case of the Books of Samuel, Kings and Chronicles, on which much of the Masonic story is based. In the New Testament, the Gospels often relate very similar information, as is the case with the crucifixion of Jesus.

The authorship of the various books is unknown. Traditionally, Moses is said to have written the first five books of the Bible – the 'Pentateuch' or 'Torah' – which are known in English as Genesis, Exodus, Leviticus, Numbers and Deuteronomy. Likewise, King David was supposedly the writer of the Book of Psalms, whilst his son, Solomon, is said to have composed several books, including Proverbs, Song of Solomon and Ecclesiastes. In the New Testament, as we will see, St Paul is credited with many of the letters to the early churches (although modern scholars question his authorship of some) and there are five items from authors called John – the Gospel of John, three letters and Revelation. We can never be sure if these are from one man or several with the same, common name.

The reader must understand that the Bible is neither an accurate historical record of world events, nor can it be completely dismissed as a collection of myths. Its contents were first passed by word of mouth and then written on scrolls, which were copied and recopied. As a result errors and omissions crept into the text – some being deliberate, so that the text would then support the author's theological viewpoint. When the books of the Bible were placed in the order in which we see them today, they were placed not in a simple chronological order, but into the following nine categories:

Old Testament

1   Books of Moses (Genesis to Deuteronomy)

2   History Books (Joshua to Esther)
3   Wisdom Books (Job to Song of Solomon)
4   Prophets (Isaiah to Malachi)

New Testament
5   The Gospels telling of the life of Jesus (Matthew to John)
6   History of the Early Christian Church (Acts of the Apostles)
7   Letters of St Paul (Romans to Hebrews)
8   Other Letters (James to Jude)
9   Apocalypse (Revelation)

Furthermore, the stories (particularly in the Old Testament) are in a very simple, almost childlike format as they were originally for illiterate, nomadic people. For example, we now know that civilisation developed over many centuries in the Fertile Crescent between the Rivers Tigris and Euphrates. In the Bible, we are told that mankind began in the Garden of Eden – but the location of this mythical place is clearly defined as between the Tigris and Euphrates. We know that farming and metalwork took many thousands of years to develop. The Bible notes this progression of mankind's skills, but makes it very simple and attributes these major steps forward to two brothers – Jabal and Tubalcain (see section on this man, who features in ritual), rather like the Roman legend of Romulus and Remus in establishing the great city.

This is not to say that that the Bible is devoid of historical facts. Numerous archaeological excavations have proved the existence of many of the main characters, including scrolls naming Belshazzar, of 'The Writing on the Wall' fame, in a Ziggurat (see section on the Tower of Babel), in modern Iraq. But perhaps proof of more obscure people from the Bible is more compelling. For example, a 2500-year-old tablet of Assyrian cuneiform held in the British Museum appears to confirm the historical books of the Old Testament. The writing on the tablet refers to Nabu-sharrussu-ukin, 'the chief eunuch' of Nebuchadnezzar II, who features in the Book of Jeremiah, Chapter 39. The tablet has been dated to twelve years prior to the siege of Jerusalem, which is covered in this book as it features in several Masonic ceremonies.

It should also be noted that the Old Testament was written by the members of one nation, Israel, and as such it has a very narrow viewpoint. As we will see later, the slaughter of their enemies, such as the Ammonites, is justified by the scriptures.

THE HISTORICAL AND GEOGRAPHICAL SETTING OF THE BIBLE

The place where the Bible and Masonic ritual is set is the 'Holy Land' or the Near East. Traditionally this area around the eastern shore of the Mediterranean was called 'The Levant' – French for 'rising', the point where the suns rises, the East – arguably the most fought-over piece of land in the world. Jerusalem, the heart of the story, has been besieged and destroyed on many occasions. Since the earliest time and up to the present, the area is of strategic value, being the land bridge between Asia, Europe, Arabia and Africa, with ports on the Mediterranean and Red Sea. As a result great empires have conquered and controlled the area at various times in our history – Egyptian, Assyrian, Babylonian, Persian, Greek, Roman and even British.

In historical terms, much of the Old Testament is set during the late Bronze and early Iron Ages. Looking around some lodges, the author is convinced that some Freemasons may well be eye-witnesses to such periods! There was no date when one Age passed to the other, just a gradual move from the use of one metal to another. In the Bible and Masonic ritual, many objects are referred

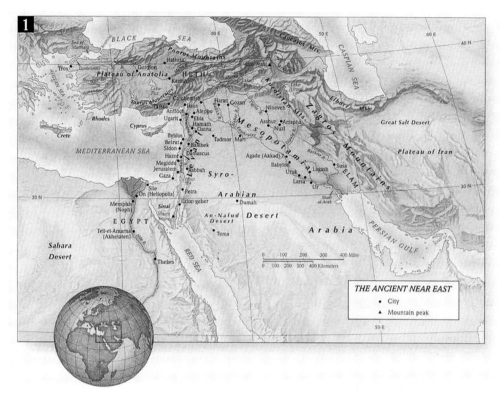

The setting of the Bible – a strategic land bridge, which many have fought over.

to as being made of 'brass', including the important pillars at King Solomon's Temple. This is a mistranslation, with bronze being the correct metal (see section on Metal Objects at the Temple).

Dates and times are notoriously difficult to pin down in the Bible. The number 40 is often used, not as an accurate measure of days or years, but to express a long period – hence the Israelites were in the desert under the Moses for 40 years and occupation by the Philistines (see Judges) and the reigns of David and Solomon each lasted for the same number of years. Forty days was the period of the rainfall in the flood story (see Noah), the time taken by Elijah to walk to Sinai (see Holy Mountains) and the period spent by Jesus in the wilderness (see Ministry of Jesus).

MASONIC DEGREES

It will help to give a brief explanation of the various orders in Freemasonry. They are diverse and jump around in Biblical and historical terms. Every Mason must go through the first three 'Craft' degrees. He can then simply stay there, with no need to progress further, but even these degrees are not in chronological order. The story in the Third Degree (the murder of Hiram Abif) comes prior to the completion of the Temple, as described in the Second Degree. Furthermore, the stories within the individual degrees jump around and travel rapidly through time. The explanation of the Second Degree Tracing Board (Masonic terms are described below) starts with the completion of the Temple, but then leaps hundreds of years backwards to Moses and the battles of Jephtha (see section on The Time of the Judges). The Holy Royal Arch, the last of the 'Solomonic' degrees, is the most diverse. The ritual mentions Adam and Abraham from the first book of the

Bible, Genesis, and later refers to God as 'the Alpha and Omega' from the last book, Revelation. There are also sections of the ritual from the Books of Numbers, Samuel, Kings, Chronicles and many others, as we will see.

The various degrees, which fill in the gaps of the story, are often linked for administrative rather than theological or chronological reasons. For example, the earliest Biblical story used as a degree is that of Noah, in the Royal Ark Mariner Degree. This degree is now administered by the Mark Masons, so to join you must first be a Mark Master Mason, the legend of which is set around 1000 BC at the time of King Solomon. The Royal Ark Mariner story is at least 3000 years earlier (although the date of the flood legend – see section on Noah – will always be a matter of great debate). The First Degree in Craft Freemasonry provides the introduction to the Order and deals with issues as diverse as King Solomon's Temple, the Golden Fleece, Roman Eagle, the importance of charity and rules of the lodge, hence it is omitted from the table below. The Second Degree is shown twice due to its two main themes. The Masonic Royal Order of Scotland is not included as it covers nearly all parts of the Masonic story.

Obviously, there is no requirement to be a Christian to participate in the degrees based on Old Testament events. The qualification for degrees based on the New Testament and Christianity is not as it would seem, with some allowing men of other faiths to join.

MASONIC DEGREES

Old Testament

Title of Degree	Parent Body	Approximate Date of Theme	Main Theme
Royal Ark Mariner	Mark	10000–4000BC	Noah
Grand High Priest	Allied	1800–1700BC	Melchizedek and Abraham
Second Degree (Craft)	Craft	1200–1100BC	Joshua and Jephtha
Order of the Scarlet Cord	Order of the Secret Monitor	1200BC	Rahab and the siege of Jericho
Order of the Secret Monitor	Order of the Secret Monitor	1006–965BC	King David
Thrice Illustrious Master 'The Silver Trowel'	Royal and Select	965BC	Solomon becomes king
Mark Master Mason	Mark	974–967BC	Preparation and building of King Solomon's Temple
Select Master	Royal and Select	969BC	Building of King Solomon's Temple
Grand Tilers of Solomon	Allied	969BC	Building of King Solomon's Temple
Third Degree (Craft)	Craft	968BC	Death of Hiram Abif

Royal Master	Royal and Select	968BC	Sacred word deposited and death of Hiram Abif
Second Degree (Craft)	Craft	967BC	Temple completed
Most Excellent Master	Royal and Select	967BC	Temple dedicated
Super Excellent Master	Royal and Select	586BC	Temple destroyed
Excellent Master	Royal and Select (Scotland)	536BC	Temple rebuilt
Red Cross of Babylon	Allied	516BC	Rebuilding authorised by King Darius
Holy Royal Arch	Chapter	534BC–70 AD	Lost word recovered to destruction of Second Temple

In Craft, Chapter and various other degrees of Masonry, efforts were made to remove the Christian content in the eighteenth century, to make it open to all men who believe in a Supreme Being; hence God is referred to as the 'Great Architect of the Universe', 'Grand Geometrician', 'Most High' or other ecumenical term. Despite the revisionists' attempts to erase the New Testament passages from the ritual, there are still many hidden Christian references and these are described in Chapters 9, 10 and 11. In the side degrees that a Mason can join after the Craft ritual, there are several that are exclusively Christian. These are not as easily identified as it would first seem. The St Lawrence Degree, part of the Allied Masonic Degrees, deals with the story of a Christian martyr. Surprisingly, any mason, of any religion, can join.

Christian Theme

Title of Degree	Parent Body	Approximate Date of Theme	Main Theme	Christians Only Degree
Rose Croix	Ancient and Accepted Rite	33 AD	Crucifixion of Jesus	Yes
Knight of Holy Sepulchre	Red Cross of Constantine	33 AD	Christ is risen	Yes
Holy Royal Arch Knights Templar Priest	HRA KTP	70–80 AD	Revelation of St John	Yes
St Lawrence the Martyr	Allied	257–258 AD	Martyrdom of St Lawrence	No
Red Cross of Constantine (RCC)	RCC	312 AD	Constantine's conversion to Christianity	Yes

Knight of Constantinople	Allied	320 AD	Knighthoods conferred at time of Constantine	No
Order of Athelstan	Athelstan	925–939 AD	Rule of King Athelstan	No
Knights Templar	Knights Templar	1099 AD	Crusades	Yes
Knight of Holy Sepulchre	RCC	1099 AD	Crusades	Yes
Knight of St John the Evangelist	RCC	1099 AD	Excavations under temple	Yes
Societas Rosicruciana in Anglia (SRIA)	SRIA	Biblical times until Medieval period	Search for wisdom and knowledge	Yes

Following on from these tables, throughout this book, Masonic degrees are listed in the order shown below. It is recognised that this does not take into account the seniority of the various orders (viz. when they were founded) but it does reflect the chronological sequence. That said, this does prove difficult when the Allied Masonic Degrees cover a timeline of over 2000 years, from Abraham to Constantine. In such cases, the earliest degree is taken into account. Whilst the Red Cross of Constantine covers the resurrection of Christ, it has been placed in accordance with the lifetime of Constantine. The 'Craft' (the first three degrees) are shown first, as all Masons must join this Order before progressing. The Royal Order of Scotland appears second as it covers a great deal of the content of the other degrees. High rank in one Order does not carry weight in another, so a 33 degree Rose Croix Mason does *not* take this rank into a Craft lodge.

1 Craft
2 Royal Order of Scotland
3 Royal Ark Mariner
4 Allied Masonic Degrees
5 Order of the Secret Monitor (including the Scarlet Cord)
6 Mark
7 Royal and Select Masters
8 Holy Royal Arch
9 Rose Croix
10 Holy Royal Arch Knights Templar Priest
11 Red Cross of Constantine
12 Order of Athelstan
13 Knights Templar (including Knights of Malta)
14 Societas Rosicruciana in Anglia

Prior to the moving to the main part of this work, it is important to understand some of the terms used in the ritual.

MASONIC TERMS EXPLAINED

Masonic Term	Explanation
Chapter/Council/Conclave	Name for a lodge in various other Masonic Orders. 'Chapter' is also used as a name for the Holy Royal Arch degree
Craft	The first three degrees (Entered Apprentice, Fellowcraft and Master Mason)
Deacon	Lodge officer, who acts as a messenger and escorts the candidates through the ceremony
Degree	A step in the Masonic system
Initiation ceremony	The ceremony of joining a lodge as a new member
Installation ceremony	Usually, the appointment of Master or head of the Masonic unit
Jewel	A medal type badge worn to show membership of different degrees, assistance in Masonic charity or membership of a lodge
Lecture	Further explanation given to a candidate after certain degrees
Lodge (or Temple)	Term for place where masons meet
Side Degree or Order	A degree or Order outside the basic Craft degrees
Solomonic Degrees	Degrees in Freemasonry having some connection with King Solomon or his temple
Pedestal	Small tables in front of the Master and the Wardens. The Bible rests on the Master's pedestal.
Tracing Board	Pictorial representation of symbols on wooden boards, used in various degrees (various examples are shown). An eighteenth-century 'PowerPoint'
Unworked Degree	Where a degree is conferred on the candidate in name only, prior to the main ceremony
Volume of the Sacred Law	Bible or other book sacred to the members
Wardens	In various degrees, the two principal assistants to the Master
Working Tools	Representations of various tools (e.g. square, chisel, mallet, axe), which are used to symbolise various moral virtues

Now we turn to the main theme of this book: the Biblical link to subjects mentioned in Masonic ceremonies. With each, the date and Biblical and Masonic references are shown. Biblical dates are often difficult to set and different books give different times so all dates should be taken as approximate. If any other significant historical event happened during the same period, this is also shown to help the reader set the subject in context.

2

THE BOOK OF GENESIS

THE CREATION OF THE WORLD

Timeline	Prehistory
Biblical reference	Genesis • Chapter 1 v1–3 (The Creation) • Chapter 1 v16 (Greater and Lesser Lights)
Masonic reference	Craft • First Degree • Second Degree • Third Degree Royal Ark Mariner • Ceremony of Elevation • Installation of Commander Holy Royal Arch • Ceremony of Exaltation Red Cross of Constantine • Knight of the Holy Sepulchre

The Biblical account of God's creation of the world, as related in the first two chapters of Genesis can be summarised as follows:

First Day	day and night
Second Day	sky and water
Third Day	sea and land with plants and trees
Fourth Day	sun, moon and stars
Fifth Day	birds and fish
Sixth Day	reptiles, animals and man
Seventh Day	rest

Whilst most Craft ritual is based on the building of King Solomon's Temple, as related in the Books of Kings and Chronicles, the stories related in Genesis are also a major influence on Masonic ceremonies. This is emphasised by the fact that the first three verses of the Bible, the initial part of the Creation story, are read out by the candidate for exaltation to a Holy Royal Arch chapter:

I   In the beginning God created the heaven and the earth.
II   And the earth was without form, and void; and darkness was upon the face of the deep. And the Spirit of God moved upon the face of the waters.
III   And God said, Let there be light: and there was light.

In the ritual, the scroll containing these words is part of the Book of the Law recovered from King Solomon's Temple, which had been devastated hundreds of years before by the Babylonians. The prayer used at the start of the Chapter ceremony is to Almighty God 'at whose command the world burst forth from chaos and all created nature had its birth'. In the Appendant Orders of the Red Cross of Constantine, part of the third verse 'Let there be light' is quoted.

In the original Hebrew, the name for God in the first sentence of Genesis is given as 'Elohim'. This word has significance during the installation ceremony of the new master ('Commander') of a lodge of Royal Ark Mariners. God is referred to in Masonic ritual by various names related to the creation – 'Great Architect of the Universe' (First Degree), 'Almighty Creator' and 'Author of the Universe' (Second Degree) and 'Divine Creator' and 'World's Great Architect' (Third Degree). Furthermore, during the explanation of the First Degree Tracing Board, and similarly in the Royal Ark Mariner degree, the 'symmetry and order' of His work is noted.

The creation story (Day four) includes familiar words, no doubt used by the ritual writers, 'And God made two great lights; the greater light to rule the day, and the lesser light to rule the night'. The initiation ceremony includes reference to Greater and Lesser Lights. According to the ceremony of initiation, the 'three great but emblematical lights are the Volume of the Sacred Law, the square and compasses.' The sacred writings are to 'rule and govern' faith. The 'lesser lights' are said to be the sun, the moon and Master of the lodge. The sun is said to 'rule the day', the purpose of the moon is 'to govern by night' and the Worshipful Master 'rules and directs his lodge'.

As can be seen, in the Biblical story, the sun was not created until day four; as a result, the 'day' of God may have been a very lengthy period. Early Hebrew also had no word for a 'period of time' and so the word 'day' was used.

ADAM AND HIS SONS: CAIN AND ABEL

Timeline	Prehistory
Biblical reference	Genesis • Chapters 1–2 (The Creation) • Chapter 3 (The serpent) • Chapter 3 v19 (Our bodies will return to dust) • Chapter 4 v1–11 (Cain kills Abel) Romans • Chapter 5 v14 (All have to die because of Adam) Hebrews • Chapter 11 v4 (Faith of Abel)

Biblical reference continued	Revelation • Chapter 12 v9 (Serpent is the devil)
Masonic reference	Craft • First Degree Tracing Board (Logic Ritual) Royal and Select Masters • Royal Master Holy Royal Arch • Mystical Lecture Societas Rosicruciana in Anglia • Second Grade 'Theoricus'

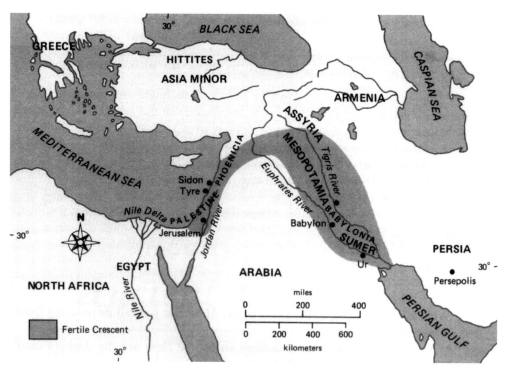

The Fertile Crescent; the location of the Garden of Eden?

As has been described in chapter 1, the Bible gives details of the location of the Garden of Eden. A stream flowed through the garden, which then divided into four rivers, one of which is the Euphrates. The River Euphrates, together with the Tigris watered the 'Fertile Crescent', the cradle of civilisation. Hence, the Bible appears to be correct, but simplifies the story, by personifying the first humans into the characters of Adam and Eve.

The Bible relates that Adam and Eve were sent out of Eden for disobeying God's commands. The serpent, which tempted Eve to eat from the 'tree of the knowledge of good and evil', appears in Revelation as the devil. As punishment for eating from the tree, God reminds Adam 'for dust thou art, and unto dust shalt thou return'. During the Royal Master degree, the candidate is reminded of this fact during a lecture on human mortality. It is also recalled during the second grade of SRIA. To stop anyone entering Eden, God placed an angel with a fiery sword at the entrance, a form of heavenly Tyler (the Masonic officer who stands outside the door of a lodge, armed with a sword).

The 'Fall of Adam' is the basis of the 'penal' or punishment sign in the Holy Royal Arch and the Mystical Lecture reminds the candidate that the 'dreadful penalty' for Adam's sin was 'no less than death'. In the New Testament in letters of the early churches in Rome and Corinth, St Paul links the death of Adam with the eternal life offered by Christ (see section on St Paul).

Adam and Eve later had two sons; Cain, a farmer and Abel, a shepherd. The story noted during the explanation of the First Degree Tracing Board relates to their offerings to God. Abel offered the finest of his lambs, whilst Cain offered poor quality fruit. Cain was chastised by God and became jealous of his brother. This led to the first murder, with Cain killing Abel.

God's questioning of Cain as to his brother's whereabouts led to the famous quote, 'Am I my brother's keeper?' Cain and Abel are the first brothers in the Bible and this is notable for Freemasons, who refer to each other as 'Brother'. The faith of Abel is noted in the New Testament in the Letter to the Hebrews. Adam and Eve later had a third son, Seth. The Bible then gives two conflicting genealogies of the human race – one from Cain and one from Seth. From these, the earth is populated and skills in agriculture and metal work are developed.

To emphasise how Masonic ritual does not follow the chronology of the Bible, Adam, who appears in its first book, is included in the Holy Royal Arch, the final 'Solomonic' degree, with the Chapter 'Hailing Sign' being derived from Adam's actions when praying. The Logic version of the First Degree Tracing Board has references to many characters from Genesis and these appear in the 'third last and grand reason' in the lecture, which explains why 'places of divine worship' face east to west. This explanation is often omitted from other versions of the Tracing Board. For example, Emulation states that the third reason is 'too long to be entered upon now' and 'is explained in the course of our Lectures.' These are given very infrequently, resulting in a significant gap in the knowledge of many Freemasons.

TUBALCAIN, HIS SIBLINGS AND THE DEVELOPMENT OF CIVILISATION

Timeline	8000–4000 BC
Biblical reference	Genesis Chapter 4 v20–22
Masonic reference	Craft • Third Degree
Historical context	8000 BC – Domestication of animals and cultivation of crops 7000 BC – First walled city, Jericho 5000 BC – Earliest known evidence of weaving 4000 BC – Bronze casting begins and first use of plough 3000 BC – Production of bronze commonplace

Prior to a Freemason being 'Raised' to the Third Degree, he has to 'prove his proficiency' in the previous two degrees (Initiation and Passing). During this short piece of ritual, he is told that Tubalcain was the 'first artificer in metals.' In the Bible, Tubalcain is a descendant of Cain and together with his brothers, Jabal and Jubal, is used by the Bible to personify the development of skills amongst humans.

Jabal developed the raising of livestock and Jubal was the first musician and played the flute and harp. Tubalcain is described as the 'instructor of every artificer in brass and iron' – a tool maker. This is the first of many mistranslations of the metal 'bronze' as 'brass' in the King James' Bible (a mistake copied into ritual during the lecture on the Second Degree Tracing Board). The setting of the pre-history in the Bible is the middle and late periods of the Bronze Age, not the 'Brass Age'.

In the Bible, Tubalcain has a sister, Naamah. Whilst no role is given to her in Genesis, Jewish legends describe her as the founder of weaving. Tubalcain was, no doubt, selected for use in the ritual as a forerunner of the craftsman most revered by Freemasons, Hiram Abif. The Hebrew word used to describe both men in the original text is *choreish-nechosheth* meaning 'a worker in brass'.

In ancient ritual, Tubalcain and his brothers built two pillars, which have since been attributed to Enoch (see below) to preserve the knowledge of the 'sciences'. This is the earliest pillar legend, with Masonic ritual now being concerned with the pillars constructed many centuries later outside King Solomon's Temple.

During the current ritual, Tubalcain is connected with 'Worldly Possessions'. This may be because the Hebrew words 'tebel' meaning 'earth' and 'kanah' meaning 'to obtain' may have been used by the ritual compilers to translate Tubalcain as 'to acquire possessions' (Jackson 1992). As with the Creation and Adam, one of the first stories in the Bible is one of the last in the ritual, with Tubalcain appearing in the Third Degree of Craft ritual.

THE GENEALOGY OF NOAH: JARED, ENOCH, METHUSELAH AND LAMECH

Timeline	10000–4000 BC
Biblical reference	Genesis • Chapter 5 (Genealogy of Pre-flood Patriarchs) Hebrews • Chapter 11 v5 (Faith of Enoch) Jude • Chapter 1 v14 (Enoch and Angels)
Masonic reference	Craft • First Degree Tracing Board (Logic Ritual) Royal Ark Mariner • Ceremony of Elevation • Tracing Board Royal and Select Masters • Select Master Degree Rose Croix • 13th Degree – Royal Arch of Enoch

Masonic reference continued	Order of Athelstan

In the genealogy of Adam's third son, Seth, the forefathers of Noah appear, namely Jared, Enoch, Methuselah and Lamech. Enoch apart, the other three only appear in the Royal Ark Mariner degree, but their names are used as an important part of the ceremony. What is amazing about these men are their apparent life spans, with Jared living 962 years, Methuselah 969 years and Lamech a mere 777 years. It is possible that the names relate to ancient tribes and not individuals. For example, the House of Tudor ruled England for 118 years (1485–1603), this was not of course one man called 'Tudor', but five monarchs. In any case, little else is noted about these men. Enoch is far more interesting.

The three books of Enoch were considered as apocryphal. They were omitted from most versions of the Bible, although the First Book of Enoch is revered by the Ethiopian Orthodox Church. This book contains many bizarre stories of angels or 'Watchers' and although it was excluded from the King James' Bible, rather oddly it appears to be quoted in the penultimate book of the New Testament, the Epistle of Jude (see section on Apostles after the crucifixion). A section of the Book of Enoch relating to the birth of Noah is quoted in the explanation of the Royal Ark Mariner Tracing Board (see image in section on Noah).

During this lecture, it is related that Enoch was informed by God that mankind is to be destroyed to wipe out all the wickedness in the world. As a result, he constructed two pillars, in which he hid the 'Archives of Wisdom', to preserve knowledge prior to the destruction of mankind (by the Flood). These pillars were approached by nine arches, a link to the arches described in the Select Master degree. These are under Mount Moriah in Jerusalem. It is unclear whether King Solomon later constructed his own nine arches or whether he utilised those constructed by Enoch (both sets of arches may just be legend and neither are mentioned in the Bible). According to the Book of Enoch, Methuselah was advised by his father that Noah would be saved from the flood.

During the explanation of the Logic version of the First Degree Tracing Board, the audience are reminded of the Biblical account of Enoch being 'translated' – this means to be taken by God to heaven, not having died. In the Royal Ark Mariner version his residence is said to be 'with angels'. Of the ten pre-flood Patriarchs (senior Biblical figures from whom the human race is descended), he is the only one not to die a physical death. Enoch appears fleetingly in two other Masonic orders. During the Rose Croix ceremony the degree of the Royal Arch of Enoch is conferred on the candidate in name only and in the Order of Athelstan, Enoch is simply described as a 'wise man'.

NOAH AND HIS SONS: SHEM, HAM AND JAPHETH

Timeline	10000–4000 BC
Biblical reference	Genesis • Chapters 6–10 (Story of Noah) • Chapter 6 v8 (Found grace in the eyes of the Lord) • Chapter 7 (the flood begins) • Chapter 8 v6–12 (Raven and dove sent out) • Chapter 8 v2–22 (God's promises) • Chapter 9 v1 ('Be fruitful, and multiply')

Biblical reference continued	• Chapter 9 v20 (First vineyard) Wisdom of Solomon • Chapter 14 v1–8 (Thanksgiving for Noah) Hebrews • Chapter 6 v19 (Anchor of hope) • Chapter 11 v7 (Faith of Noah) II Peter • Chapter 2 v5 (Preacher of Righteousness) I Enoch • Chapter 106 (Noah's birth)
Masonic reference	Craft • First Degree Tracing Board (Logic Ritual) • Installation Ceremony Royal Ark Mariner • Ceremony of Elevation • Tracing Board • Installation of Commander Mark • Tracing Board

Noah is the son of Lamech and in the confused genealogy of Genesis he could be a half-brother of Tubalcain (whose father was a man with the same name). In a very early ritual of 1723, Noah is the main character in the Craft ritual, not King Solomon, and his sons try to raise his dead body from the grave. The story of Noah and the flood is preserved in the Royal Ark Mariner degree. In the ceremony the head of the lodge is known as 'Worshipful Commander Noah' and he refers to the Wardens as his 'sons', Japheth and Shem. Candidates for the degree are called 'Noachida', that is to say 'Son of Noah.'

Noah does make a fleeting appearance in Craft ritual on some versions of the explanation of the First Degree Tracing Board, where he is described as a 'Teacher of Righteousness'. This is a very similar description to the Second Epistle of St Peter, where Noah is called a 'Preacher of Righteousness'.

As we have seen, the Lord became angry with his creation and decided to destroy the 'old world' (as described in the Second Epistle of St Peter and during the presentation of the Working Tools in the Royal Ark Mariner ceremony). Noah, however, was ordered to build the Ark as he had 'found grace in the eyes of the Lord' and this quotation from Genesis is used in the explanation of the Tracing Board in the same degree.

The Ark is described in the Bible as 150m long, 25m wide and 15m high. There were three decks, a door in the centre and a small window on the top. The Working Tools of the Royal Ark Mariner (axe, saw and auger) are concerned with wooden ship building, but only the axe is mentioned in the Bible and this is not related to the construction of boats. According to the Kings James' Bible, the Ark was made of 'Gopher' wood. It is unclear what is meant by a Gopher tree, but it has been suggested that this may be another name for acacia. This has a Masonic connection (see Hiram Abif). Some Bibles state that it was made of cypress wood.

Noah took all manner of animals in the Ark, together with his family, including his three sons, Shem, Ham and Japheth. Given the number of animals in the Ark, it may have been a very unpleasant place inside. Rain fell for 40 days and the earth was covered with water – only the inhabitants of the Ark survived. The drowning suffered by the Antediluvians (pre-flood inhabitants of earth) is alluded to in one of the several signs used by Royal Ark Mariner masons.

Many will be familiar with the story of Noah releasing a raven, which flew away, and then sending a dove three times to establish if there was any dry land. On the first occasion, the dove simply returned as water covered everywhere. The posture in which Noah stood whilst he waited for the dove and his method of bringing the bird back into the Ark are the origin of signs used by Royal Ark Mariner masons. After seven days, the Dove returned with an olive leaf in its beak – the first indication that the waters were receding. After another week, the Dove was released from the Ark again and she did not return. Noah was then sure he could soon leave the Ark 'in safety and in peace' as the ritual describes.

The dove and olive branch remain universal symbols of peace. The Noah connection is maintained in Craft lodges by the presence of doves on the wands of the two Deacons. Some Installation Rituals describe the duties of the Deacons as keeping peace in the lodge.

Many theories surround the flood legend, with accounts of an ancient deluge appearing in many parts of the world, including amongst Native Americans. In ancient Mesopotamia, the flood story's hero is Gilgamesh. Evidence of a huge flood has been found near Babylon, in thick layers of mud from 4000 years ago. Furthermore, after the last ice age some 10,000 years ago, sea levels rose and caused the Mediterranean Sea to flood and break over to the Bosporus. This flooded the fertile inhabited area around a freshwater lake, which became the Black Sea.

The theory of the flooding of the Black Sea area would fit with the Ark landing on Mount Ararat. In the first century AD, the Jewish historian, Josephus (see section on the Destruction of the Temple for more on this man), stated that the name of the landing site was *Apobaterion*, meaning 'the place of descent'. The same word in the Royal Ark Mariner ritual is translated as 'a sacrifice after landing'. It should be noted that in the Koran, the whole earth is not flooded. Noah lived in the area of the Fertile Crescent and the Ark landed not too far away on Mount Ararat or 'Mountains of Armenia' as the area is also referred to in the ritual. This would appear to confirm the theory that it was a large regional flood around the Black Sea, rather than a universal deluge.

Once on dry land, Noah built an altar and offered up a sacrifice to God, whereupon God placed the rainbow in the sky, in token of his covenant that he would never again destroy mankind by means of a flood. The colours of the rainbow are used on the apron and jewel of this degree. God then instructed Noah and his sons to 'be fruitful, and multiply' and these words from Genesis are used at the very start of the ceremony of Advancement.

Later, as related in the Bible and Masonic ritual, Ham 'fell from grace'. His father had fallen asleep naked in his tent (such tents are depicted on the Royal Ark Mariner Tracing Board) after becoming drunk on wine. Rather than covering Noah and maintaining his dignity, Ham left the tent to inform his two brothers. They were more respectful and walked backwards to lay a coat over him without looking. This incident is the first mention of wine in the Bible – 'Taking wine' is a Masonic tradition at the meal held after the lodge meeting, known as the 'Festive Board'. Masons, therefore, have much to thank Noah for. It should also be noted that again the Bible appears to be relating the development of human knowledge in a simplified way – archaeological evidence suggests that the first wine was produced in the area around Georgia and Armenia between 8000 BC and 6000 BC.

As a result of Ham's lack of action to help his drunken father, he was (rather harshly) cursed by Noah. As the father of Canaan, Ham's descendents were to be slaves of the children of Shem and Japheth. According to Genesis, the descendants of Noah's sons re-populated the Earth as follows:

Japheth   European and Asian people, including modern day Turkey, Spain, and Portugal and inhabitants of the north Mediterranean coast and islands.

Shem   Arabs and Hebrews, including northern Mesopotamia and the founders of the city of Ur, where Abraham was born.

Ham   Africa, Egypt and Libya. His descendents also included Babylonia (Babel) and the Canaanites and Philistines.

It should be noted that Canaan was the Promised Land, which was later invaded and ruthlessly purged of inhabitants by the Israelites (see Joshua). In addition, the Philistines and Babylonians were also future enemies of Israel. The cursing of Ham story may have been added to justify the wars against these peoples.

According to the Royal Ark Mariner ritual, Noah built his altar using the porphyry stone, which he had used as the ark's anchor. The stone is formed of cooled magma and can only be found in a few places in the world. The name is derived from the Greek for purple. It was used by Constantine, Emperor of Rome (see section on Constantine), to build a pillar to celebrate the founding of his new capital, Constantinople. There is a Masonic link here through the Red Cross of Constantine degree. In relation to Noah, there is no Biblical mention of an anchor or porphyry stone. The mention of them in the Royal Ark Mariner degree would appear to be Masonic legend.

The Royal Ark Mariner degree is administered by the Grand Lodge of Mark Master Masons. The Mark Tracing Board has a nautical feature, a rope and anchor. This anchor also appears on Royal Ark Mariner Tracing Board and on some versions of the First Degree Tracing Board. In all cases it symbolises 'hope'. This appears to be taken from the Book of Hebrews: 'Which hope we have as an anchor of the soul.' (See St Paul).

The Royal Ark Mariner degree is possibly one of the most Biblical of the degrees. The story is taken directly from the Bible, but this is the only Masonic degree where the Bible is not physically present in the lodge. The ritual gives a clear reason, 'at the period whence we deduce the origins of this Degree, the Sacred Writings were not in existence.' This is factually correct. Written Hebrew texts started to appear many centuries later around the time of King David. Oddly, given that this degree is open to Freemasons of any religion, it contains more quotations from the New Testament than any other non-Christian degree (see section on New Testament references in degrees open to candidates of all faiths).

The Royal Ark Mariner degree also makes use of the Apocrypha. It has already been shown that the Book of Enoch is quoted during the explanation of the Tracing Board (see section on Enoch). The prayer during the Elevation ceremony for a new member appears to be based on part of the Wisdom of Solomon. This is in the form of a prayer thanking God for the salvation of Noah. It also contains the phrase 'Thy providence', which appears in the ritual.

THE TOWER OF BABEL

Timeline	4000–2000 BC
Biblical reference	Genesis • Chapter 10 v8–12 (Nimrod) • Chapter 11 v1–9 (Tower of Babel)
Masonic reference	Old Craft, Mark and Royal Ark Mariner ceremonies Worshipful Society of Freemasons – The Operatives

Historical context	3100 BC – Upper and Lower kingdoms of Egypt are united
	2800 BC – Pyramid age in Egypt begins
	2400 BC – Sargon forms first Mesopotamian empire Hittite invasions of Mesopotamia throughout the period

Earth having been re-populated, the Bible states that at this time all people spoke the same language and the next major event concerns one of the greatest building projects ever undertaken – to build a tower to heaven.

Surprisingly, the construction of the Tower of Babel no longer features in Masonic ritual. It did, however, feature in early Royal Ark Mariner and Mark Degree rituals. Furthermore, in ritual from the early part of the eighteenth century, the Tower of Babel appears to have been afforded the same status in ritual as King Solomon's Temple. It was claimed in the Old Mark Degree ceremony that 'at the building of the Tower of Babel, the Art and Mystery of Masonry was first introduced, and from thence handed down to Euclid.'

The location 'Babel' is Babylon in the plain of Shinar – the area between the Tigris and Euphrates – the cradle of civilisation. Babylon, of course, features later in the Masonic story, with the Jews being exiled there many centuries later and this early account may set the scene for future claims of Babylonian evil. Around 1700 BC, Babylon was the largest city in the world.

The building of the Tower did not please God and to frustrate their efforts He scattered the people across the face of the earth. He also made the people speak different languages, so their efforts to cooperate were frustrated. This is the origin of the word to 'babble'.

The Tower of Babel (1563) by Pieter Bruegel the Elder.

During the first 'Indentured Apprentice' and second 'Fellow of the Craft' degrees of the Operatives or Worshipful Society of Freemasons, the story of Nimrod is included. The Bible has few details of this man; he is described as a 'mighty hunter' who was the great grandson of Noah. Nimrod founded a great empire and the Bible states that he ruled Babylon and surrounding cities. As a result, legends have connected him with the building of the Tower of Babel, even though this is not mentioned in the scriptures.

The Tower of Babel legend is probably connected with the building of Ziggurats. These were flat topped pyramids built in ancient Mesopotamia by various civilisations, including the Sumerians, Assyrians and Babylonians. They were not places of worship, but meant to be the dwelling place of the Gods – as was King Solomon's Temple.

Abraham would have been familiar with these structures; the remains of the enormous Ziggurat at Ur, his birthplace, can still be seen.

RAIDERS FROM THE EAST: BIBLICAL WARFARE (PART 1)

Timeline	1800–1700 **BC**
Biblical reference	Genesis • Chapter 14 v1–24 (Four kings versus five kings) • Chapter 19 v24–25 (Cities of the Plain destroyed) Deuteronomy • Chapter 29 v23 (Four cities destroyed) Job • Chapter 1 v15 (Sabean raiders) • Chapter 1 v17 (Chaldean raiders) • Chapter 3 v17 ('Wicked cease from troubling') • Chapter 5 v17 (Chastening of the Almighty) • Chapter 8 v20 ('Perfect man') • Chapter 18 v14 ('King of terrors') • Chapter 29 v3–4 (The candle of God) • Chapter 34 v13 (Great Disposer) • Chapter 34 v22 ('Workers of iniquity') Hebrews Chapter 7 v1 ('The slaughter of the kings')
Masonic reference	Craft • Third Degree Allied Masonic Degrees • St Lawrence the Martyr • Grand High Priest Order of the Secret Monitor • Third or Supreme Ruler Degree

Masonic reference continued	Mark • Tracing Board Holy Royal Arch • Mystical Lecture • Installation Ceremony Holy Royal Arch Knights Templar Priests • Installation of a Knight Templar Priest Societas Rosicruciana in Anglia Fifth Grade 'Adeptus Minor'
Historical context	Hammurabi founded Babylonian empire in 1750 BC.

Genesis contains an account of early warfare between two alliances of kings – four based in and around Babylonia and five who ruled the 'Cities of the Plain' at the southern end of the Dead Sea or 'Salt Sea' as it is described in the Bible. This story forms a major part of the Grand High Priest ritual. Indeed, it is a New Testament book, Hebrews, which describes 'the slaughter of the kings', a phrase which appears in the Grand High Priest ritual.

The 'Four Kings' were as follows:

1 Chedorlaomer, king of Elam, an area to the north of the Persian Gulf and now in modern day Iran. The leader of this alliance.
2 Amraphel, who ruled Shinar in southern Babylonia. He is possibly the famous ruler Hammurabi (1750 BC), who is remebered for the Code of Hammurabi.
3 Aroich, king of Ellasar, which may be the city of Larsa near the Persian Gulf.
4 Tidal, ruler of Gutium in southern Mesopotamia. The city has been named as *Goyim* (Hebrew for 'nations') resulting in the Bible wrongly giving the ruler the title 'Tidal, king of nations'.

The 'Five Kings' was an alliance of the following:

1 Bera, king of Sodom
2 Birsha, king of Gomorrah
3 Shinab, king of Admah
4 Shemeber, king of Zeboiim
5 Unnamed king of Bela, a city also known as Zoar

The five Canaanite 'Cities of the Plain' had been defeated by Chedorlaomer and paid tribute for twelve years, but they then rebelled and a new war ensued. Chedorlaomer's alliance of four kings was again victorious and the kings of Sodom and Gomorrah fled and hid in tar pits. Abraham's nephew Lot was taken captive from Sodom and had to be freed by his uncle (see section on Abraham). The secret sign and 'test word' of the Grand High Priest are based on this story and the broken alliance with King Chedorlaomer is particularly significant in the ritual.

Four of the Cities of the Plain were later destroyed by God for their wickedness. The destruction of Sodom and Gomorrah is well known, but the Book of Deuteronomy explains that Admah and Zeboiim suffered the same fate. Only Zoar survived because Lot had made it his place of residence. In Hebrew Zoar means 'small' or 'insignificant'.

The author in the Dead Sea (note salt deposit) near Zohar – the Biblical 'Zoar'.

Whilst the Book of Job is nearly 20 books after Genesis in the Bible, the setting is at the same time as the raids from the east (as described in the first chapter, it is placed in the 'wisdom' section of books). The book is dated to this time because God is known by the name 'Shaddai' – the name used for Him by Abraham and Jacob. Job lived in the land of Uz, which was located in or around modern-day Israel or Jordan. He also suffered raiders from the area of the Persian Gulf, firstly an attack by the Sabeans (Arabs possibly from Sheba – see section on Queen of Sheba) and then by the Chaldeans – the name given to the Babylonians in the King James Version of the Bible.

At the beginning of the Book of Job, the main character is described as a righteous and prosperous man. Satan appears in the story and suggests that Job is only faithful to God as his life is pleasant. Then, as a result of the raids, Job's family was slain and all his property looted. He was also inflicted with painful boils, which covered his body from head to foot. Throughout his suffering, he refused to blame God and kept his faith, despite his friends advising him that his fate must be as a punishment for some form of sin. During his sufferings, Job lamented that he wished for the time when God's 'candle shined upon my face.' This is used in the Knights Templar Priest degree along with several other references to light. God eventually spoke to Job and his faith was rewarded – he had ten more children and his wealth was doubled.

The Book of Job is quoted during the explanation of the Mark Tracing Board, which includes the phrase 'the wicked cease from troubling and there the weary be at rest.' (This also appears in the Order of the Secret Monitor installation). During the Mark ceremony, the ritual further refers to a 'peaceful haven' after 'a well-spent life'. This alludes to the grave, as does the verse from Job. In the Craft Third Degree ceremony there is a reference to 'trampling the king of terrors beneath our feet.' The 'king of terrors' is used to refer to death in Job as it is also in the 5th Grade of SRIA, which also uses the phrase 'Perfect Man' during the ceremony. This may have been taken from the Book of Job: 'Behold, God will not cast away a perfect man, neither will he help the evil doers.'

Job also observes that no place where the 'workers of iniquity' can hide themselves. This phrase appears in several other places in the Bible, especially in the Book of Psalms. In Masonic terms, it is used during the Addresses on the Significance of the Colour of the Robes, which is given at the end of a Chapter installation ceremony. Job's friend Eliphaz observed that we should be happy to be corrected by God and therefore we should not despise the 'chastening of the Almighty'. This appears to be the origin of the phrase 'the chastening hand of the Almighty', which also appears in Holy Royal Arch ritual.

In the discussions relating to the power of God in Job, it is asked, 'Who hath given him a charge over the earth? Or who hath disposed the whole world?' This may be the origin of the title 'The Great Disposer of All' used in the St Lawrence the Martyr ceremony. A similar title for God is used in the Koran and by the Christian writers John Calvin and John Wesley.

MELCHIZEDEK, THE FIRST HIGH PRIEST

Timeline	1800–1700 BC
Biblical reference	Genesis • Chapter 14 v18–24 (Blesses Abraham) Psalms • Psalm 110 v4 (Melchizedek priest forever) Hebrews • Chapters 5–7 (Jesus compared to Melchizedek) • Chapter 7 v3 ('Neither beginning of days')
Masonic reference	Allied Masonic Degrees • Grand High Priest Holy Royal Arch • Mystical Lecture Holy Royal Arch Knights Templar Priest • Installation of a Knight Templar Priest Red Cross of Constantine • Consecration of Viceroy
Historical context	Hammurabi founded Babylonian empire in 1750 BC

Melchizedek, a ruler and priest in Canaan, at first seems to be a rather obscure character, who appears in several side degrees. He is described in the Bible as 'the king of Salem' and 'priest of the most high God'. The section of Genesis relating to Melchizedek contains the first mentions of the following important issues:

War in the Holy Land
Priesthood

The use of bread and wine to bless
Jerusalem, referred to as 'Salem'

Unlike many other biblical characters, Melchizedek is given no genealogy and is without 'beginning of days' (a phrase quoted in the Holy Royal Arch). This has resulted in him being compared to Jesus in the Book of Hebrews, as he was a 'high priest forever'. The name is also an important feature of the Holy Royal Knights Templar Priest degree (where much of Chapter 7 of Hebrews is quoted) and in the Red Cross of Constantine degree, the officer elected to be 'Viceroy' or the second senior position, takes the name of Melchizedek prior to his installation.

During the explanation of the Logic version of the First Degree Tracing Board, at the point where the lecture relates to Moses, it states, 'But we never hear or read of any place being set apart for the public solemnisation of divine worship until the happy deliverance of the Israelites from their Egyptian bondage.' It would appear that this may not be entirely correct; Melchizedek must have had some form of dwelling or temple. Abraham (or Abram as he was then known) gave him a large quantity of goods, taken during his victories. These must have been stored somewhere and a clue may be contained in the Grand High Priest degree, where part of the lodge room represents Melchizedek's tent.

This story shows that Jerusalem has been a holy place since earliest times. The place where Abraham was about to sacrifice Isaac may not have been the wilderness as it is usually depicted. According to a Jewish legend, Melchizedek is Shem, the son of Noah (this is noted in John Wesley's *Commentary on the Whole Bible*). Given the allegedly enormous life spans in those days as related in the Bible, this has a possible internal logic.

Abraham and Melchizedek (1625) by Peter Paul Rubens.

ABRAHAM AND ISAAC

Timeline	1800–1700 BC
Biblical reference	Genesis • Chapter 11 v26 (Birth of Abraham) • Chapter 13 v18 (Camp at Mamre) • Chapter 14 (Battle of the Kings and Blessed) • Chapter 15 v5 (God's promise to Abraham) • Chapter 22 v1–14 (Faith in offering Isaac) • Chapter 22 v2 (Abraham and Mount Moriah) • Chapter 22 v17 (Blessed) Acts • Chapter 7 v2–8 (Summary of Abraham's life) Romans • Chapter 4 (Abraham's life and faith) Hebrews • Chapter 7 v1 ('Slaughter of the Kings') • Chapter 11 v8–19 (Faith of Abraham) • Chapter 11 v20 (Faith of Isaac) James • Chapter 2 v21–23 (Faith of Abraham)
Masonic reference	Craft • First Degree Tracing Board (Emulation/Logic Ritual) Allied Masonic Degrees • Grand High Priest degree Holy Royal Arch • Historical Lecture Rose Croix • Ceremony of Perfection

Abraham is, arguably, one of the most significant figures in human history. He is the father of three great monotheist religions, Judaism, Christianity and Islam.

Hence, although he lived thousands of years ago, his actions still have a major impact on the world we live in. Like civilisation itself, Abram (as he was known until God changed his name) was born near the banks of the Euphrates and he lived in the city of Ur. At the age of 75, he was commanded by God to leave this city, so that he could be shown a land that would become a great nation. Together with his wife, Sarah and nephew, Lot, he journeyed through Haran (north west Mesopotamia), down the 'King's Way' or 'King's Highway' (central route through the Holy Land) to Canaan (the Holy Land). This was the land promised to him.

At Bethel, he erected a pillar to God (see the account of Jacob's ladder two generations later). Following famine, Abraham had to 'sojourn' in Egypt. 'Sojourn' will be a familiar word to Companions of the Holy Royal Arch, where the ritual features three 'sojourners'. When they returned to Canaan, Abraham and Lot were so successful in breeding cattle, they became very rich. So much so, that the land could not sustain them both and Lot moved to the south of the Dead Sea, to the area around the city of Sodom.

The next major event in Abraham's life is the battles of Four Kings against Five (see section on Raiders from the East). After the victory of the four Mesopotamian kings, the wealth of Sodom and Gomorrah was captured, together with Lot and his family. Abraham and his small force of 318 men pursued the captors to Dan in the north and defeated them at Hobah, near Damascus, where Lot was freed – this incident is described as 'the slaughter of the kings' in the Letter to the Hebrews.

On his return, Abraham was met by the king of Sodom and Melchizedek (see above). Abraham had made a promise to God to have nothing to do with the King of Sodom, but he was blessed by Melchizedek. The story of the battle of the Kings and blessing form the basis of the Grand High Priest ceremony – and it is clearly based on the later account in Hebrews from the New Testament. In the Masonic order the candidate takes the role of Abraham 'on his journey over the plains, when returning from the slaughter of the kings'. Abraham's camp with Mamre the Amorite (a people who lived to the west of the Dead Sea) and his meeting with the king of Sodom in the Valley of Shaveh are significant in the ritual, despite the Biblical obscurity of these stories. Abraham refused an offer of goods from the king of Sodom, as Abraham had promised God

that he would take nothing from him. Some of the offered goods were taken by Mamre and his brothers, Eschol and Aner, who had assisted Abraham. These minor Biblical characters are also recalled in the ceremony.

God promised that Abraham would become the father of a great nation and that Canaan would be given to him. This is noted in the explanation of the First Degree Tracing Board and Rose Croix ritual. Abraham was very old and had no sons, so with his wife's consent; he had a son, Ishmael, by a slave woman, Hagar. At God's promise, Sarah became pregnant and when Abraham was 100 years old, she gave birth to Isaac. Sarah became very jealous of Hagar and Ishmael and they were sent away. Ishmael became the father of the Arab nations and a prophet of Islam.

To test Abraham's faith, God commanded him to offer up Isaac as a burnt sacrifice on Mount Moriah

Sacrifice of Isaac (1635) by Rembrandt.

(the King James Version gives the location as 'one of the mountains' in the 'land of Moriah'). Abraham did as he was told and bound his son, but as he was about to kill him with a knife, he was prevented from doing so by an angel, who said, 'Lay not thine hand upon the lad.' His faith had been proved and God provided a ram to sacrifice in place of Isaac. The location of this incident is said to be in the Dome of the Rock in Jerusalem (see section on Islamic Conquest of the Holy Land).

This act of faith is one of the three reasons why the First Degree Tracing Board (Emulation, Logic and others) states that 'our lodges stand on holy ground, because the first lodge was consecrated on account of three grand offerings made thereon, which met with Divine approbation.' In this sense, the 'first lodge' is King Solomon's Temple, which was built on Mount Moriah, the place where:

• Abraham offered up his son as a sacrifice
• King David appeased the wrath of God (see section on Araunah)
• King Solomon dedicated the Temple

The testing of Abraham also features in the New Testament in the Book of Hebrews (see section on St Paul). It is also included in the Holy Royal Arch ritual during the Historical Lecture. God then promised that Abraham's descendents will be as numerous as 'stars in the heavens or the sand upon the seashore' (Logic First Degree Tracing Board).

Abraham then settled in Beersheba, south west of Jerusalem. Beersheba is often seen as the southernmost city of Ancient Israel, with Dan being the northern point. Isaac had two sons, Esau and Jacob, who will be described in the next section.

JACOB, THE MAN WHO BECAME ISRAEL

Timeline	1600–1300 BC
Biblical reference	Genesis • Chapter 27 v43 – Chapter 28 (Sent to Padan Aran) • Chapter 28 v11–22 (Jacob's Ladder) • Chapter 32 v24–32 (Wrestles with angel) • Chapter 32 v28 (Name changed to 'Israel') • Chapter 33 v17 (Succoth) • Chapter 33 v20 (Altar called 'El-elohe-Israel') • Chapter 37 v9–10 (Joseph's dream) • Chapter 41 v5 (Shibboleth = 'ear of corn') • Chapter 49 (Descendants and their emblems) Numbers • Chapter 2 (Tribes of Israel) • Chapter 10 v11–28 (Tribes order of march) Hosea • Chapter 12 v3–4 (Wrestles with angel) John • Chapter 1 v51 (Jesus recalls Jacob's Ladder)

Biblical reference continued	Acts • Chapter 7 v8–15 (Jacob and Joseph) I Corinthians • Chapter 13 v13 (Faith, Hope and Charity) Hebrews • Chapter 11 v21 (Faith of Jacob)
Masonic reference	Craft • First Degree Tracing Board • Second Degree Mark • Tracing Board Royal and Select Masters • Super Excellent Master Holy Royal Arch • Historical Lecture • Symbolical Lecture • Installation of Joshua Rose Croix • Ceremony of Perfection Holy Royal Arch Knights Templar Priests Societas Rosicruciana in Anglia • Second Grade 'Theoricus' • Fourth Grade 'Philisophus'

Jacob is the grandson of Abraham, being the second son of Isaac. Whilst King Solomon's story forms a great part of Masonic ritual, Jacob or 'Israel' as he is later known, features in the following ways:

• Jacob's Ladder   First Degree Tracing Board, Second Degree Working Tools (long version) and Rose Croix
• Journey to Padan Aran   First Degree Tracing Board (Logic)
• Wrestle with angel   First Degree Tracing Board (Logic) and the 5th Degree in the Knights Templar Priests
• Descendants form the tribes of Israel   ensigns on Chapter staves and noted in Super Excellent Master degree

In consequence, Jacob has a very visual influence in lodges. His ladder is prominent in every Craft Lodge, as the First Degree Tracing Board is displayed for the vast majority of the time. The ladder also features on the Mark Tracing Board, which is the centre piece of a lodge of Mark Master Masons and in Holy Royal Arch chapters, the staves and banners are also highly visible as they dominate the centre of the room.

First Degree Tracing Board with Jacob's Ladder.

Returning to the story of Jacob, the Bible states that he tricked his father, Isaac, into giving him and not the oldest son, Esau, his birth right. Esau was a hunter, who had rough skin and was very hairy. To deceive his father, Jacob, in collusion with his mother, covered his arms with goat skins and offered food that Esau had been asked to bring. Isaac, who was very old and nearly blind, was tricked and the birth right was obtained.

Esau was furious and threatened to kill Jacob. He also complained that there was little wonder that Jacob had acted in this manner as his name sounds like the Hebrew word to 'trick'. To save Jacob from Esau's wrath and also to prevent him marrying a local Hittite, he was sent to his Uncle Laban's home in Padan Aran – this is not a town, but is the 'Plain of Aran' – northwest Mesopotamia. Laban was the brother of Isaac's wife, Rebecca. His journey, detailed in the Bible, features a number of occurrences of interest to Freemasons.

The journey began at Isaac's residence at Beersheba, where Abraham had settled, and Jacob headed north. The ladder appeared as he lay down to rest at the close of his first day's journey. This was at Bethel, north of Jerusalem, although some have claimed that this occurred on Mount Moriah (the later location of King Solomon's Temple).

Jacob took a stone for a pillow and in a dream he observed the ladder, featured on the Tracing Boards. In the dream he saw angels ascending and descending the ladder and God appeared to him and gave him the land for his descendants. To commemorate this vision he set up a pillar of stone. In Masonic ritual, the three main staves are emblematic of 'faith, hope and charity', but this is not from the Biblical account of the ladder. The three virtues first appear together in the Bible in the New Testament, in a letter from St Paul to the Church in Corinth (see section on St Paul). In Freemasonry, as well as in St Paul's view, charity is the most important. These three virtues are noted as 'pillars of the new law' in the Red Cross of Constantine ceremony of a Knight of the Holy Sepulchre. This is a degree restricted to Christians. It should be noted that Jesus links Himself to the Ladder story in the Gospel of St John.

Jacob eventually arrived at his uncle's home, where he had to work for seven years to earn the hand of his youngest daughter (and Jacob's cousin), Rachel. Uncle Laban, however, tricked Jacob into marrying his older daughter, Leah, and Jacob was faced with another seven year's work for his unscrupulous relative. Despite his problems, Jacob's work was good and his flocks grew. This eventually caused a dispute between him and his uncle and as a result, he fled and returned south to resolve the conflict with his brother, Esau.

The fresco *Jacob's Ladder* (1726–1729) in the Palazzo Patriarcale, Udine by Giovanni Battista Tiepolo.

On that journey, he came to the River Jabbok (see map in section on Jephtha), a tributary of the Jordan, and throughout the night he wrestled with a mysterious man (the Book of Hosea describes him as an angel). The angel could not defeat Jacob and so struck his hip and put it out of joint. This is the reason some Jews will not eat the sinew of an animal's thigh. The angel then blessed Jacob and changed his name to 'Israel'. Jacob or Israel named the place Peniel (or Penuel), which means 'I have seen God face to face.'

Having left there, he met Esau and the two made their peace. Jacob then camped at a place where he built animal shelters and named it 'Succoth' meaning 'resting place'. This is the first mention of the place where holy vessels were cast some centuries later by Hiram Abif, as noted on the Second Degree Tracing Board (see section on Metal objects at the temple). Jacob then erected an altar to God and called the place *El-elohe-Israe*. This incident is recalled in the Installation of the officer referred to as Joshua in the Holy Royal Arch. In this ceremony, the words are translated as 'God, God of Israel.' (As was noted during the section on Job, the name of God was still *Shaddai* or *El Shaddai* until the time of Moses – see Chapter 3).

Jacob settled at Bethal and, by his two wives and two concubines, he had twelve sons: namely, Reuben, Simeon, Levi, Judah, Dan, Naphtali, Gad, Asher, Issachar, Zebulun, Benjamin and Joseph, the latter being the owner of the coat of many colours or the 'Technicolor Dream Coat' of the musical. As you will recall, his brothers were jealous of their father's love for his favourite son and sold him into slavery in Egypt. Joseph had not endeared himself to his family by telling them of his dream, where the sun, moon and stars had bowed down to him. Jacob scolded him for seeing himself as above his family. This story is recalled in the second grade of SRIA.

Despite being condemned to a life of slavery, the dream did come true and Joseph rose to be one of the Pharaoh's most trusted advisors and saved the Egyptians from starvation during a seven-year famine. He interpreted Pharaoh's dreams, including his vision of 'ears of corn'. This is translated from the Hebrew word 'Shibboleth', which is used in the Second Degree (see section on Psalms for further explanation). During this time, the brothers and Jacob came to Egypt to obtain food and Joseph, unrecognised by them at first, eventually revealed himself to them. Much of this story is summarised in the New Testament, in Chapter 7 of the Book of Acts.

When the land of Canaan was apportioned to the Twelve Tribes (see section on Joshua), tribal areas were not simply named after the sons of Jacob. Levi headed the priests and they, being spread across the land, were not given a specific area. As a result, Manasseh and Ephraim, two sons of Joseph and therefore grandsons of Jacob, were given full tribe status. This latter list of the Twelve Tribes, viz. ten sons (all except Levi and Joseph) and two grandsons of Jacob are featured on the staves of a Royal Arch Chapter. The tribes were divided into four groups, headed by Judah, Reuben, Ephraim and Dan. The standard of Judah is a lion, Reuben a man, Ephraim an ox and Dan an eagle. Again, these banners can be seen in the Chapter room, where they are hung on the wall behind the Three Principals. In the Super Excellent Master degree, the formation of tribes around the Ark of the Covenant is used in the ritual. The degree relates to the time shortly before the fall of Jerusalem to the Babylonians, when the temple treasures will be captured. The positions of the Tribes are based on the account in Numbers, Chapter 10:

East   Judah, Issachar and Zebulun
South Reuben, Simeon and Gad
West   Ephraim, Benjamin and Manasseh
North Dan, Asher and Naphtali

Tribe	Link to Masonic Ritual
Judah	Bezaleel, the builder of the Ark of the Covenant Used in Red Cross of Babylon degree ritual
Ephraim	Joshua, the successor to Moses, was an Ephraimite, the same tribe involved in the war with Jephtha
Benjamin	Used in Red Cross of Babylon degree ritual
Dan	Aholiab, Bezaleel's assistant
Naphtali	Hiram Abif's mother

The twelve tribes are mentioned in the fourth grade of SRIA, as are the twelve apostles (see section on Ministry of Jesus). Twelve and seven (as we will see later), are symbolic numbers throughout the Bible.

The death of Jacob/Israel is the end of the Book of Genesis. We leave that book with the Israelites well respected in Egypt. As the generations passed, the Egyptian view of these foreign settlers was to change and we move on to the story of Moses.

3

The Time of Moses

Moses

Timeline	Around 1200 BC
Biblical reference	Exodus • Chapter 3 (Burning bush and removal of shoes) • Chapter 4 v1–5 (Staff turns into serpent) • Chapter 6 v2–3 (God uses name Jehovah) • Chapter 6 v3 (God not previously known as Jehovah) • Chapter 6 v6 (God's 'out stretched arm') • Chapter 6 v16–20 (Descendant of Levi) • Chapter 12 v31–51 (Israelites leave Egypt) • Chapter 13 v21 (Pillars of fire and cloud) • Chapter 14–15 (Crossing of Red Sea) • Chapter 15 v1 (Song of Moses) • Chapter 16 (Manna from Heaven) • Chapter 17 v1–7 (Water from rock) • Chapter 17 v8–16 (Battle against the Amalekites) • Chapter 20 (Ten Commandments) • Chapter 24 v1–9 (Moses and 70 elders) • Chapters 25–31 (Instructed to build the Tabernacle) • Chapter 32 (Golden Calf) • Chapter 33 v23 (God's face must not be seen) • Chapter 34 (New tablets – Ten Commandments) Numbers • Chapter 10 v29–33 (Hobab the guide) • Chapter 11 v16–25 (Moses and 70 elders) • Chapter 16 (Korah, Dathan and Abiram) • Chapter 21 v6–9 (Brass serpent to heal snake bites) • Chapter 26 v8–10 (Korah, Dathan and Abiram) • Chapter 33 v3 (Rameses was Pharaoh) • Chapter 33 v3 (Israelites left with a 'high hand')

Biblical reference continued	Numbers • Chapter 10 v29–33 (Hobab the guide) • Chapter 11 v16–25 (Moses and 70 elders) • Chapter 16 (Korah, Dathan and Abiram) • Chapter 21 v6–9 (Brass serpent to heal snake bites) • Chapter 26 v8–10 (Korah, Dathan and Abiram) • Chapter 33 v3 (Rameses was Pharaoh) • Chapter 33 v3 (Israelites left with a 'high hand') Deuteronomy • Chapter 5 1–21 (Ten Commandments) • Chapter 5 v32 (Turn not to the right or the left) • Chapter 6 v2 ('…keep all His statutes') • Chapter 6 v5 (Love the Lord with 'all thy soul') • Chapter 23 v1–3 (Men excluded from worship) • Chapter 28 v26 ('…fowls of the air, and unto the beasts of the earth') • Chapter 34 (Death of Moses) Psalms • Psalm 68 v4 (Name of God) Acts • Chapter 7 v22 (Moses and wisdom of Egyptians) • Chapter 7 v36 ('…wonders in the land of Egypt') Hebrews • Chapter 11 v23–29 (Faith of Moses) Jude • Chapter 1 v11 (Korah was a sinner)
Masonic reference	Craft • First Degree Tracing Board (Logic Ritual) • Second Degree • Third Degree Royal Ark Mariner • Tracing Board • Closing Prayer Allied Masonic Degrees • Grand High Priest Order of the Secret Monitor • Second or Prince Degree Mark • Opening Prayer

Masonic reference continued	Royal and Select Masters • Select Master • Royal Master • Super-Excellent Master • Thrice Illustrious Master (Silver Trowel) Holy Royal Arch • Ceremony of Exaltation • Installation of Zerubbabel, Haggai and Joshua • Historical Lecture • Mystical Lecture • Questions Before Toasts Rose Croix • Ceremony of Perfection Holy Royal Arch Knights Templar Priests • Installation of a Knight Templar Priest Red Cross of Constantine • Knight of the Holy Sepulchre Knights Templar
Historical context	1200 BC Hittite power wanes 1279 BC Rameses II becomes king of Egypt

Moses was traditionally believed to be the author of the first five books of the Bible – Genesis, Exodus, Leviticus (book of law for Levite priests), Numbers (in Hebrew called 'In the Wilderness') and Deuteronomy (meaning the Second Book of Law). Moses could not have written the last chapter of the latter, which relates to his death. More recent studies have concluded that the books are a complex interweaving of four distinct sources. Whatever the authorship these books are, according to the Select Master degree, the 'Books of the Law' kept in the replica Ark of the Covenant hidden in a secret vault.

In addition to a fleeting mention in some versions of the First Degree Tracing Board ritual, as one of the 'two grand parallel lines', Moses receives the greatest Craft attention on the Second Degree board. Here the story of the pillars of fire and cloud, which led the Israelites out of Egypt, is retold. Surprisingly, despite its nautical links, the most comprehensive Masonic telling of Moses' story is on the Royal Ark Mariner Tracing Board. The phrase on this Tracing Board, 'Moses worked many wonders in Egypt and at last led the Israelites to the shores of the Red Sea' is very similar to part of the summary of the Old Testament related by Stephen, the first Christian martyr, in the Book of Acts.

The second book of the Bible is Exodus and this contains much of the story of Moses, who was a descendant of Jacob's son Levi. Moses was placed in a basket of reeds on the Nile as Pharaoh had ordered all newborn Hebrew boys to be killed. By chance he was found and adopted by Pharaoh's daughter. He then rose to a high position within Pharaoh's court and may have learnt many of the secrets of the Egyptians and taken these rites and ceremonies into Judaism. Indeed, in Acts, Stephen observed that 'Moses was learned in all the wisdom of the Egyptians'. Freemasons will recall that

Moses before the Burning Bush

the opening paragraph of the explanation of the First Degree Tracing Board claims that Masonic 'usages and customs' are very similar to those used by the ancient Egyptian 'priests or Magi'.

Moses, however, had to escape from Egypt after he killed a slave driver, who was beating a Hebrew. He fled to the desert and became a shepherd for a number of years. When driving a flock of sheep near Mount Sinai or Horeb (these are possibly the same location – see section on Holy Mountains), he saw the bush, which was burning, but not consumed by the flames. As he approached God said to him, 'Put off thy shoes from off thy feet, for the place whereon thou standest is holy ground.'

At this point God named Himself as 'YHWH' (or with vowels 'Yahweh') to Moses, although this has also been translated as 'Jehovah' or in English as 'I am that I am'. The lecture on the Royal Master degree states that this account of the name being given to Moses is 'Masonic tradition' but it is clearly outlined in the Bible.

In ancient Israel, it was seen as a sin to even pronounce the sacred name of God or 'Tetragrammaton' (Greek for 'a word having four letters'). This may be the origin of the Chapter ritual, where the name must be pronounced by three members. In various Masonic rituals, the triangle is a symbol of the deity, but this does not appear to have any Biblical origin. Prior to Moses, God had been known to Abraham, Isaac and Jacob as 'Shaddai' or 'El Shaddai' (possibly meaning 'God of the Mountain'), names which feature in Royal Arch Chapter ritual. In the King James' Version of the Bible, 'El Shaddai' is translated as 'God Almighty'. Keats (2008) observed that 'El Shaddai' is a tautology as both words 'El' and 'Shaddai' were used by the ancient Hebrews as a name of God.

The account of Moses being given the name of God is quoted in the Chapter installation to the office of 'Joshua'. It should be noted that this Joshua is not the man of the same name, who appears in the story of Moses. The second Joshua appears many centuries later at the time of the building of the Second Temple. The burning bush also appears in the lecture of the Royal Master degree, the explanation of the Royal Ark Mariner tracing board and in the Rose Croix ritual.

This incident relating to Moses and the removal of footwear is the likely origin of the practice of candidates for the three degrees of Craft Masonry having to remove their footwear and be 'slipshod'. In the first degree, right foot, in the second, left and the third, both feet. Freemasons consider that lodges stand on holy ground (see Abraham).

As recounted on the Royal Ark Mariner Tracing Board, to give Moses confidence, God turned a staff into a serpent and then changed it back again. This is also quoted from the Bible during the 'Standard' ritual version of the Chapter Installation of Zerubbabel. With renewed self-belief, Moses returned to Egypt and asked Pharaoh to let his people go. Pharaoh was determined to keep the Israelites as slaves, but after ten plagues, with the death of the first-born being the final woe inflicted on the Egyptians, he allowed them to leave. According to some versions of the explanation of the First Degree Tracing Board, the Israelites left with a 'high hand' (that is to say, they went boldly) and under the 'out stretched arm' of God. These phrases are taken from the books of Exodus and Numbers.

It is unclear which Pharaoh was the ruler of Egypt at this time. Rameses II and Dudimose have been suggested, but there is no conclusive proof, although the Book of Numbers names the Pharaoh involved as the former. When the Israelites left Egypt, God showed them His chosen route by the two miraculous pillars described on the Second Degree Tracing Board: a pillar of cloud to lead them by day and a pillar of fire at night.

Once the Israelites had left, Pharaoh again changed his mind and pursued them to the shores of the Red Sea with 600 chariots. The pillar of cloud initially blocked the Egyptian army and the miraculous crossing took place, with God parting the waves for the Israelites and then destroying the pursuing army with the water. This incident is noted during the Chapter installation ceremony and is shown on the Royal Ark Mariner Tracing Board, with an observation that for the second time, as with the story of Noah, the Lord had used the power of the waters to destroy wickedness.

Furthermore, the actions of Moses to signal the dividing of the waters is significant to candidates elected to the office of Haggai in a Royal Arch Chapter.

Once across, the Israelites sang the 'Song of Moses' as quoted in the Royal Ark Mariner Tracing Board lecture: 'I will sing unto the Lord, for he hath triumphed gloriously; the horse and his rider hath he thrown into the sea.'

After crossing the Red Sea, the Israelites wandered through the desert and soon began to complain about lack of food. This is when God provided the manna from heaven for them to eat. A pot of manna was later kept in the Ark of the Covenant (as noted in the Select Master degree). According to the Bible, the manna was like small white seeds and tasted like wafers with honey. Next, the Israelites complained about the lack of water. God commanded Moses to strike a rock and water flowed from it. This is referred to in the closing prayer of the Royal Ark Mariner degree. Soon after this incident, the Israelites fought the Amalekites (see section on Joshua for the relevance of this story to Masonic ritual).

A further incident occurred in the wilderness involving snakes. Due to the wickedness of the Israelites, the Lord sent 'fiery serpents' to bite them. When they repented, God told Moses to make a brass serpent, which was used to heal those bitten. It has been suggested that this story may be the origin of the serpent emblem on the Rose Croix collar (Jackson 1979).

Three months after leaving Egypt, the Israelites camped near Mount Sinai and Moses went up the holy mountain and received the Ten Commandments from God. These tablets were also held in the Ark of the Covenant (see section below on the Ark). Part of the Second of the Ten Commandments, 'Thou shalt not make unto thee any graven image, or any likeness of any thing that is in heaven above' appears to form the basis of the obligation in the Super-Excellent Master degree. Here the candidate promises not to 'pay religious adoration to idols' or to 'worship the sun, moon or stars'.

The 'Holy Commandments' are mentioned during the Opening Prayer of a Mark Lodge and during the Installation of Haggai in a Royal Arch Chapter. At the end of Chapter 5 of Deuteronomy, where the Ten Commandments are described, God ordered the Israelites, 'Ye shall observe to do therefore as the Lord your God hath commanded you: ye shall not turn aside to the right hand or to the left.' The latter part is the apparent origin of the instruction in the Second Degree, not to turn to the 'right nor the left from the path of virtue'.

In addition to the Ten Commandments, God gave Moses many laws regarding religious and moral conduct. In Deuteronomy, there are bizarre rules forbidding certain types of men from taking part in worship – men with injuries to their testicles ('stones'), part of their penis ('privy member') missing and 'bastards'. The hated Ammonites (who later fought Jephtha) are expressly excluded. Deuteronomy also includes many punishments for disobeying God and one is very similar to the punishment from the Second Degree (see also David and Jeremiah): 'thy carcase shall be meat unto all fowls of the air, and unto the beasts of the earth.'

God also commanded Moses to construct the tent or tabernacle to hold the Ark of the Covenant. This is the first place 'set apart for the public solemnisation of divine worship' as described on the Logic version of the First Degree Tracing Board.' God gave Moses detailed instructions to build the tabernacle and Ark of the Covenant (see section on the Ark). He also instructed Moses to call together 70 elders and this is the origin of the Grand Sanhedrin, which is noted in Royal Arch Chapter ritual. The Sanhedrin was the 'supreme court' of ancient Israel. The Chapter ritual gives the membership as 72 – this figure could be the result of a mistranslation from the Greek text or 70 elders, together with Moses and Aaron.

The first two tablets containing the Ten Commandments were smashed by Moses in anger when he came down from Mount Sinai and found the Israelites had made a golden calf and were worshipping it. God later made a second set and these are the ones held in the Ark of the Covenant. When Moses received these, he was not allowed to look at the face of God. This may be the origin of a Holy Royal Arch sign. The Lord then told the Israelites that they must 'serve the Lord thy God with all thy heart and with all thy soul'. This phrase is used in the Silver Trowel ceremony with the additional instruction to love

Moses Presenting the Tablets of the Law (1648) by Philippe de Champagne.

'thy neighbour as thyself'. The Grand High Priest ceremony opening prayer asks God to 'enable us to keep all His statutes'. This is also taken from Deuteronomy.

God did not lead the Israelites directly to the Promised Land, because of their various acts of wickedness. Instead they were made to wander in the wilderness of the desert for 40 years, until the generation who had left Egypt had died. At one point they were guided through the desert by Hobab, Moses' father-in-law and seemingly an expert on survival in the hostile environment. Hobab features in the Order of the Secret Monitor.

Throughout the journey there were challenges to the leadership of Moses and Aaron. Korah, Dathan and Abiram angered God by refusing to follow Moses and they were swallowed up by the ground and buried alive as a punishment. This story is contained in two Masonic ceremonies – Knights Templar Priest and the Grand High Priest, where it is the basis of one of the secret signs. It is also noted in the New Testament in the Epistle of Jude. Moses himself had disobeyed God and was only allowed to see the Promised Land from afar on Mount Nebo. He died at 120 years old, having never entered the land shown to him.

According to ritual in the Knight of the Holy Sepulchre, an Appendant Order of the Red Cross of Constantine, Moses, Solomon and Zerubbabel were the founders of Freemasonry. In the Holy Royal Arch ceremony he is noted as the first Grand Master of Freemasonry. There is no historical basis for this claim.

THE HOLY MOUNTAINS: SINAI, HOREB, MORIAH AND TABOR

Biblical reference	Genesis • Chapter 22 v2 (Isaac to be sacrificed on Moriah) • Chapter 22 v14 (Mountain of Vision) Exodus • Chapter 3 (Burning bush) • Chapter 17 v6 (Water from the rock) • Chapter 19 v4 (Taken on eagles' wings) • Chapter19 v18–20 (God on Sinai) • Chapter 31 v18 (Ten Commandments) Joshua • Chapter 19 v22 (Mount Tabor) I Kings • Chapter 19 v1–13 (Elijah on Horeb) II Chronicles • Chapter 3 v1 (Temple built on Mount Moriah) Matthew • Chapter 17 v1–9 (Transfiguration of Jesus) Mark • Chapter 9 v2–13 (Transfiguration)

Biblical reference continued	Luke • Chapter 9 v28–36 (Transfiguration) Acts • Chapter 7 v30–38 (Moses on Mount Sinai)
Masonic reference	Craft • First Degree Tracing Board (Logic Ritual) • Grand Lodge opening ceremony Royal Ark Mariner • Tracing Board Rose Croix Ceremony of Perfection

The author at the summit of Mount Sinai.

Various translations of the Bible use Sinai and Horeb as the name of the same mountain. This is where Moses saw the burning bush and was commanded to return to Egypt by God as featured in the explanation of the Royal Ark Mariner Tracing Board. Fitting in with its watery theme, the prayer of the Royal Ark Mariner degree alludes to Moses striking the rock and water springing from it. This incident also occurred on the mountain.

Once in the wilderness, Moses returned to Mount Sinai with the Israelites. God descended onto the mountain and Exodus describes a mass of smoke and fire appearing as He did so. Only Moses was allowed to approach God, who told him to remind the Israelites of how he destroyed the Egyptian army and helped them escape as if they were 'on eagles' wings'. This is used in Rose Croix ritual. Most importantly, the Ten Commandments were handed to Moses upon the mountain. In the Logic Ritual version of the First Degree Tracing Board, this is described as the Lord revealing the 'Moral, Ceremonial and Judicial Laws'. In his summary of the Old Testament in the Book of Acts, Stephen mentions Mount Sinai twice, recalling the burning bush and Ten Commandments.

The Book of Kings confirms that Mount Sinai was a considerable distance from Israel. The Bible states that Elijah's journey to the mountain took 40 days and 40 nights. As with Moses, God spoke to Elijah there (see section on Division of Israel).

During the opening ceremony of a Grand (State or National) or Provincial (county) lodge, the Junior Grand Warden represents Boaz on Mount Tabor, the Senior Grand Warden Jachin the Assistant High Priest on Mount Sinai, and the Deputy Grand Master Hiram Abif on Mount Moriah. This appears to be a Masonic legend to link the ritual with three Holy Mountains. There is no Biblical link with any man called Jachin being on Sinai. As the Assistant High Priest (see section on Jachin), he would have been on Mount Moriah, the site of the temple and not hundreds of miles away in the wilderness. Mount Moriah is called the 'Mountain of Vision' during the explanation of the Royal Ark Mariner Tracing Board. This is due to Abraham naming the mountain where he had been prepared to sacrifice his son, Isaac (see section on Abraham) *Jehovah-jireh,* which means 'In the mount of the Lord it shall be seen.'

Mount Tabor is mentioned in the Book of Joshua as the border of three of the Israelite tribes, including the Naphtali, the tribe of Hiram Abif's mother. Again, there is no Biblical connection between the mountain and Boaz, who was from Bethlehem, south of Jerusalem. Tabor is located in the northern part of ancient Israel, west of the Sea of Galilee. In the third century, Tabor was identified as the site of the Transfiguration of Christ, where Jesus spoke with Moses and Elijah (see section on Ministry of Jesus), although the Bible is unclear on the location. Later it was the site of a Crusader church and a Roman Catholic chapel now stands at the summit.

Hence, the only correct location in the Grand Lodge ceremony appears to be that stated in the ritual for Hiram Abif (see below). He was the chief architect at the construction of King Solomon's Temple and this was constructed on Mount Moriah (see King Solomon's Temple).

THE TENT OR TABERNACLE BUILT BY BEZALEEL AND AHOLIAB

Timeline	Around 1200 BC
Biblical reference	Exodus • Chapter 25–27 (Tabernacle, Ark and Altar) • Chapter 25 v30 (Shewbread) • Chapter 25 v31 (First reference to candles) • Chapter 25 v32 (Six candles)

Biblical reference continued	• Chapter 31 (Aholiab and Bezaleel) • Chapter 35 v30–35 (Bezaleel's skills) • Chapter 36–39 (Description of the Tabernacle) • Chapter 40 v38 (Cloud by day, fire by night) Leviticus • Chapter 24 v5–7 (Ingredients of showbread) Numbers • Chapter 9 v15–23 (Cloud of God over the tent) Acts • Chapter 7 v45–47 (Tent used until time of David) Hebrews • Chapter 9 v2–8 (Description of the Tabernacle)
Masonic reference	Craft • First Degree Tracing Board (Logic Ritual) • Third Degree Holy Royal Arch • Ceremony of Exaltation • Historical Lecture • Questions Before Toasts Holy Royal Arch Knights Templar Priests Knights Templar

The tent or tabernacle built by Moses in the wilderness was the first place 'set aside for the public solemnisation of divine worship' as described during the explanation of the First Degree Tracing Board. The instructions given by God to Moses on Mount Sinai were extremely detailed and can be seen in the Bible chapters shown above.

To summarise, the Bible relates that the tabernacle consisted of an inner and outer section, all surrounded by a courtyard. The inner tabernacle had ten curtains of the best linen with Cherubim (winged figures) depicted thereon. These curtains were hung with gold loops and were protected by an outer covering made of goat hair. The frame was constructed of acacia wood, with silver bases.

On entering the tent, the Ark of the Covenant could not be seen as it was hidden by veils consisting of blue, purple and red curtains. When standing before the Ark of the Covenant, the High Priest would atone for the sins of the Israelites once a year. This is described in the Royal Arch ceremony and in some versions of Chapter ritual a part of the Book of Hebrews, which further describes the tabernacle, is used as a closing prayer. The Day of Atonement at King Solomon's temple also features in the Craft Third Degree ceremony. The tent also contained a golden table, on which were gold vessels for holding drink and twelve loaves of bread (which were eaten at the end of each week by the priests). This 'shewbread' or 'showbread' was also used at the temple and is referred to in the Royal Master Degree. The loaves must have been large, as modern translations of the Bible show them as containing four litres of flour each.

The tent was illuminated by an ornate lamp stand, the Menorah, and Exodus contains the first Biblical reference to candles, so important in a Masonic lodge. In a Craft lodge, three candles are lit, by the sides of the Master and two Wardens. God instructed Moses that the candlestick must have three candles on each side. In Holy Royal Arch chapters, six candles are used and this may be based on this account.

Further curtains were used to form a courtyard around the tent and the altar, situated in front of the tabernacle, which was used to make sacrifices. As has been explained, in early Bibles, the tabernacle was depicted as having a black and white floor. This was called a 'Mosaic Pavement' possibly named after Moses and the tradition was taken up by Masonic lodges.

God selected Bezaleel, a skilful craftsman, to build the tabernacle and the Ark in accordance with His commands. Bezaleel was a member of the Tribe of Judah and a grandnephew of Moses. Aholiab (or Oholiab), from the Tribe of Dan was to be his assistant. Both these men are celebrated during the toasts at a Chapter Festive Board as they presided with Moses over the 'First or Holy Lodge' (as it is described in the Holy Royal Arch ritual), which was held in the wilderness of Sinai. The two men are also noted in the Historical Lecture in the same degree and during the Knights Templar ceremony. They were once far more important, as together with Moses they represented the officers of a Chapter. These are now named after Zerubbabel, Haggai and Joshua (see sections on these men).

God's presence was indicated by the pillar of cloud by day and fire by night in front of the tent. When the pillar of cloud lifted, the Israelites broke camp and moved on. The pillar remained at different locations for various lengths of time, from one day, to a month or even a year. Most importantly for Freemasons, the tabernacle became the ground plan for the temple later built by King Solomon at Jerusalem. According to Stephen, as noted in the Book of Acts, the tent remained in use until the time of King David.

THE ARK OF THE COVENANT

Timeline	Around 1200 BC
Biblical reference	Genesis • Chapter 49 v10 (First reference to Shiloh) Exodus • Chapter 16 v31–36 (Pot of Manna) • Chapter 25 v10–22 (Plans for the Ark) Numbers • Chapter 7 v89 (Presence of God on the Ark) Deuteronomy • Chapter 10 v1–5 (Ten Commandments in the Ark) • Chapter 31 v26 (Book of the Law in the Ark) Joshua • Chapter 6 (Fall of Jericho) • Chapter 18 v1 (Tabernacle set up at Shiloh) Judges • Chapter 21 v19 (Shiloh near Bethel)

Biblical reference continued	I Samuel • Chapter 3 v21 (Lord at Shiloh) • Chapter 4 v3 (Ark used in battle) • Chapters 4–6 (Philistines capture the Ark) I Kings • Chapter 8 v9 (Contents of Ark) I Chronicles • Chapter 28 v2–3 (King David's plan for the Temple) II Chronicles • Chapter 5 v2–10 (Ark in the Temple) • Chapter 35 v3 (Ark in reign of Josiah) II Maccabees • Chapter 2 v4–8 (Ark hidden in a cave) II Corinthians • Chapter 5 v1 ('House not made with hands') Hebrews • Chapter 9 v4 (Further contents of the Ark) II Peter • Chapter 1 v21 (Prophecies from Holy Spirit) Revelation • Chapter 11 v19 (Ark in Heaven)
Masonic reference	Craft • First Degree Tracing Board Royal Ark Mariner • Tracing Board Mark • Ceremony of Advancement Royal and Select Masters – all degrees Holy Royal Arch • Ceremony of Exaltation • Historical Lecture Rose Croix • Ceremony of Perfection Red Cross of Constantine • Installation of a knight

The Ark was constructed by Bezaleel and Aholiab (see section on Tent or Tabernacle above). It was a small chest, shown in the Bible as two and a half cubits (43″/110 cm) in length, and one and a half cubits (27″/70 cm) in width and depth. It was constructed of wood and overlaid with gold. The top section, known as the 'Mercy Seat' was made of solid gold, including the two Cherubim on the top.

The Ark of the Covenant served two religious purposes. Firstly, according to the Book of Numbers, the presence of God lived between the wings of the two cherubim on the top of the Ark. Second, it was a container for important Israelite artefacts – the two tablets of stone engraved with the Ten Commandments and at various times, other items, including the Book of Law written by Moses, a pot of Manna and Aaron's Rod. Due to its importance, it had to be kept in a special place. Hence, the tabernacle (see above) and King Solomon's temple (see below) were constructed to house the Ark. According to the Select Master degree, a replica Ark also contained the 'Books of the Law' (see Moses).

In addition to its religious uses, the Ark was used to lead the Israelites into battle. This was in a similar manner to the use of Roman Eagles or the carrying of Regimental colours or standards in Napoleonic times.

It had great power and contact with it could cause instant death. When it was captured by the Philistines for seven months, they decided to return it as it caused grave misery to their people. According to various translations of the Bible, it resulted in the Philistines suffering piles, tumours, plagues of vermin and possibly an outbreak of Bubonic Plague. When placed before an idol of their god, Dagon, it caused the statue to fall on its face. At Jericho, the Ark's power was used to defeat the enemy and cause the collapse of the city's walls (see section on Joshua).

During the time of Joshua and the Judges, the Ark was kept at the town of Shiloh in the hills of Ephraim, near Bethel, where Jacob's Ladder appeared. Shiloh was the religious centre of the Israelites prior to the capture of Jerusalem by King David. In Genesis, 'Shiloh' appears to be a person, rather than the place. The reference to this Shiloh as a 'lawgiver' resulted in Christians believing it referred to Jesus. In the Christian degree of the Red Cross of Constantine, Shiloh is the 'City of God' a place where the knights hope to rest. In a further Christian degree, the Rose Croix, the reference to 'Shiloh' may refer to a 'place of rest'.

Solomon before the Ark of the Covenant (1747) by Blaise Nicolas Le Sueur.

The last reference to the Ark being kept in the Temple is in II Chronicles. This is recorded as being during the celebration of the Passover at the time of the reign of King Josiah (see section on The Division of Israel).

In Masonic terms, the Ark has the most prominence in the Royal and Select Master degrees. In the ceremonies of that order, a half size copy of the Ark rests in the centre of the Council. During the Select Master degree, King Solomon, King Hiram of Tyre and Hiram Abif produce a replica of the Ark and its contents and deposit it in a secret vault. According to the ritual, they carved their initials on three sides and on the fourth, Hebrew characters representing 'Anno Lucis 3000' to denote that the Ark was constructed 3000 years after the creation of the world (see Masonic dating below). This replica Ark has no Biblical basis.

In the Royal Master degree a detailed description of the Ark is given. Reference is also made to the '*Shekinah*', the divine presence of God and the '*Bath Kol*' which gave answers when consulted. The *Bath Kol* in Hebrew means the 'daughter of the voice' and is a form of divination or seeing into the future, with the voice of God heard as an echo (Goodman, 2006). It is mentioned in Jewish scripture, but it is not recorded in the Bible. The *Shekinah* can be equated with the Holy Ghost in the New Testament and St Peter refers to the prophecies being from the Holy Spirit of God.

The Ark is also shown on the Royal Ark Mariner Tracing Board and in the Koran, when it features in the story of King Saul (Koran 2.248). After the capture of Jerusalem by the Babylonians (see Fall of Jerusalem), the Ark was lost, but in the final book of the Bible, Revelation, it is said to be in God's Temple in heaven, but the Book of Maccabees (see Destruction of Second Temple) states that the Prophet Jeremiah hid it in a cave. Many legends have surrounded its whereabouts, including the Hollywood film, 'Raiders of the Lost Ark' and claims that it is housed in a small church in Ethiopia.

AARON AND THE BIBLICAL IMPACT ON MASONIC DRESS: CONSECRATION, CEREMONIES AND FURNITURE

Timeline	Around 1200 BC
Biblical reference	Exodus • Chapter 4 v14 (God appoints as speaker for Moses) • Chapter 25 v7 (Jewels for breastplate) • Chapter 28 v1 (Ordination of Aaron) • Chapter 28 v4–5 (Breast plate and mitre) • Chapter 28 v9–11 (Precious stones on breastplate) • Chapter 28 v30 (Urim and Thummim) • Chapter 30 v1–2 (Double cube altar) • Chapter 30 v10 (Day of Atonement) • Chapter 30 v22–33 (Anointing Oil) • Chapter 39 v1–21 (Precious stones on breastplate) • Chapter 40 v9–15 (Use of anointing oil) Numbers • Chapter 6 v22–27 (God's blessing on the Israelites) • Chapter 16 v46 (Use of incense)

Biblical reference continued	• Chapter 16 v47–48 (Aaron saves the Israelites) • Chapter 17 (Aaron's Rod buds) Leviticus • Chapter 8 v1–12 (Oil and Breast plate) • Chapter 16 v4 (Ceremonial washing) I Samuel • Chapter 14 v42 (Casting of lots) Ezra • Chapter 2 v63 (Urim and Thummim) Nehemiah • Chapter 7 v65 (Urim and Thummim) Hebrews • Chapter 9 v4 (Further contents of the Ark)
Masonic reference	Craft • Third Degree Tracing Board Royal Ark Mariner • Tracing Board Allied Masonic Degrees • Grand High Priest degree Royal and Select Masters • Select Master • Degree of Thrice Illustrious Master (Silver Trowel) Holy Royal Arch • Ceremony of Exaltation • Installation of Joshua • Address on Significance of Colours of Robes Red Cross of Constantine • Consecration of Viceroy Societas Rosicruciana in Anglia • Second Grade 'Theoricus'

Aaron is another Biblical character who, like Jacob, appears fleetingly in various Masonic degrees, but does have a major impact. He was the great-grandson of Levi and brother of Moses and became the first High Priest of the Israelites. Even after God had shown His power by turning the staff into a serpent (see Moses above), as featured on the Royal Ark Mariner Tracing Board, Moses still lacked confidence to speak to Pharaoh. Therefore, God appointed Aaron as his spokesman.

Through Moses, God explained to Aaron how to bless the Israelites. These words are quoted during three Masonic ceremonies: Grand High Priest, Silver Trowel and the consecration of the Viceroy (second senior officer) in the Red Cross of Constantine ceremony:

> The Lord bless thee, and keep thee:
> The Lord make his face shine upon thee, and be gracious unto thee:
> The Lord lift up his countenance upon thee, and give thee peace.

After the attempt by Korah and others to usurp Moses' authority (see section on Moses), Aaron saved many Israelites from God's wrath. On the orders of Moses, he took a censer with incense and made atonement for the sins of the people. This stopped a great sickness spreading, although over 14,000 died. This incident forms part of the Installation Ceremony of the officer known as 'Joshua' in a Chapter.

Aaron's rod also features both in the Bible and Masonic ritual. Firstly, it features in the story of the plagues inflicted in Egypt, where he stretched out his rod to turn water into blood and bring about the plagues of frogs and flies. Second, the budding of Aaron's rod occurred once the Israelites had left Egypt. When they were wandering in the wilderness, God decided to select one of the Tribes to form the priesthood. All the heads of the families, including Aaron, had to carve their name on a rod and place it in the Tabernacle. Moses was told by the Lord that one of the rods would bud and the following day, Aaron's rod was found to have blossomed and produced almonds. This rod was later kept in the Ark of the Covenant and these contents form an important part of the Select Master degree. This list of contents is taken from the Book of Hebrews in the New Testament. The rod features on the Royal Ark Mariner Tracing Board, to the right of the

Aaron anointed as High Priest by Moses. Note the breastplate and mitre.

Perfect Ashlar, but it is not mentioned in the official explanation (an image of the Tracing Board is shown on p.37).

As the first Jewish High Priest, Aaron is celebrated in the Order of the Grand High Priest. When Aaron was ordained as a priest, he had to wear a symbolic mitre and breastplate, as described in the Book of Exodus. A replica breastplate is worn in some Royal Arch Chapters by the officer known as 'Companion Joshua', with its jewels representing the twelve tribes of Israel. The form of the breastplate is the basis of one of the signs in the Grand High Priest ceremony. Indeed, in the Allied Masonic Degrees, the Grand High Priest wears both a mitre and a breastplate.

In Biblical times, contained within the breastplate were the mysterious *Urim* and *Thummim*. These are noted in the Royal Arch Chapter ritual, but it is unclear whether they were gemstones, runes or other objects. According to the Jewish historian, Josephus (see section on Destruction of the Second temple), these mysterious items answered 'yes' or 'no' by the way they shone. Throughout the Bible they are used to establish the will of God, at least until the time of Ezra and Nehemiah (both names are used as officers in a Chapter). In the Book of Samuel, it is described as casting lots. Interestingly, casting lots is mentioned in the legend used in Chapter ritual to decide which workman should descend into the secret vault.

The dress of the High Priest is detailed in the Book of Exodus. His coat was to be multi-coloured, made from fine thread – not simply white (as noted in the second grade of SRIA). The mitre, which was likely to have been some form of turban in Biblical times, features as a badge on top of the sceptre carried by Companion Joshua in a Royal Arch Chapter. Around the base of the turban or mitre was a crown of gold, with the inscription 'Holiness to the Lord'. These words feature on the sceptre and on the Master Mason Certificate presented by the United Grand Lodge

The author in his Royal Arch Chapter (Frederick Chapter of Unity). Note the double cube pedestal and staves with ensigns of the Tribes of Israel.

of England. They are also used during the Chapter installation ceremony, when the significance of the colours of the robes is explained. In Hebrew the words are *Kodesh la-Adonai* and these appear on some versions of the Third Degree tracing board and during the Grand High Priest ceremony.

During their time in the desert, the Lord commanded the Israelites to place a 'ribbon of blue' upon the borders of their clothing. This is to remind them to follow the Ten Commandments. Later Bible translations describe several 'tassels'. The Masonic apron may well have been based on this description. There is clearly a border of blue and two groups of seven tassels. Additionally, these tassels may allude to the seven years taken by King Solomon to build the temple. The only Old Testament reference to 'aprons' is when Adam and Eve sew fig leaves together to protect their modesty. This is not linked to Freemasonry!

In the battle against the Amalekites, Aaron was one of the men who held up Moses' arms. This resulted in a variation of the Second Degree 'Hailing Sign' (see section on Joshua). Aaron's work as the priest had further influence on Masonic ritual in relation to the double cube pedestal used in a Royal Arch Chapter. The altar Aaron had to use in the Tabernacle is described in the Bible as a cubit in width and breadth and two cubits high; a double cube.

This altar was to be used by Aaron once a year to make an offering to atone for the sins of the Israelites. The Day of Atonement is an important element of the explanation of the Third Degree Tracing Board, which relates the duties of the High Priest at the time of King Solomon. The lecture notes the 'washings and purifications' carried out by the High Priest and these rules are contained in Leviticus.

The Book of Exodus notes the use of oil to consecrate priests, including Aaron and his sons. The Royal Ark Mariner Tracing Board clearly shows the vase, which holds the 'oil of consecration' and when new lodges or chapters are consecrated, oil is used as part of the ceremony. Oil is also used in the Allied Masonic Degree of 'Grand High Priest' to anoint the new member. As with his brother, Moses, Aaron was not permitted by God to enter the Promised Land. We now turn to Joshua, who became the new leader of the Israelites.

The Israelites Secure the Promised Land

Joshua and Rahab: Biblical Warfare (Part II)

Timeline	1200 BC
Biblical reference	Exodus • Chapter 17 v8–16 (Battle against the Amalekites) Numbers • Chapter 14 v6 (Caleb was a spy with Joshua) • Chapter 14 v24 (Faith of Caleb) • Chapter 26 v65 (God's reward for Caleb and Joshua) Joshua • Chapter 2 (Rahab assists the Israelite spies) • Chapter 6 (Fall of Jericho) • Chapter 7 (Valley of Achor) • Chapter 10 v1–27 (Sun stands still) Judges • Chapter 2 v6–9 (Death of Joshua) Hosea • Chapter 2 v15 (Valley of Troubles) Matthew • Chapter 1 v5 (Rahab in genealogy of Jesus) Acts • Chapter 7 v45 (Joshua's conquest of Holy Land) Hebrews • Chapter 11 v30 (Faith led to fall of Jericho)

Biblical reference continued	• Chapter 11 v31 (Faith of Rahab) James • Chapter 2 v25 (Faith of Rahab)
Masonic reference	Craft • Second Degree ceremony Order of the Secret Monitor • Second or Prince Degree • Royal Order of the Scarlet Cord Holy Royal Arch Knights Templar Priests • Order of the Scarlet Cord or Knight of Rahab • Installation of a Knight Templar Priest • Installation of High Priest
Historical context	1200 BC – Collapse of Hittite Empire

After the death of Moses, Joshua took command of the Israelites. This is not the Joshua who features in the Holy Royal Arch, which is set many centuries later. It should also be noted that 'Joshua' and 'Jesus' are English translations of the same Hebrew name. Confusingly, the Book of Acts (King James' Version), in Stephen's summary of the Old Testament, refers to 'Jesus', meaning Joshua, conquering the Holy Land.

The first Joshua, Moses' successor, features prominently in Craft ritual during the explanation of the second part of the Second Degree sign – the 'Hailing Sign' or 'Sign of Perseverance'. Some Freemasons will have witnessed a strange version of this sign, with the palm facing forward, in lodges using Logic Ritual or Scottish workings. There is a clear reason for this – the origin of this sign is from a completely different battle to that quoted in other versions of the ritual.

Joshua was born in Egypt prior to the Exodus in around 1200 BC. According to the Bible, Joshua was born into the Tribe of Ephraim. The Ephraimites would become known as the most militaristic of the tribes of Israel; a 'clamorous and turbulent people' as they are described during the explanation of the Second Degree Tracing Board. A century later they would be involved in the Israelite civil war fought against Jephtha and the Gileadites, which forms part of the Tracing Board ritual.

Joshua became one of Moses' most trusted assistants and accompanied him part of the way up Mount Sinai, where Moses was given the Ten Commandments. He was also the commander during their first battle after leaving Egypt. During this fight against the Amalekites, when Moses held up his hands, the Israelites were victorious, but not so when he put them down. So when Moses tired, Aaron and Hur held up his hands until complete victory was gained. This is the source of the Logic Ritual story.

No doubt due to his strategic vision and warrior skills, Joshua was used as a spy and was sent into Canaan, the 'Promised Land'. To prove the fertility of the area, the spy patrol cut down grapes, figs and pomegranates and took them back to Moses. The incident is described in the ceremony of a Knight Templar Priest. This obscure story seems to be quoted to fit with a later quotation from the Book of Hosea, which mentions vineyards (see section of the Division of Israel). Whilst the land was flowing with 'milk and honey', it was also inhabited and the occupants would have to be ruthlessly defeated to enable the Israelites to take over this land. Intelligence on the Canaanites was, therefore, vital.

Joshua was appointed by Moses to succeed him as leader of the Israelites and Joshua commanded the subsequent crossing of the River Jordan and conquest of Canaan. God had allowed

Destruction of the Walls of Jericho by Robert Leinweber. Note the Ark of the Covenant and the trumpets.

the generation that had rejected Him to perish in the desert. Only Joshua and Caleb, another of the twelve spies who had remained faithful to the Lord, had been allowed to journey to their new land. The loyalty of Joshua and Caleb is noted in the Order of the Secret Monitor.

In addition to Divine support, Israel had picked the right time to seize this territory. Egypt, which had previously controlled the area, was weak and the small city states in Canaan were engaged in internal feuds. Furthermore, the Egyptians had almost bled the area dry of resources. Into this weakened land, the Israelite Army was thrust.

Joshua's first major battle was the siege of Jericho, which was situated on the west side of the River Jordan. This was a fortified city and one of the oldest settlements in the world, having been founded around 8000 BC. To assess the morale of the inhabitants, two Israelite spies were sent into the city and they operated from the house of Rahab, a prostitute. Her house formed part of the city walls and therefore provided an escape route. The king of the city sent men to arrest the spies, but Rahab hid them under bundles of cotton on the open roof of her home. Her faith is described in the Book of Hebrews and she betrayed her city as she knew it was God's will that it would fall. She informed the spies that morale was very low in the city, as the inhabitants had heard of the many victories of the Israelites, She enabled the men to leave the city by climbing from her window using a scarlet cord. When she asked that her family be saved, the spies told her to tie the cord to her window to identify her house when their army entered the city.

God commanded the Israelites to march around the walls for seven days carrying the Ark of the Covenant and trumpets. On the seventh day, the trumpets sounded and the walls collapsed. The scarlet cord saved Rahab's family, but all the other inhabitants were slain. The story of Rahab is celebrated in the Masonic Royal Order of the Scarlet Cord (see Mighty Men of David for further information on this Order) and despite her profession she was accepted by the Israelites. She later married an Israelite called Salmon and their son was Boaz, who is much celebrated in Masonic ritual (see section on Boaz and Ruth). Rahab is also part of the genealogy of Jesus and her faith is used as an example twice in the New Testament – in Hebrews and James.

The entire city of Jericho was destroyed in accordance with God's command. Only objects made from precious metals were not burned. These were to be presented to the Lord, but an Israelite named Achan stole a Babylonian coat, together with gold and silver from the city and hid them under his tent. For his sins, he was stoned to death in a place which became known as the Valley of Achor. This place name came to be used as a proverbial phrase as the 'Valley of Troubles'. In this sense, it features in the Book of Hosea and this section is read out during the installation of a High Priest (senior officer) in a Tabernacle (lodge) of Knights Templar Priests.

The conquest continued and the Israelites faced a combined force of southern Canaanites, headed by the Amorite king. At Gibeon, six miles north of Jerusalem, after an all-night march, Joshua fought this army. The enemy panicked at the sight of Joshua's army and were either put to the sword or killed by hailstones sent by God. As night was setting in and victory was not complete, Joshua prayed to the Lord for the Sun to stand still. The Lord granted his request until the Amorites were utterly defeated (see section on Church and Freemasonry for Galileo's opinion on this story). This battle forms the basis of the Second Degree sign in Taylor's, Emulation and other versions of Craft ritual.

This need for daylight to complete the battle may appear odd to us, when we have night-vision equipment and battles can be fought at any time of the year. It should be recalled that, until the twentieth century, battles were rather like cricket matches – they had to be performed during daylight and not in the winter months. This is the origin of the 'Retreat Parade' – the Army is not defeated, it is simply retiring in good order to fight again tomorrow. Likewise, until the invention of canned foods, massed armies could only operate effectively when food was plentiful in summer and autumn.

Once the Promised Land had been occupied, Joshua allocated the land to the Tribes of Israel (the details are contained in the section on Jacob). When Joshua died at 110 years old, he was buried in the hills allocated to his own tribe, the Ephraimites. In his farewell address, he commanded the Israelites to continue to obey the Lord and follow the Law of Moses.

The conquest, however, was not complete. Many cities, notably Jerusalem, were not in Israelite hands. They did control the previously sparsely populated areas and a secure foothold had been achieved. The settlement of the Holy Land marked a significant change. The Israelites had previously led a nomadic existence but they now became farmers, producing, as the Second Degree Tracing Board notes 'corn, wine and oil'; the latter being olive oil. The surplus produced encouraged trade and this later led to alliances being formed with other countries, to the benefit of all concerned (see section on Hiram, King of Tyre). It also attracted invaders, the most significant of these being the Philistines. The Book of Joshua now ends and we move to the Book of Judges, with its heroes, Jephtha, Samson and others, who had to fight the Philistine invaders.

THE TIME OF THE JUDGES:
BIBLICAL WARFARE (PART III)

Timeline	1100 BC
Biblical reference	Genesis • Chapter 19 v30–38 (Ammonites come from incest) Numbers • Chapter 10 v1–9 (Trumpet calls)

Biblical reference continued	Deuteronomy • Chapter 20 (Rules of Warfare) Judges • Chapter 3 v16 (Bronze Age sword) • Chapters 6–8 (Story of Gideon) • Chapter 10 v6–17 (Ammonites attack) • Chapter 11 v1–11 (Jephtha leader of Gileadites) • Chapter 11 v19 (Message to King Sihon) • Chapter 11 v29–40 (Promise and defeats Ammonites) • Chapter 12 v1–6 (Ephraimites defeated) • Chapter 12 v7 (Death of Jephtha) • Chapter 16 v23–30 (Heroic Samson) • Chapter 21 v25 (A lawless time) I Kings • Chapter 10 v26 (Solomon's Chariots) • Chapter 22 v34 (Weaknesses with armour) II Chronicles • Chapter 26 v14–15 (Siege towers) Isaiah • Chapter 54 v17 (Servants of the Lord protected) Hebrews • Chapter 11 v32–34 (Faith of Jephtha)
Masonic reference	Craft • Second Degree Tracing Board • Emulation 'Additional Explanation' Royal Ark Mariner • Ceremony of Elevation Order of the Secret Monitor • Scarlet Cord 3rd Grade
Historical context	1200 BC – Collapse of Hittite Empire

The Book of Judges could more accurately be called the 'Book of Rulers'. This was a lawless time and the Bible states 'every man did that which was right in his own eyes.' According to the Bible, during this period of Israelite history God appointed various 'Judges' to unite the Israelites against their common enemies; both the foes still inside Canaan, who were aggrieved about the occupation of their land and those outside, who desired to occupy parts of the 'Promised Land'. The Judges included some notable Biblical characters – Gideon, Samson and Deborah, the first woman Judge. In Masonic ritual, the most important judge is rather less well known. He was a soldier named Jephtha. That said, a number of the other Judges appear in various side degrees.

Throughout the time of the Judges, the Israelites are punished with invaders when they turn to idol worship and other sins. When they repent, a deliverer is sent, often from an unlikely source. For example, Jephtha was the son of a prostitute. He lived near Mount Gilead, to the east of the River Jordan. When his father died, his half-brothers ejected him from the household, so he could not share in his father's possessions. As a result, he fled to the land of Tob, to the north of Gilead, and there became the successful leader of a small army.

When the city of Gilead was threatened by the Ammonites, who inhabited the land on their south eastern border, the city rulers appealed for Jephtha's help. They appointed him to be the head of their army and Jephtha used his veteran troops to strengthen the Gileadite forces. Prior to fighting the Ammonites, Jephtha appealed to Sihon, king of the Amorites, to allow the Gileadites to pass peacefully through his territory, near the River Jabbok (see section on Metal for the Temple). The king rejected the plea and Jephtha had to destroy his army. The verse relating to the message to Sihon is read out during the Scarlet Cord ritual.

The victory over the Amorites allowed him to face the main enemy, the hated Ammonites. Throughout the Bible, the Ammonites are rivals of Israel (see Fall of Jerusalem and the reasons for the death of Gedaliah) and Genesis states that their country was founded by Ben-Ammi, who was born as a result of incest, Lot's daughter having had sex with her drunken father after the destruction of Sodom and Gomorrah. The story of their origin appears to be justification for the warfare against them.

It is at this point that Jephtha made a vow that he was later to regret; if God delivered the Ammonites into his hands, he would sacrifice the first creature that met him on his return. Victory was his and the Ammonites were crushed. Unfortunately for Jephtha, instead of a dog or other animal, his only child, his daughter, came to meet him. Jephtha kept his promise to God.

The story connected to the Second Degree Tracing Board begins after the death of Jephtha's daughter, where a dispute arises with the Ephraimites over the 'spoils of the Ammonitish war'. These are shown in the Bible as 20 towns to the south of Gilead between Heshbon and Aroer.

Jephtha, having fought a war against the Ammonites on an eastern front, now found himself with an attack from the west, with Ephraimites crossing the Jordan. As has been previously observed in the section on Joshua, the lecture on the Tracing Board notes that the Ephraimites were a 'clamorous and turbulent people'. It is easy to forget that the Ephraimites were Israelites and their warlike nature had served them well, with great military leaders amongst their number in the past.

Few countries have escaped civil war with its terrible suffering and here Israelite fought Israelite. The Ephraimites were defeated and 42,000 were slain, either on the battlefield or attempting to flee back across the Jordan. There is some discussion as to whether 'forty and two thousand' means 42,000 or 2040. The former would appear to be correct given the Hebrew numbering system.

The Biblical and Masonic account notes the use of *Shibboleth* as a test word to establish if a man was an invader. The Gileadites guarding the fords across the Jordan asked each man attempting to cross to pronounce this word. Unfortunately for the Ephraimites, their accent caused them to say *Sibboleth* (no 'h') and they were discovered and killed. This is the first recorded use of this tactic, which has been employed throughout history. For example, during the British commando raid on the U-boat pens at St Nazaire in the Second World War, the passwords were 'Weapons War Week'. Few Germans could say this phrase without being discovered!

A further ancient battlefield communication method is shown in the Book of Numbers. Here various trumpet calls are listed to gather the leaders, position the Twelve Tribes or warn of attack. This is very similar to bugle calls still used today, such as 'Last Post' and 'Reveille'. In this sense, the trumpets are signalling devices and not musical instruments. A herald with a trumpet can be seen on the Royal Ark Mariner Tracing Board (see Zedekiah below).

The use of siege weapons is mentioned during the reign of King Uzziah around 700 BC (see After Solomon below). The Second Book of Chronicles describes them as 'engines, invented by

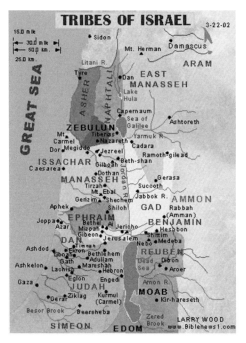

Notable places in relation to Jephtha – the River Jordan runs north to south with Mount Gilead (area shown as Gad on the map) south of the River Jabbok. The Ammonite territory can be seen to the east of the Jordan. The Ephraimites occupied the land to the west and the 'spoils of the Ammonitish war' are Aroer and other nearby towns (in the Reuben tribe area).

cunning men, to be on the towers and upon the bulwarks, to shoot arrows and great stones withal'. These tactics were used extensively during the Crusades (see below) and continued until the Middle Ages.

The weapons employed during the battles at this time were a short sword, javelins, bows and arrows and chariots. Sling shots, such as used by David to kill Goliath, were also used. As weapons improved, armour and helmets became thicker to afford protection. Armour was particularly weak around the seams or joins in the sleeves. In the Book of Kings, King Ahab of Israel was killed when an arrow hit him 'between the scale armour and the breastplate'.

The support of God was seen as the best protection and the short passage from Isaiah, which is read out during the Royal Ark Mariner degree, states, 'No weapon that is formed against thee shall prosper, and every tongue that shall rise against thee in judgment thou shalt condemn. This is the heritage of the servants of the Lord, and their righteousness is of me, saith the Lord.' More practically, the Bronze Age sword is described in the Book of Judges as a one-cubit-long, double bladed weapon.

The chariot was a two-man mobile platform, with a driver and an archer or javelin thrower. Throughout the Bronze and Iron Ages, chariots remained an important weapon. There are many references to them in the Old Testament, with them being used by Israel and her enemies. For example, King Solomon is said to have had 1400 chariots at his disposal. The Assyrians developed the defence tactic against chariot attack – well drilled and disciplined infantry armed with long, heavy spears.

The Bible has its own 'Geneva Convention' and the rules for warfare are shown in Deuteronomy. This includes the conduct for sieges, where the occupants of a city are to be given to opportunity of surrender prior to the siege commencing. If a city was taken after a siege, all men were to be slain and all women and children taken as slaves (see p.120 for a Masonic link to siege warfare). Despite their brutality, the rules are environmentally friendly. Trees, particularly those bearing fruit, were not to be cut down unnecessarily; they could only be felled to build siege towers.

The battles of Jephtha occurred around 150 years before the building of King Solomon's Temple. In considering the use of the 'Shibboleth' and the number of Ephraimites apparently killed, we should consider how stories become exaggerated or amended during our own recent history. Many readers will have seen the film *Zulu* with its portrayal of Welsh soldiers fighting in South Africa. In fact, only a quarter of the soldiers were Welsh, the burly and brave middle-aged Colour Sergeant was really just 24 years old, and the malingerer, Private Hook, was a first-rate soldier, later a Sergeant, who guarded the Crown Jewels. Film makers frequently amend the historical facts to please the audience.

Whether or not the numbers killed were exaggerated, Jephtha's victories were short lived. Less than 30 years later the 'Sea Peoples' (historically a coalition that included the Philistines) landed

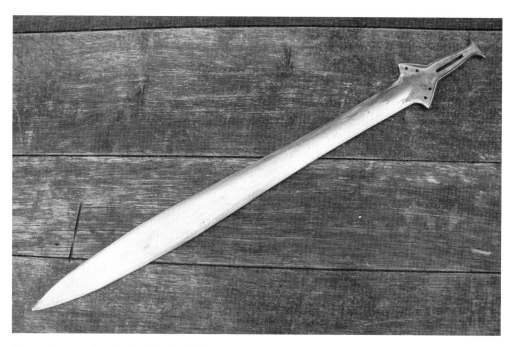

Bronze Age sword as described in the Bible.

on Israelite territory. These invaders possibly came from Cyprus or islands in the Aegean Sea. As punishment for sins, God placed the Israelites under the rule of their enemies for 40 years. This is the time of Samson, who defeated thousands of Philistines with his legendary strength, before succumbing to the charms of Delilah. Samson was the last leader in the Book of Judges and he is mentioned simply as the 'heroic Samson', in the 3rd Grade of the Scarlet Cord ritual. This has several references to the military exploits of Biblical and other characters.

It will be recalled that Samson's colossal strength was lost when his hair was cut. He was captured by the Philistines and blinded. When chained in the temple of the false god, Dagon, Samson prayed to the Lord, who returned his strength. He then pushed down the two supporting pillars of the temple, killing himself and many Philistines. The Scarlet Cord also has a reference to 'the daring Gideon' in praise of the Israelite Judge who defeated many enemies and whose story fills three chapters of the Book of Judges.

BOAZ AND RUTH

Timeline	1100 BC
Biblical reference	Ruth • Chapter 2–4 (Ruth and Boaz) • Chapter 4 v7–8 (Boaz removes a shoe) I Kings • Chapter 7 v21 (Pillar named Boaz) II Chronicles • Chapter 3 v17 (Pillar named Boaz)

Biblical reference continued	Matthew • Chapter 1 v5 (Boaz in genealogy of Jesus) • Chapter 1 v5 (Rahab was mother of Boaz)
Masonic reference	Craft – All degrees Order of the Secret Monitor • Scarlet Cord 1st Grade

Boaz is one of the most significant characters in Freemasonry. In the Bible, the name is given to the left hand pillar that stood in the entrance of King Solomon's Temple and in some versions 'Boaz' is said to mean 'in strength'. Masonic ritual uses these details and links them to a man named Boaz, who lived in the time of the Judges and features in the Book of Ruth. This is at least 100 years before the building of the Temple. It should be noted that the Bible makes no connection between the name of the pillar and the man named Boaz.

In Biblical terms, Boaz was the son of Salmon and his wife, Rahab, who had assisted the Israelite spies during their time within the city of Jericho (see Joshua and Rahab). He is described in the First Degree ceremony as 'a Great Grandfather of David, a prince and ruler in Israel'. The genealogy is correct and in the New Testament, Boaz (shown as 'Booz') is one of the forefathers of Jesus. He was not, however, a prince or ruler, although in the Talmud, which contains details of Jewish laws and customs, he is described as a learned judge. The King James Version of the Bible refers to Boaz as a 'mighty man of wealth' and in the story of Ruth, he is a kind and rich farm owner.

Ruth was a Moabite, a tribe who lived to the east of the Israelites. With her widowed Israelite mother-in-law, Naomi, Ruth left Moab and went to live near Bethlehem. Here she met Boaz, a distant relative of Naomi. Boaz was impressed by Ruth's loyalty to her mother-in-law and allowed her to gather grain from his fields. They soon became close friends and eventually married. Later they had a son, Obed, who was the father of Jesse, the father of David. This story is the major feature of the lecture during the 1st Grade of the Scarlet Cord.

There is no clear explanation as to why, in Masonic terms, King Solomon should choose to name one of the pillars of his temple after his great-great-grandfather. This appears to be a further embellishment of the Biblical story to fit Masonic ritual.

When Boaz purchased land he took off his shoe and handed it to the seller. The Bible explains that this as being an Israelite custom to show that the deal was agreed. This, together with the removal of shoes at the burning bush (see Moses) may be the basis for the Masonic tradition of entering the lodge 'slip-shod' (without shoes) before taking the obligation in certain degrees.

SAMUEL

Timeline	1100–1050 BC
Biblical reference	I Samuel • Chapter 1 v19–20 (Elkanah father of Samuel) • Chapter 2 v19 (Samuel taken to Shiloh) • Chapter 3 v1–21 (God calls Samuel) • Chapter 16 v1–13 (God points out David as king) Hebrews • Chapter 11 v32–34 (Faith of Samuel)

Masonic reference	Scarlet Cord • Preparation for Installation Holy Royal Arch • Installation of Haggai • Installation of Zerubbabel Red Cross of Constantine • Installation of a Knight

Samuel was the last 'Judge' of Israel, although his story is after the end of the Book of Judges. He was the son of Elkanah and this name features in the Scarlet Cord installation. Whilst Samuel is an important Biblical character, he only appears in two small sections of Masonic ritual, in readings in the Chapter Installation Ceremonies of Haggai (Calling of Samuel) and Zerubbabel (David selected as King).

Samuel was a boy servant of Eli, an elderly priest, who was responsible for the Ark of the Covenant, which was kept at Shiloh, a town to the north of Bethel near Mount Ephraim. The Ark was kept at this location prior to the capture of Jerusalem (see sections on the Ark of the Covenant and David). The town of Shiloh is significant in the Red Cross of Constantine ceremony.

During one night, Samuel believed Eli was calling his name. Eli was wise and realised that it was God calling Samuel. He therefore instructed him on what to say and Samuel's words are quoted during the Chapter Installation ceremony; 'Speak Lord, for Thy servant heareth.' Samuel eventually united Israel against the hated Philistine invaders.

The Infant Samuel (1776) by Joshua Reynolds. 'Speak Lord, for Thy servant heareth.'

It was during the time of Samuel's early life that the Philistines captured the Ark of the Covenant, but returned it after suffering terrible illnesses (see Ark above). Samuel later led the united Israelite army to defeat the Philistines at Mizpah. He also appointed Israel's first two kings – Saul and David. Samuel died during the reign of the latter.

DAVID, JONATHAN AND SAUL

Timeline	1006 BC – David becomes king 965 BC – Death of David
Biblical reference	I Samuel • Chapter 10 (Saul made first king of Israel) • Chapter 16 (David chosen by God) • Chapter 17 (David and Goliath) • Chapter 18 (King Saul fears David) • Chapter 19 (Saul tries to kill David) • Chapter 20 (Jonathan signals using arrows) • Chapter 22 v11–23 (Saul slays the priests) • Chapter 23 v13–18 (David and Jonathan's covenant) • Chapter 31 (Death of Saul and Jonathan) II Samuel • Chapter 1 v19 (How are the mighty fallen) • Chapter 2 (David made King of Judah) • Chapter 5 v1–5 (David king of all Israel) • Chapter 5 v6–10 (Capture of Jerusalem) • Chapter 5 v11–12 (Hiram's masons sent to Israel) • Chapter 6 (Ark brought to Jerusalem) • Chapter 7 (Plans to build a temple) • Chapter 7 v13 (Son of David will build Temple) • Chapter 8 (Further conquests in Israel) I Kings • Chapter 1 v1–4 (David cannot keep warm) • Chapter 1 v28–53 (Appoints Solomon as king) • Chapter 2 v1–11 (Death of David) • Chapter 5 v3 (Forbidden from building temple) I Chronicles • Chapter 11 v1–3 (David king of all Israel) • Chapter 16 v2–3 (Sacrifices when Ark moved) • Chapter 17 v12 (Son of David will build Temple) • Chapter 22 v1–4 (Preparation for the temple) • Chapter 22 v5–12 (Forbidden from building temple) • Chapter 22 v14–16 (Funds to build the Temple) II Chronicles • Chapter 13 v5 (Covenant of Salt)

Biblical reference continued	Matthew • Chapter 1 v1–6 (David in genealogy of Jesus) Luke • Chapter 4 v32 (David in genealogy of Jesus) Acts • Chapter 7 v45–46 (David pleased God) Hebrews • Chapter 11 v32–34 (Faith of David) Revelation • Chapter 22 v16 (Jesus is a descendant of David)
Masonic reference	Craft • Second Degree Royal Ark Mariner • Installation of Commander Order of the Secret Monitor Mark • Tracing Board Royal and Select Masters • Degree of Thrice Illustrious Master (Silver Trowel) Holy Royal Arch • Historical Lecture • Installation of Zerubbabel
Historical context	1100 BC – Phoenicians develop alphabetic script

King David is important to Freemasons as he is the father of Solomon, and he, David, made the decision to build the temple at Jerusalem. He is also credited as being the author of the Book of Psalms, the longest book in the Bible. This book is so important to Masonic ritual that it is covered in a separate section. For Christians, Jesus is a 'son of' (meaning from the family of) David. This is clearly described in the first verse of the New Testament.

David was the son of Jesse, who lived with his large family in Bethlehem at the time of the rule of Saul, the first king of Israel. God commanded Samuel to visit Jesse the 'Bethlehemite' as the next king would be found amongst his sons. Samuel was particularly impressed by Eliab, the eldest son, who was strong and handsome, but he was rejected, as were his brothers, Abinadab and Shammah. The three brothers are named during the Installation Ceremony in a Royal Arch Chapter.

To Samuel's surprise, David was chosen. He was the youngest son, who had to be called home as he was caring for a flock of sheep. David was then anointed as the future leader of Israel, as Saul had fallen out of favour with God. God explained his decision to select the shepherd boy, and not the older, stronger sons because 'the Lord seeth not as man seeth; for man looketh on the outward appearance, but the Lord looketh on the heart'. This story is included in the Installation of the most senior officer (Zerubbabel) of a Holy Royal Arch Chapter. The explanation of the Mark Tracing Board paraphrases the quotation as 'God seeth not as man seeth.'

Later, King Saul was troubled by an evil spirit and David's harp playing helped to relieve this problem. He was also selected as Saul's armour bearer, an important role, as the Israelites were at war with the Philistines at the time. Saul's forces were facing the Philistines in the Valley of Elah, to the south west of Jerusalem. It was here that Goliath, who is described as being over 6 cubits tall (approximately 9 feet), appeared. Goliath continually challenged the Israelite soldiers, but it was David, who was still a boy, who volunteered to fight him.

David brought Goliath down by striking him on the forehead with a stone from his slingshot. David then cut off Goliath's head, using his enemy's sword. The Philistine army was defeated and the Bible notes that they were pushed back towards the Mediterranean coast. The battle with Goliath has a Masonic connection as Goliath threatened David that he would feed his body to 'the fowls of the air' and the 'wild beasts of the field'. David responded that he would do the same to the Philistine army. These horrible punishments are also included in the 'physical penalty' formerly included in the Second Degree obligation.

The killing of Goliath resulted in a strong bond between David and Saul's son, Jonathan. This relationship is celebrated in the Masonic Order of the Secret Monitor. Saul, however, became increasingly jealous of David and made many attempts to kill him, but these were thwarted with the help of Jonathan. In one memorable event, Jonathan signalled to David by firing three arrows

David with the Head of Goliath (1609–1610) by Michelangelo Merisi da Caravaggio.

and shouting a coded message to his servant 'the arrows are beyond you.' This was a pre-agreed message to David, which told him that he was still in danger. This incident is symbolised on the Jewel worn by members of the Order of the Secret Monitor.

Saul's wickedness continued and he had the priests at the town of Nob slain because they had assisted David – another incident that features in the Secret Monitor ceremony. Soon after, David and Jonathan entered into a covenant before God. Saul and Jonathan later died in battle against the Philistines, near Mount Gilboa, to the west of the River Jordan. Saul was badly wounded by archers and asked his body guard to kill him rather than allow him to be captured. He refused and Saul 'fell upon his own sword'. The phrase 'How the are mighty fallen' is a Biblical reference to his death. The fact that Saul was the first king of Israel is quoted in the Super Excellent Master degree, which deals with the last king, Zedekiah.

Saul being dead, David became King of Judah and soon after was appointed King of all Israel. The Bible states that God gave Israel to David and his sons forever by a 'covenant of salt' – this means a binding agreement and this may be the origin of the Arab tradition of sharing salt with a guest, which is used in the Royal Ark Mariner installation ceremony. The section of I Chronicles relating to David becoming king is recited in the installation ceremony of the Order of the Secret Monitor. In the Bible, the territory of Israel is often defined as from Beersheba in the south to Dan in the north. It was David who completed the invasion of the 'Promised Land' as started by Joshua, with the capture of Jerusalem. Here, David's forces gained access to the city by stealth, not a traditional siege, via a water pipe.

With Jerusalem captured, David was now a powerful force to be reckoned with and he received messengers from Hiram, King of Tyre, who controlled the important coastal area to the north of Israel. An alliance was subsequently formed, which was to continue during the reign of Solomon and which features heavily in Masonic ritual, with King Hiram cast as one of the 'Three Grand Masters'.

The alliance was based on benefits for both countries. Israel had much 'corn, wine and oil', as noted during the lecture on the Second Degree Tracing Board, but King Hiram's cities were often built on land reclaimed from the sea – very poor arable land. On the other hand, the Israelites were tent dwellers and the expert masons and craftsmen of Tyre, Sidon and Phoenicia could assist their building projects. Furthermore, the cities of Phoenicia controlled the forests of the Lebanon with its sought-after cedarwood, together with other important ancient goods – purple dyes from the Murex snail and fine linen. (See sections on materials for the Temple below).

The Phoenicians were expert sailors, with experience of trading throughout much of the known world. The Israelites controlled ports on the Mediterranean, notably Joppa, and access to the Red Sea, through the port at Ezion Geber. This opened trading routes to Arabia, Africa and India. David could provide the access; Hiram could provide the sailors and boats to exploit it. But quite why they imported apes and baboons is yet to be established!

Jerusalem being secured, David ordered the transfer of the Ark to his new capital. This was accompanied by burnt offerings and the king presented every Israelite with 'a loaf of bread, and a good piece of flesh, and a flagon of wine'. This is noted in the Secret Monitor ceremony. David was very much aware that he was living in a house constructed of the finest cedar, but the Ark was still kept in a tent. The plans would be put into effect by Solomon. The workmen sent by King Hiram built a palace for David and this is the first mention of 'masons' in the Bible. David further secured the borders of Israel, with victories over the Philistines, Syrians, Ammonites and others.

David displeased God by having an adulterous relationship with the beautiful Bathsheba, the future mother of Solomon. David deliberately caused the death of her husband, Uriah, one of his army commanders, by ensuring that he was placed in the most dangerous part of a battle. This being done, David took Bathsheba for his wife and her second child was Solomon.

According to the Bible, David prepared for the construction of the Temple by providing a great amount of treasure, manpower and materials. God, however, forbade him from building a house in

His name as he had 'shed blood abundantly' and 'made great wars'. God told David that one of his sons would build the Temple and II Samuel is quoted in the Holy Royal Arch Historical Lecture – 'He shall build me an house, and I will establish his throne for ever' appear to be the basis of the phrase used in the Second Degree, 'In strength will I establish this mine house to stand firm forever.' Solomon, his son, was appointed King (when David was elderly) and charged to complete the transformation of Jerusalem from a fortified village into a capital city with a palace and temple. This hand-over of power is the setting of the Silver Trowel, a ceremony for Masters of Councils of Royal and Select Masters (see section on Mighty Men).

At the start of the First Book of Kings, David is shown to be very elderly. He was constantly cold, no matter how many blankets his servants covered him with and this is noted in the Silver Trowel ceremony. The Masonic ritual does not, however, relate the full story as told in the Bible, which notes that the king was given a beautiful virgin to lie with (the unfortunately named *Abishag*) to warm him up. But David's age appears to have caught up with him. The Bible makes it clear that he did not have sex with her.

When David died, he was buried in Bethlehem, the 'City of David'. He had created a great kingdom, with a strong alliance with his powerful neighbour, Hiram, King of Tyre. We shall now turn to other areas of David's life that influence Masonic ritual – the Book of Psalms, the purchase of land of Araunah the Jebusite and his 'Mighty Men', including the power politics of his time.

BOOK OF PSALMS

Timeline	1000 BC
Biblical reference	Psalms • Psalm 11 (Trust in the Lord) • Psalm 15 (Behaviour pleasing to God) • Psalm 18 (A song of victory) • Psalm 19 v1 ('Heavens declare the glory of God') • Psalm 22 v1 ('My God, my God, why hast thou forsaken me?') • Psalm 23 (Valley of the shadow of death) • Psalm 24 v4 (Clean hands and a pure heart) • Psalm 25 v21 (Integrity and uprightness) • Psalm 33 v9 (Commanded and it stood fast) • Psalm 40 v5 ('Wonderful works' of God) • Psalm 40 v7 ('Volume of the book') • Psalm 44 v1 ('We have heard with our ears') • Psalm 50 v14 'Most High') • Psalm 55 v4 ('Terrors of death') • Psalm 57 v1 ('Shadow of Thy wings') • Psalm 65 v4 (People chosen by God) • Psalm 68 v4 (Name of God) • Psalm 69 v2 (Shibboleth = 'fall of water') • Psalm 78 v2 (Stories with secret meanings) • Psalm 78 v4 ('Wonderful works' of God) • Psalm 79 (Prayer for Jerusalem) • Psalm 80 v1 (Lord lives between cherubims) • Psalm 83 v18 (Jehovah the Most High) • Psalm 84 v10 (Temple doorkeeper)

Biblical reference continued	• Psalm 103 v12–17 (Several Masonic references) • Psalm 106 v17 (Earth swallowed Dathan) • Psalm 106 v47–48 ('save us...gather us') • Psalm 107 v8, 15, 21 and 31 ('Wonderful works') • Psalm 107 v29–33 (References to water) • Psalm 110 v4 (Melchizedek priest forever) • Psalm 111 v4 ('Wonderful works' of God) • Psalm 118 v22 (Headstone rejected) • Psalm 119 v105 ('Thy word is a lamp') • Psalm 119 v133 ('Let not any iniquity have dominion over me') • Psalm 119 v158 ('Holy will and word') • Psalm 121 v4 (God neither slumbers nor sleeps) • Psalm 122 (Prayer for Jerusalem) • Psalm 132 v13 ('His habitation') • Psalm 133 (Brethren dwell in unity) • Psalm 134 v1–3 (Night guards at the temple) • Psalm 136 v8–9 (Sun to rule by day) • Psalm 137 v1 ('By the rivers of Babylon')
Masonic reference	Craft • First Degree • Second Degree • Third Degree • Installation Ceremony Royal Ark Mariner • Ceremony of Elevation Allied Masonic Degrees • Grand High Priest • Knight of Constantinople Order of the Secret Monitor • Second or Prince Degree • Third or Supreme Ruler Degree • Scarlet Cord 1st, 2nd and 3rd Grades Mark • Ceremony of Advancement • Tracing Board Royal and Select Masters • Royal Master • Most Excellent Master • Super Excellent Master • Degree of Thrice Illustrious Master (Silver Trowel) Holy Royal Arch • Ceremony of Exaltation

Masonic reference *continued*	• Installation of Joshua • Installation of Zerubbabel Holy Royal Arch Knights Templar Priests • Installation of Knight Templar Priest Red Cross of Constantine • Knight of the Holy Sepulchre • Knight of St John the Evangelist Knights Templar Societas Rosicruciana in Anglia • Sixth Grade 'Adeptus Major'

It was around the time of Saul and David, about 950 BC, that the Hebrew language was first written down. Prior to this, all the Bible stories had been passed on by word of mouth or recorded in other ancient languages. Freemasons, who have to learn their ritual off by heart, will appreciate the time that these story tellers must have spent on memorising many books. These ancient 'books' were papyrus scrolls, with a small piece of wood at each end. The Dead Sea scrolls are examples of this medium.

In relation to writing, David is significant in the Bible, as he is believed to be the author of the Book of Psalms, which consists of 150 short religious poems. The word 'psalm' is derived from the Greek meaning 'songs sung to the harp'. The Book of Psalms has always been popular with Christians and over 30 psalms are quoted in or form part of Masonic ceremonies. The following have been identified as being linked to the ritual:

Psalm 11 – Rather aptly, the first Psalm used features in the Second or Prince Degree of the Order of the Secret Monitor, which is concerned with the life of King David. Verses 1, 2, 4 and 5 are recited during the ritual and these relate to honest people putting their trust in God and punishments for the wicked.

Psalm 15 – In the Allied Masonic Degrees, the Bible must be opened at Psalm 15 during the Knight of Constantinople ceremony and five verses are used as the closing prayer in the Silver Trowel. The Knight of Constantinople degree teaches the lessons of humility and this Psalm gives examples of behaviour pleasing to God. This includes being an upright man, speaking the truth, keeping promises and not being involved in gossip. It also forbids the charging of interest by money lenders.

Psalm 18 – Seventeen verses of this Song of Victory are quoted during the Silver Trowel ceremony. The Psalm refers to God as a rock, a protector and a light in the darkness. The degree is set during the time of David and the final verse contains a promise that God will be merciful to David and his descendants forever. Verse 35 refers to the 'shield of thy salvation' and this is possibly the origin of the 'Shield of David' or, as it is more commonly known, the 'Star of David'. This is referred to in Hebrew as *Magen David* in the first grade of the Scarlet Cord. The symbol is not described in the Bible, but the shape features on the Chapter Jewel.

Psalm 19 – The wording of the first verse is very similar to parts of the lecture on the Working Tools in the Royal Ark Mariner ceremony – 'The heavens declare the glory of God; and the firmament sheweth his handiwork.'

Psalm 22 – According to the Gospel of St Matthew, the first verse was quoted by Jesus whilst on the cross – 'My God, my God, why have you forsaken me?' In the Knight of St John the Evangelist ceremony it is rendered in Aramaic (possibly Jesus's mother tongue) as 'Eloi, Eloi lama sabachthani'.

Psalm 23 – This is arguably the most famous Psalm ('The Lord is my Shepherd') and the phrase 'valley of the shadow of death' is used in at least four Masonic ceremonies, including the Third Degree prayer, during the Super-Excellent Master degree, as a section of King David's speech in the Silver Trowel and as part of the sixth grade of SRIA. All degrees study, in some way, human mortality. It is worth including this short, but beautiful, Psalm I in its entirety:

> The Lord is my shepherd; I shall not want. He maketh me to lie down in green pastures; he leadeth me beside the still waters. He: restoreth my soul; he leadeth me in the paths of righteousness for his name's sake. Yea, though I walk through the valley of the shadow of death, I will fear no evil; for thou art with me; thy rod and thy staff they comfort me. Thou preparest a table before me in the presence of mine enemies; thou anointest my head with oil; my cup runneth over. Surely goodness and mercy shall follow me all the days of my life; and I will dwell in the house of the Lord forever.

Psalm 24 – The opening prayer in the Most Excellent Master degree is based on this Psalm, particularly the references to 'clean hands and a pure heart' and being 'found worthy to stand in His holy place.'

Psalm 25 – During the Installation Ceremony in a Craft lodge, the Junior Warden is informed that the plumb rule is an emblem of 'uprightness' and 'points out the integrity' required in ruling the lodge. Both integrity and uprightness appear in verse 21 of this Psalm.

Psalm 33 – Verse 9 of this Psalm is used in the prayer during the Royal Ark Mariner degree and is rendered as 'Who didst speak and it was done, Who didst command and it stood fast.' Verse 7 refers to the 'waters of the sea' and the Psalm may have been selected due to this nautical reference as the degree is based on the story of Noah.

Psalm 40 – The named used for the Bible by Freemasons – the 'Volume of the Sacred Law' – may be derived from the phrase 'volume of the book' which appears in this Psalm and is later quoted in the Letter to Hebrews (see section on St Paul). This Psalm also has the first mention of the 'wonderful works' of God (see also Psalms 78, 107 and 111), as recalled in the Craft Second Degree, where the candidate is told to 'estimate the wonderful works of the Almighty Creator.'

Psalm 44 – The first section of the first verse – 'We have heard with our ears, O God, our fathers have told us' is paraphrased during the Exaltation Ceremony in a Holy Royal Arch Chapter.

Psalm 50 – This Psalm uses the title 'Most High' for God. It is included in the Book of Common Prayer (see section of the same name). This book had considerable influence on Chapter ritual (see also Psalm 83).

Psalm 55 – The phrase 'terrors of death' from this Psalm is used in the lecture on 'Faith' in the Knight of the Holy Sepulchre ceremony. This oration makes clear that such terrors cannot destroy faith. The phrase 'terrors of death' also features in the Knights Templar Priest degree.

Psalm 57 – The Closing Prayer of the Scarlet Cord includes a reference to being safe with God under the 'shadow of His wing' to rest 'secure from harm'. This appears to be a paraphrase of verse one, but the expression 'shadow of Thy wings' also appears in Psalms 17, 36 and 63.

Psalm 65 – This is a hymn of thanksgiving and the verse including the phrase 'Blessed is the man whom thou choosest' is read out during the Knights Templar Priest ceremony.

Psalm 68 – The name of God is shown as *Jah* (see section on Moses). This is used during the installation of the principal officer in a Holy Royal Arch chapter.

Psalm 69 – In the Second Degree, the word 'Shibboleth' is said to represent 'an ear of corn near a fall of water'. The 'ear of corn' is from the story of Joseph and his dreams (see section on Jacob), but The Hebrew word 'Shibboleth' is also found in this Psalm, where it relates to 'the floods'.

Psalm 78 – This is not used directly in Masonic ritual, but may be relevant as it relates to telling stories with secret meanings – the King James' Version refers to them as 'dark sayings'. (See section on Parables of Jesus). This is the second Psalm to include a reference to the 'wonderful works' of God as used in the Fellowcraft ceremony.

Psalm 79 – In verse 2 this Psalm contains the punishment of being fed to the 'fowls of heaven' and the 'beasts of the earth'. As with David's threat to Goliath (see above) this may be the origin of the physical penalty associated with the Second Degree in Craft masonry.

Psalm 80 – The first verse of this Psalm is included in the lecture during the Order of Grand High Priest, where it describes God as dwelling 'between the cherubims' (see section on Ark of the Covenant). (The Biblical use of the word 'cherubims' is grammatically incorrect as 'Cherubim' is already the plural of 'cherub'.) The 'Divine Presence' on the Ark of the Covenant is further explained during the lecture on the Royal Master degree.

Psalm 83 – God is described as 'Jehovah' who is 'the most high over all the earth'. This name of God and his title from this Psalm are significant in the Holy Royal Arch.

Psalm 84 – The Bible is opened at this Psalm during each of the Grades in the Scarlet Cord. Part of verse 10, 'I had rather be a doorkeeper in the house of my God, than to dwell in the tents of wickedness,' is also read out in the First Grade ceremony.

Psalm 103 – This Psalm contains several Masonic references from at least four different ceremonies. In verse 12 there is a reference to east and west, a constant theme in Masonic degrees. In verse 14, it states that God 'knoweth our frame, he remembereth that we are dust'. This may be linked to the human 'perishable frame' as noted in the Third Degree and the fact that that we will all crumble to dust, which is recalled in the Royal Master ceremony. The next verse refers to the 'flowers of the field', which are recalled in Working Tools section of the Royal Ark Mariner degree. Finally, 'children's children' are mentioned in verse 17 and this phrase is used in the Address to the Brethren during the Installation Ceremony of a new Master.

Psalm 106 – This Psalm reiterates the story from the Grand High Priest and Knights Templar Priest ceremonies (see section on Moses) where God caused the earth to swallow up Dathan for challenging the authority of Moses and Aaron. Verses 47 and 48 are slightly amended when used as the Closing Prayer in the Grand High Priest ceremony – 'May the Lord save us and gather us from among the nations.' (Psalms uses 'heathen' instead of 'nations'.)

Psalm 107 – Verse 29 and verse 33 are paraphrased to form the Closing Prayer in the Royal Ark Mariner degree, in particular, 'maketh the storm to cease', the 'waves to be still' and 'water springs into dry ground'. This Psalm has four references to the 'wonderful works' of the Lord, as recalled in the Craft Second Degree.

Psalm 110 – This contains a reference to Melchizedek being a priest forever. (See section on Melchizedek.) Melchizedek features in the Order of the Grand High Priest and the Red Cross of Constantine.

Psalm 111 – This includes a further reference to the 'wonderful works' of God.

Psalm 118 – This Psalm was quoted by Jesus and relates to the headstone being rejected. It is particularly significant in the Mark Degree. (See sections on the Ministry of Jesus and Stone for the Temple).

Psalm 119 – The longest Psalm in the Bible is a hymn of praise to God's commandments. It is quoted twice in the Knights Templar Priest ritual. There is a slight change to one verse. The Bible states 'not let any iniquity have dominion over me' whilst in the ceremony the last word is 'thee'. On each of the seven pillars used in the ceremony is a lamp, hence the use of the verse 'Thy word is a lamp unto my feet, and a light unto my path.' In the 1840 English 'Psalter' ('Book of Psalms') verse 158 is translated to include 'Thy Holy will and word', which features during a prayer during the Chapter installation ceremony.

Psalm 121 – This is used in the Silver Trowel and refers to God guarding his people. The Psalm states that the Lord will 'neither slumber or sleep'. A very similar reference appears during the explanation of God's 'All Seeing Eye' on the Mark Tracing Board and during the Second Grade of the Scarlet Cord.

Psalm 122 – This Psalm is used as the opening prayer in the Silver Trowel and it is quoted during the Knights Templar ceremony and in the Second Degree of the Order of the Secret Monitor. It is a prayer for peace in Jerusalem and David also prays for his 'brethren' (used to denote members of Craft lodges) and 'companions' (used to denote members of a Chapter). The Psalm also contains 'Peace be within thy walls' and a similar phrase appears in the Address to the Brethren during the Craft Installation ceremony.

Psalm 132 – The Closing Prayer in the Mark Degree appears to utilise the expression 'His habitation' from this Psalm, which states that the Lord has chosen 'Zion' (Jerusalem) as his home.

Psalm 133 – The short Psalm is recited during the Installation of a Master (Supreme Ruler) in the Order of the Secret Monitor. Additionally, in Craft masonry during the First Degree ceremony, some lodges have the Bible open at this Psalm, which includes the line: 'Behold, how good and how pleasant it is for brethren to dwell together in unity!' This phrase is an unattributed quote in the Grand High Priest ritual. The use of the word 'Brethren' makes the Masonic connection obvious.

Psalm 134 – The first three verses of this Psalm are quoted during the Grand High Priest ceremony. It is unclear why these verses were selected as it is a prayer for the night guard at the temple.

Psalm 136 – As with the Book of Genesis, this Psalm contains a reference to the sun ruling the day and the moon ruling the night. These words are paraphrased during the Masonic initiation ceremony.

Psalm 137 – This verse seems to have been written long after the time of David and alludes to the exile in Babylon (see section on the Destruction of Jerusalem). The first verse has been used in popular music – 'By the rivers of Babylon, there we sat down, yea we wept, when we remembered Zion.'

ARAUNAH THE JEBUSITE

Timeline	1000 BC
Biblical reference	Numbers • Chapter 1 (People are counted) • Chapter 26 (People are counted) Judges • Chapter 19 v10 (Jerusalem known as 'Jebus') II Samuel • Chapter 24 v1–15 (Numbers the people) • Chapter 24 v16–25 (Threshing Floor) I Chronicles • Chapter 21 (Numbers the people and Threshing Floor)
Masonic reference	Craft • First Degree Tracing Board (Emulation and Logic Ritual) Holy Royal Arch Historical Lecture

Included in the explanation of the First Degree Tracing Board and during Chapter ritual, is the story of David 'numbering' his people, an act which incurred the wrath of God. The moral of the story is unclear as in the Book of Numbers Moses is shown to have twice counted the Israelites at God's command. It appears, however, that David was being punished for his pride in having a survey conducted of the number of fighting troops available to him. It should also be noted that the Book of Chronicles states that Satan 'provoked' David into this action. God offered David the choice of three awful punishments:

1   Seven years of famine
2   Three months at the mercy of Israel's enemies
3   Three days pestilence throughout the land

David chose the latter and 70,000 men died. The Angel of the Lord was to destroy Jerusalem, but God stopped the angel as it was standing on a threshing floor located on Mount Moriah. This location, on the top of a hill, would have been ideal for separating wheat from the chaff – the purpose of a threshing floor. The area belonged to Araunah (called 'Ornan' in Chronicles), who is described in the Bible and Chapter ritual as a 'Jebusite'. The Jebusites were the rulers of Jerusalem before David had captured the city and it is recorded in the Book of Judges that Jerusalem was originally known as 'Jebus'.

In gratitude, David bought this piece of land on Mount Moriah and this was later selected as the location of King Solomon's Temple. It should be recalled that this is the same place as Abraham had intended to sacrifice Isaac. According to the explanation of the First Degree Tracing Board, 'our lodges stand on holy ground, because the first lodge was consecrated on account of three grand offerings made thereon.' These three offerings are the sacrifice of Isaac, David's prayers on the threshing floor and the consecration of King Solomon's Temple – the 'First Lodge' according to Craft ritual or, rather confusingly, the 'Second or sacred lodge' in the Holy Royal Arch.

THE MIGHTY MEN AND OTHER CHARACTERS IN THE STORY OF KING DAVID

Timeline	1000 BC
Biblical reference	I Samuel • Chapter 26 v5–12 (Abishai and Saul's spear) II Samuel • Chapter 3 (Joab kills General Abner) • Chapter 7 v2 (Nathan the prophet) • Chapter 8 v16 (Joab is captain in David's army) • Chapter 11 v14–25 (Joab and Uriah) • Chapter 15 v24 (Zadok and the Ark of the Covenant) • Chapter 18 v2 (Abishai commands a third of army) • Chapter 20 v23 (Joab is captain in David's army) • Chapter 21 v1–9 (David spares Saul's grandson) • Chapter 21 v17 (Abishai saves David) • Chapter 23 v8–12 (The mighty men) • Chapter 23 v15–17 (Water from the well for David) • Chapter 23 v20 (Benaiah fights a lion) • Chapter 24 v2–4 (Joab advises against numbering) I Kings

Biblical reference continued	• Chapter 1 v5–7 (Joab supports Adonijah) • Chapter 1 v8 (Benaiah and Zadok loyal to Solomon) • Chapter 1 v24–26 (Nathan warns of Adonijah's plot) • Chapter 1 v32–40 (Zadok anoints Solomon as king) • Chapter 2 v28–34 (Benaiah kills Joab) • Chapter 4 v5 (Nathan was father of Zabud) I Chronicles • Chapter 2 v49 (Machbenah) • Chapter 11 v6 (Joab is captain in David's army) • Chapter 11 v22 (Benaiah fights a lion) • Chapter 12 v13 (Machbanai) • Chapter 15 v18 ('Brethren of the second degree') • Chapter 18 v15 (Joab is captain in David's army) • Chapter 20 v1 (Joab fights the Ammonites) • Chapter 21 v1–6 (Joab advises against numbering the people) • Chapter 27 v34 (Joab promoted to General) • Chapter 29 v29 (Nathan wrote history of David) II Chronicles • Chapter 31 v13 (Benaiah is an overseer) Matthew • Chapter 26 v52 (Those who live by the sword)
Masonic reference	Craft • Third Degree Order of the Secret Monitor • Second or Prince Degree • Scarlet Cord – All grades Royal and Select Masters • Degree of Thrice Illustrious Master (Silver Trowel) Holy Royal Arch Knights Templar Priests • Installation of a Knight Templar Priest

The stories of several obscure Biblical characters from this period are celebrated most notably in the Second or Prince degree of the Order of the Secret Monitor and members of the lodge take the names of Abishai, Adino, Eleazar and Shammah. Zadok, the first high priest appointed in the new capital, Jerusalem, and Nathan, the prophet at this time also feature in Masonic ritual. They feature in the Thrice Illustrious Master or Silver Trowel degree and the Royal Order of the Scarlet Cord. Most significantly, however, one of the names of the Mighty Men is a very important feature of the Third Degree.

The Silver Trowel is a North American degree, recently introduced into England for Installed Masters of a Council of Royal and Select Masters. The Scarlet Cord was an appendant rite of the Order of the Secret Monitor, which has recently been re-established, having been suspended in 1929. The qualification requires an applicant to hold the rank of 'Prince' in the Order of the Secret Monitor and be a member of the Benevolent Fund.

During David's reign, God sent a three-year famine to punish Israel for Saul's actions. The Gibeonites wanted to kill the descendants of Saul to appease the Lord. Seven sons were hanged, but David saved Mephibosheth as he had made an agreement with Jonathan. (Mephibosheth was son of Jonathan and therefore the grandson of Saul). This story is related in the Order of the Secret Monitor.

According to the Bible, David does much battle with the Philistines and his generals and warriors ('Mighty Men') are described. A significant character is General Abishai, who commanded a third of the Israelite army. Earlier in the life of David, Abishai and his future king had managed to creep into Saul's camp at night. Abishai had urged David to kill the sleeping King Saul, but David refused as Saul had been chosen by God. Instead, they took Saul's spear to show they had entered his trench. Abishai later saved David from being killed by a Philistine. As a reward, David removed him from front-line fighting, describing Abishai as the 'light of Israel' (meaning 'greatest leader'). This incident is related in the Knights Templar Priest ceremony.

The 'Mighty Men' included Adino, Eleazar and Shammah and they are claimed to have killed hundreds of Philistines single handedly. Adino reputedly killed 800 men with his spear! When King David was desperate for a drink during battle, these men broke through the Philistine ranks, just to bring him water from a well near the gates of Bethlehem. David refused to drink it, saying that it would be like drinking the blood of his brave warriors. This is featured in the third grade of the Scarlet Cord.

Three further characters from the story of David feature in the Scarlet Cord. Two 'Mighty Men' and a High Priest give their names to the three wings of the fund; Joab for the old age section, Zadok for sickness and Benaiah (or Banaiah) for education.

Joab was a nephew of King David, who held the rank of captain in the Israelite Army and fought against the hated Ammonites. He advised David not to count (the Bible uses the verb 'number') the people, but was ordered by the king to do so. This resulted in God punishing Israel (see section on Araunah). Joab was a successful soldier and was promoted to general after leading an assault on a fortress on Mount Zion in Jerusalem. Unfortunately, he was also involved in the treacherous politics of the time and assisted King David by placing General Uriah in the most dangerous part of a siege, to ensure Uriah was killed (see section on David for motives).

Earlier in his career, Joab had murdered Abner, another of David's generals, in revenge for the death of his brother. Jesus said, 'All that take the sword will perish by the sword' and Joab was to suffer a similar fate as that of his victims. He was later killed by another Israelite officer, Benaiah (see section on King Solomon), who also features in the Scarlet Cord.

General Benaiah was another of David's 'Mighty Men', who is reputed to have killed an eight-foot-tall Egyptian and fought with a lion for the amusement of the king. From a Masonic view point, he is interestingly described in the Bible as being part of the 'brethren of the second degree' when the Ark of the Covenant was transferred to Jerusalem at the time of King David. This title relates to the second tier of priests and is not connected with the Masonic Fellow Craft ceremony. Benaiah also served King Solomon and was head of the army after the death of Joab. Another man called Benaiah, who lived some centuries later when Israel was divided, is described as an 'Overseer', a title used in the Mark Degree.

Zadok was not a military man. He was the first high priest to hold the position in the new capital city of Israel during the reign of King David. When Nathan, the prophet, warned David that his eldest son, Adonijah, had attempted to claim the throne, Zadok and Benaiah were loyal to Solomon. On David's command, Zadok anointed Solomon as his successor. Joab had sided with Adonijah and this appears to have sealed his fate. Benaiah killed Adonijah shortly before disposing of Joab. These deaths secured Solomon's position as king. The story of Adonijah's attempted coup is related in the Silver Trowel.

The names David, Zadok and Nathan are titles used by the senior officers during the Silver Trowel ceremony. Nathan appears throughout the story of David, telling the king of God's displeasure at his unfaithfulness with Bathsheba and informing David that he would have to allow his son to build the temple (see section on David). The Bible states that Nathan recorded a history of the king. Nathan is further linked to the Royal and Select Masters ceremony as he was the father of Zabud (see Officers of King Solomon), who plays an important role in the Select Master degree.

Finally, we come to a man described as the eleventh member of a band of King David's warriors. This is Machbenah or Machbanai (it is spelt in several ways). This name literally means 'the builder is smitten' and this is how it appears in the Third Degree as one of the most important phrases in the ceremony, describing the death of Hiram Abif (see later section). It demonstrates the ritual writers' knowledge of Hebrew and their willingness to search the Bible for words and phrases relevant to the ceremonies.

As we saw in the section on David, when the king was elderly, he handed over power to his son, Solomon. We now turn to the time of Solomon, an extremely important character in many Masonic degrees.

The Builders of King Solomon's Temple

Solomon, King of Israel

Timeline	962 BC – Solomon becomes king 938 BC – Death of Solomon
Biblical reference	I Kings • Chapter 1 v28–48 (Solomon made king) • Chapter 1 v35 (Benaiah made head of the army) • Chapter 2 v12–46 (Solomon takes control) • Chapter 4 v29–30 and v34 (Wisdom of Solomon) • Chapter 5 v12 (Alliance with King Hiram) • Chapter 6 (Solomon builds the Temple) • Chapter 10 v1–10 (Visit of Queen of Sheba) • Chapter 10 v18 (Ivory throne) • Chapter 11 (Numerous wives and resulting sins) • Chapter 11 v42–43 (Reign and death) II Chronicles • Chapter 1 v9–12 (Given wisdom by God) • Chapter 2 (Preparation for the Temple) • Chapter 3 (Solomon builds the Temple) • Chapter 9 v1–9 (Visit of Queen of Sheba) • Chapter 9 v30–31 (Reign and death) Matthew • Chapter 1 v6–7 (Solomon in genealogy of Jesus) • Chapter 6 v29 (Jesus speaks of glory of Solomon) Acts • Chapter 7 v47 (Solomon built the temple)
Masonic reference	Craft – All degrees

Masonic reference continued	Royal Ark Mariner • Tracing Board Allied Masonic Degrees • Grand Tilers of King Solomon Mark – All ceremonies Royal and Select Masters • Select Master • Royal Master • Most Excellent Master • Degree of Thrice Illustrious Master (Silver Trowel) Holy Royal Arch • Historical Lecture • Symbolical Lecture • Mystical Lecture • Questions before Toasts Holy Royal Arch Knights Templar Priests Red Cross of Constantine • Knight of the Holy Sepulchre Order of Athelstan Knights Templar

King Solomon is, arguably, the most important Biblical character in Masonic ritual. The Grand Master is said to represent the 'Royal Solomon' in the opening ceremony of a Grand Lodge. Most degrees are described as 'Solomonic' – that is connected with the period of Solomon or subsequent rulers around that period. It would be far easier to state which degrees he does not feature in, rather than those in which he does. According to ritual in the Knight of the Holy Sepulchre, an Appendant Order of the Red Cross of Constantine, Solomon, together with Moses and Zerubbabel, were the founders of Freemasonry.

Having been selected as his successor by David, Solomon was anointed king by the high priest, Zadok, in the presence of Nathan, the prophet and General Benaiah (see section on Mighty Men). The Silver Trowel ceremony relates the Biblical account of this incident, which occurred at Gihon Spring, the main water supply for Jerusalem. (This Gihon must not be confused with the River Gihon, which is noted in Genesis as being one of the four rivers near the Garden of Eden).

Solomon initially forgave his elder brother Adonijah for his attempted coup, but after the death of David, Solomon had General Benaiah kill Adonijah. Solomon also had Benaiah dispose of Joab following advice from his father just before his death that Joab had been involved in much betrayal and murder – some of this on David's orders! Joab had been a trusted advisor of David (see Mighty Men). For his loyalty (and ruthlessness), Benaiah took over Joab's role as head of the Israelite army. At this point the Bible reads like a plot from the 'Godfather' series of films.

A time of peace then followed and Solomon continued the successful alliance with Hiram, King of Tyre, developed by his father, David. The trade links between the two are shown in the Bible and in the Royal Master degree the Biblical claim that Solomon had an ivory throne is reiterated. This clearly demonstrates the use of Hiram's Phoenician trade routes with India or Africa. Many of these imported goods were used by Solomon to build a magnificent temple for the Lord. This is covered extensively in Chapters 6 and 7 of this book. Solomon's riches were such that nearly 1000 years after the king's death, Christ referred to it during His teachings.

On the Royal Ark Mariner Tracing Board (see image on section on Noah) a five-pointed star is shown. This is believed to be the jewel or badge of office worn by the Master of a lodge during the eighteenth century. It is claimed to be the 'Seal of Solomon' (although this reference was removed in the 2010 version of the ritual). This description does not appear to be correct as the Jewish Star of David has six points (see section on Psalms). There is no reference to the 'seal' in the Bible. It has been suggested (Knight and Lomas 2003), that this five-pointed star refers to Venus; the orbit of the planet, when observed from earth, does make five points. Venus is the 'bright and morning star' and this is the name Jesus referred to himself by in Revelation (see section on that book).

Solomon's wisdom is renowned (see next section) but as he grew old he upset God by marrying foreign wives, including women of the hated Ammonites. These wives led him to follow other gods and God's punishment was that Solomon's kingdom would be torn apart when the throne passed to his son (see section on the Division of Israel). Solomon reigned for 40 years, during which the kingdom of Israel reached its zenith. When he died he was buried in Bethlehem with his father, David. The kingdom then passed to his unpopular son, Rehoboam. It should be noted that St Matthew (unlike St Luke) places Solomon and Rehoboam in the genealogy of Jesus.

THE WISDOM OF KING SOLOMON AND THE BOOK OF PROVERBS

Timeline	1000 BC
Biblical reference	I Kings • Chapter 3 v9–10 (Solomon prays for wisdom) • Chapter 3 v16–28 (Solomon's wisdom) Proverbs • Chapter 2 v1–9 (Rewards of wisdom) • Chapter 3 v1–6 (Advice to children) • Chapter 3 v13–20 (Value of wisdom) • Chapter 3 v17 ('All her paths are peace') • Chapter 4 v9 (Crown of glory) • Chapter 4 v18 (Shineth more unto the perfect day) • Chapter 4 v26–27 (Keep to the path of virtue) • Chapter 9 v1–6 (Pillars of wisdom) • Chapter 10 v29 (The way of the Lord) • Chapter 10 v31 (Evil tongue cut out) • Chapter 13 v9 ('The light of the righteous') • Chapter 15 v3 (All Seeing Eye of God) • Chapter 15 v33 (Wisdom and humility) • Chapter 17 v6 ('Children's children')

Biblical reference continued	• Chapter 18 v10 (Strong tower) • Chapter 22 v28 (Landmarks) • Chapter 25 v4 (Removing dross from silver) • Chapter 25 v18 (Maul described as a weapon) • Chapter 30 v8–9 (Hiram Abif's prayer) Ecclesiastes • Chapter 9 v8 (White garments) • Chapter 12 v1–8 (The problems of old age) • Chapter 12 v13 (The 'whole duty of man') Wisdom of Solomon • Chapter 8 v7 (Cardinal Virtues) • Chapter 14 v1–8 (Thanksgiving for Noah)
Masonic reference	Craft • First Degree • Second Degree • Third Degree • Installation Ceremony Allied Masonic Degrees • St Lawrence the Martyr Mark • Ceremony of Advancement • Tracing Board Royal and Select Masters • Royal Master • Super-Excellent Master • Degree of Thrice Illustrious Master (Silver Trowel) Holy Royal Arch • Ceremony of Exaltation Holy Royal Arch Knights Templar Priests • Installation of a Knight Templar Priest Societas Rosicruciana in Anglia • First Grade 'Zelator' • Fifth Grade 'Adeptus Minor'

King Solomon's wisdom is legendary. He was granted wisdom by God and the famous story of him offering to divide a baby in two when two women claimed to be the mother is related in the First Book of Kings. Masonic lodges are said to be supported by three Great Pillars, symbolising wisdom, strength and beauty. These pillars are represented in lodges by elaborate candlesticks by the chairs occupied by the Master in the east, Senior Warden in the west and Junior Warden in the

The Judgement of Solomon (1649) by Nicolas Poussin.

south. The pillars are in the form of the Ionic, Doric and Corinthian orders of architecture respectively. Unsurprisingly, the 'wisdom', or Ionic pillar, is said to represent King Solomon.

In some versions of Chapter ritual, the wisdom of Solomon is said to be represented by the 'Bible'. This is one of the rare occasions when the Bible is referred to by name. It is usually called by an ecumenical term, such as 'Sacred Writings' or 'Sacred Volume'; this should be the case in the Holy Royal Arch, which is not exclusively Christian. It is unclear why the ritual is worded in this way. In the Royal Order of Scotland, the Holy Book is also referred to as 'the Bible'.

King Solomon is traditionally believed to be the author of the Books of Proverbs, Ecclesiastes and the Wisdom of Solomon. Indeed, the Hebrew title of Proverbs is the 'Proverbs of Solomon'. Sections of the Book of Proverbs, which relate to the benefits of wisdom, are quoted during ceremonies, particularly some versions of Chapter ritual. Chapter 2 observes the reward of wisdom and the first seven verses are read out in the Silver Trowel ceremony. One verse observes that God is a 'buckler' (a shield) to the upright. According to Proverbs, wisdom will deliver a 'crown of glory'. Wisdom is also the subject of Chapter 10, v31 and some Craft lodges open the Bible at this page during the initiation ceremony – 'The mouth of the just bringeth forth wisdom: but the froward tongue shall be cut out.'

This verse is linked to the ancient penalty of having the 'tongue torn out by the root' ('froward' is an old English word meaning 'turning away from', as in turning away from the right path). Part of the same Proverb is used in the Knights Templar Priest ceremony, 'The way of the Lord is strength to the upright: but destruction shall be to the workers of iniquity.'

Chapter 3 contains advice on behaviour. The first six verses are used in the Silver Trowel and they relate to obeying and trusting God and being kind and truthful. The chapter goes on to observe the value of wisdom and this is quoted during the first grade of the Societas Rosicruciana in Anglia ceremony. Speaking of wisdom, the Proverb notes that 'Her ways are ways of pleasantness, and all her paths are peace.' This is also the origin of the last line of the famous hymn, 'I Vow to Thee My Country.'

In Chapter, Mark and Royal Master ceremonies, God is said to have an 'all seeing eye' and whilst this phrase does not appear in the Bible, it appears to be linked to Proverbs, Chapter 15: 'The eyes of the Lord are in every place, beholding the evil and the good.'

In the Knights Templar Priest ceremony there are seven pillars and Proverb 9 is quoted, which relates that Wisdom has 'hewn out her seven pillars'. These pillars appear to be represented twice on the Royal Ark Mariner Tracing Board, firstly behind the image of Enoch and second, as a very small triangle of pillars under the representation of the nine arches. The number seven features continually throughout the Bible and Masonic ritual (see Ezekiel).

The Knights Templar Priest degree obviously has a military element, given the warrior status of the original Knights Templar (see section on this Order) and may be the reason for the use of Proverb 18, which observes that 'the name of the Lord is a strong tower.' As we saw in the section on Psalms, each of the pillars in the Knights Templar Priest ceremony have a lamp placed on them and this is the reason for the use of the section of Proverb 13: 'The light of the righteous rejoiceth: but the lamp of the wicked shall be put out'.

According to the Masonic legend of Hiram Abif, the 'maul' (from the Middle English 'mealle', a mace, club or heavy hammer) is the weapon that finally kills the temple architect. The maul appears in Proverbs in a similar manner: 'A man that beareth false witness against his neighbour is a maul, and a sword, and a sharp arrow.' The same chapter also includes a reference to removing 'dross from silver'. This may be the basis to a prayer in the Rose Croix ceremony, part of which includes the phrase that the members 'may be enabled to distinguish the precious metal from the dross'.

During the explanation of the Working Tools in the Second Degree ceremony, candidates are advised 'to walk justly and uprightly before God and man, neither turning to the right nor left from the paths of virtue'. This appears to be from Chapter 4 of Proverbs, which gives very similar advice: 'Ponder the path of thy feet … Turn not to the right hand nor to the left.' During the lecture on the Super-Excellent Master degree the candidate is advised to enlighten his mind, to become 'wiser and better, shining more and more unto the perfect day'. The latter part of the sentence is also taken from Chapter 4.

When a lodge is opened in the degree of St Lawrence the Martyr, the ritual directs that the Bible must be opened to show Chapter 15 v33 of the Book of Proverbs; 'The fear of the Lord is the instruction of wisdom; and before honour is humility.' A further example of the use of Biblical phrases in ritual is the use of the expression 'children's children' in the Craft Installation Ceremony. This is also from Proverbs.

'The Ancient Landmarks of the Order' are noted in the Charge to the Initiate and during the obligation of a new Master, who promises to uphold them. These ancient customs are not clearly defined and there is debate as to what exactly is a Masonic landmark. In any case, this may be based on Proverbs – 'Remove not the ancient landmark which thy fathers have set.'

Ecclesiastes appears in various rituals, but a large part of Chapter 12, which relates to the problems of growing old, is read out in some lodges during the Third Degree ceremony. It is also part of the fifth grade of SRIA and the first line of the chapter 'Remember now thy Creator in the days of thy youth' is used in the Silver Trowel as part of King David's dying speech to his son. These verses contain poetic language describing the arms as 'keepers of the house', legs as 'strong men', teeth as 'grinders' and white hair as the blossom on an 'almond tree'. A reference to 'let thy garments be always white' may be the reason that some officers and the candidate are clothed in white surpluses during the ceremony. Chapter 12 also declares that the 'whole duty of man' is to 'fear God' and 'keep his Commandments'. When a new Master of a Craft lodge is installed, he is told that the Bible explains the 'whole duty of man'. Chapter 3 of Ecclesiastes is the basis of the 1965 hit record *Turn, Turn, Turn* by The Byrds. Hence, in addition to his important role in Freemasonry, King Solomon holds the record for being the most ancient composer of a Number One single in the American charts!

The Biblical book entitled Wisdom of Solomon does not appear in the King James' Version of the Bible, but it is included in Roman Catholic versions. Interestingly, it includes a reference to prudence, temperance, fortitude and justice. These appear twice during the initiation ceremony (see section on St Thomas Aquinas). There is also a thanksgiving prayer for the salvation of the Ark (see section on Noah).

HIRAM, KING OF TYRE AND SIDONIA

Timeline	Reign 969–936 BC
Biblical reference	I Kings • Chapter 5 v1–11(Assistance given to Solomon) • Chapter 5 v12 (Alliance with Solomon) • Chapter 9 v26–28 (Assists Solomon's navy) • Chapter 10 v22 (Further naval assistance) II Chronicles • Chapter 2 v3–9 (Request for craftsmen and materials) • Chapter 2 v10 (Agreed price)
Masonic reference	Craft • First Degree Tracing Board • Second Degree Tracing Board • Third Degree Allied Masonic Degrees • Grand Tilers of Solomon Mark • Ceremony of Advancement Royal and Select Masters • Select Master • Royal Master • Most Excellent Master Holy Royal Arch • Historical Lecture • Symbolical Lecture • Mystical Lecture • Questions before Toasts Holy Royal Arch Knights Templar Priests Rose Croix • 22 Degree – Prince of Libanus Knights Templar

King Hiram ruled an area known by several names – Tyria, Sidonia and Phoenicia, although its precise boundaries are unknown. It covered many of the most important cities and areas of the Holy Land:

Tyre – Founded around 3000 BC, this famous port had fabulous defences which broke many an attempted siege. The name is derived from the word for 'rock'. It was built on two islands and then land reclaimed from the sea. From a Masonic point of view, it is important as the seat of King Hiram and also as the birthplace of Hiram Abif's father.

Sidon – another Mediterranean port and one of the oldest cities in the world (it features in Genesis, Chapter 10). Its name means 'fishing' and in his accounts of Ancient Greece, Homer noted the Sidonians' skill in workmanship and embroidery and this is verified in the Biblical description of Hiram Abif's skills. In the Mark Degree, reference is made to various punishments used by the Sidonians (see section on Organisation of Temple Workforce).

Gebal – also known by the Greek name 'Byblos'. This city developed the modern alphabet and its Greek name originates from the practice of exporting papyrus ('byblos') from the port. Hence it is linked to the word 'Bible'. In the Select Master Degree, 22 skilled craftsmen from the city are employed to assist King Solomon in constructing a secret vault under the Temple.

Lebanon – the forests of this area have been renowned from ancient times for cedar. (See section on Wood for the Temple). The ancient name for the area can be seen in the title of the Rose Croix degree 'Prince of Libanus'.

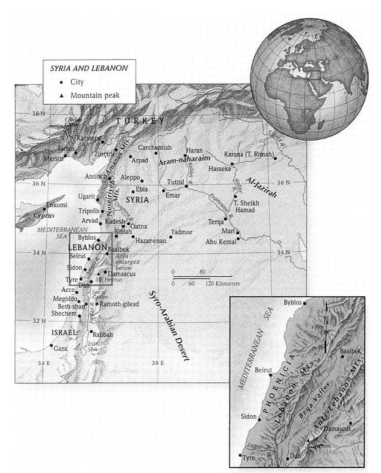

Lebanon – Tyre, Sidon and Byblos (known then as Gebal) are shown. Note that 'Jbail' is the modern name for Byblos/Gebal.

The name 'Phoenicia' from Greek, means 'Land of Purple' and the area was famed for the dyes created from the Murex sea snail. These dyes could give various shades of purple, blue and red. (See section on dyes).

As has been described in the section on King David, there were sound reasons for an alliance between King Hiram and the ruler of Israel. The Biblical accounts show that Hiram's sailors manned the navy of King Solomon at Ezion Geber and other Red Sea ports.

For Christians, it is important to note that King Hiram was a Gentile, a non-Jew, and yet he was still able to make a major contribution to the construction of the Temple. In Masonic lodges, he is represented by the Senior Warden in Craft Lodges and, according to the explanation of the First Degree Tracing Board, is said to be emblematic of 'strength' as he assisted King Solomon with 'men and materials'. This is clearly shown in the Biblical account. In various degrees, including the Knights Templar ceremony, he is one of the 'Three Grand Masters', who presided over the building of the temple. In the Select Master Degree, where the second highest officer plays the part of King Hiram, he is present to show the 'fellowship of kings' with Solomon.

HIRAM ABIF

Timeline	1000 BC
Biblical reference	I Kings • Chapter 7 v12–14 (Hiram Abif and his skills) II Chronicles • Chapter 2 v7 (Solomon requests a Master Craftsman) • Chapter 2 v13 (Hiram Abif named) • Chapter 2 v13–14 (Hiram Abif and his skills) Proverbs • Chapter 25 v18 (Maul described as a weapon) • Chapter 30 v8–9 (Hiram Abif's prayer) Ecclesiastes • Chapter 9 v5–10 (The dead know nothing) I Corinthians • Chapter 15 v55 (Death, where is thy sting?)
Masonic reference	Craft • First Degree Tracing Board • Second Degree Tracing Board • Third Degree Allied Masonic Degrees • Grand Tilers of Solomon Mark • Ceremony of Advancement • Lecture on the Degree

Masonic reference continued	Royal and Select Masters • Select Master • Royal Master • Most Excellent Master Holy Royal Arch • Historical Lecture • Symbolical Lecture • Mystical Lecture • Questions before Toasts Holy Royal Arch Knights Templar Priests Red Cross of Constantine • Installation of Knight • Knight of St John the Evangelist Knights Templar

From the late eighteenth century, the legend of Hiram Abif replaced that of Noah in Craft Rituals. Whilst Hiram and his skills are noted in the Books of Kings and Chronicles, his murder, burial in a shallow grave and subsequent re-interment near the 'Holy of Holies' are not. This minor Biblical character is, together with King Solomon, one of the most important in Masonic ritual.

It should first be clarified that there is nothing suspect in the fact that he is called 'Hiram' in Kings and 'Huram' in Chronicles (see section on The Translation of the Bible into English). Ancient Hebrew had no vowels and thus it is very difficult to establish the exact spelling or pronunciation of words. His surname 'Abif' is from Chronicles, Chapter 2, v13, where the verse does not seem to make sense, ending with 'Huram my father's' – the original would have read 'Huram Abi'. The section on the Translation of the Bible into English gives further details of the translation of his name.

The use of the word 'Abi' or 'Abif' meaning 'father' does not literally mean he was the biological parent of the person giving him that title. It means 'teacher' or 'counsellor' or one held in high esteem. As a Master Craftsman, it is an obvious title for Hiram to have been given. In the same sense, in Genesis Chapter 45, Joseph, son of Jacob, is made a 'father to Pharaoh'.

The Bible does give us numerous clues as to Hiram Abif's background. His father came from Tyre and his mother was a member of the tribe of Naphtali (from Kings) and lived in Dan (from Chronicles). This would strongly indicate that she lived in the town of Dan in the Naphtali tribal area (see map in section on Jephtha), on the northern border of Israel, rather than in the area occupied by the tribe of Dan in the south. It is the Book of Kings which describes him as a 'widow's son' – an important Masonic reference. Masons are often known as 'Sons of the Widow' and this is alluded to in various forms of the 'Sign of Distress' given in the Third Degree.

Hiram Abif would have been well suited to assist King Solomon. He may well have been bi-lingual, able to speak the language of Tyre and of Israel. His Tyrian background would have resulted in him having an apprenticeship in many crafts, whilst his Israelite mother would have taught him the law of Moses and belief in one God.

Hiram is described in Chronicles, which is read out in the Mark Degree, as being skilled in working with all manner of metals, stone, timber, dyes and linen. He was also an expert engraver. As such, he was no doubt involved in all areas related to the building of the Temple, including casting bronze vessels (Second Degree Tracing Board), building a secret vault (Select Master), inspecting craftsmanship (Royal Master) and placing the keystone in the sacred arch (Mark).

During the Craft Third Degree ceremony, Hiram Abif is described as praying in the Temple at 'High Twelve', or noon. This is when the rest of the work force has gone to refreshment. In the Royal Master degree, this legend is taken further and he meets Adoniram. In this account, Hiram Abif ensured that the sacred word was not lost by hiding a copy of it under the Holy of Holies, written in three languages (Syrian, Chaldean and Egyptian). During a moving ceremony, he informs Adoniram of this plan. The later discovery of the word is celebrated in the Exaltation Ceremony of a Royal Arch Chapter. During the Royal Master degree there are two Biblical quotations used when Hiram Abif is contemplating death. The first is from Ecclesiastes: 'The dead know not anything: their love, their hatred, their malice, their envy, is forgotten! Neither have they, henceforth, a portion in anything that is done under the sun'. (The ritual also uses part of a subsequent verse, which relates to there being no work or device in the grave).

The second is from the New Testament, from the first letter to the Corinthians 'O death, where is thy sting? O grave, where is thy victory?' These familiar words are used in the popular hymn, 'Abide with me'. They would not have been familiar at the time of Hiram Abif, as they were written over 1000 years after his death. (The Silver Trowel ceremony attributes these words to an even earlier character, King David).

Hiram Abif was all too timely in considering his own death. Freemasons will recall that fifteen Overseers employed at the temple, aggrieved that they were not in possession of the secrets of a Master Mason, conspired to attack Hiram Abif to force them from him. In the end, only three conspirators carried out the plan and waited for him at the three entrances of the Temple, where he had gone to pray, whilst the workforce were on a break. Despite being viciously assaulted by being struck about the head with workmen's tools (a level and plumb rule) and further threatened with a heavy maul (here a large wooden hammer), Hiram Abif steadfastly refused to disclose the secrets. It is also stated that to do so, he would require the assistance of the other two Grand Masters – Solomon, King of Israel and Hiram, King of Tyre. This is another link to Royal Arch Chapter ritual, where the sacred word can only be pronounced by three working together.

Whilst at the east entrance (main entry) to the temple Hiram was struck on the forehead with the maul and

Third Degree Tracing Board with references to Hiram Abif's death, including coffin shape, skull and crossbones, sprig of Acacia and the murder weapons (bottom centre).

died. The story of the murder is Masonic legend; the only Biblical feature is the use of a maul as a weapon, which is derived from the Book of Proverbs. During the Third Degree ceremony, the candidate plays the role of Hiram Abif. In the Christian order of the Red Cross of Constantine, the three attacks on the chief architect are compared to the three points of condemnation against Christ at the tribunals of Caiaphas the High Priest, Herod the King and Pilate the Roman Governor. The three blows represent the striking of Jesus' cheek, the beating with a stick and the crown of thorns. This is described in the Appendant Order of a Knight of St John the Evangelist.

The murder having been committed in King Solomon's Temple in Jerusalem, Hiram Abif's body was removed some distance and buried in a shallow grave. With this knowledge Freemasons may view the Second Degree Tracing Board in a different light – it shows two of the three crime scenes – the south and east entrances to the Temple, where the assaults on Hiram Abif took place.

Panic ensued when Hiram Abif could not be found and the twelve Overseers involved in the original conspiracy informed King Solomon of the evil plan. Three teams or 'lodges' of Fellowcrafts were then despatched to find him. One group returned having found nothing, but the second found Hiram Abif's body. To mark the spot, they placed a sprig of Acacia at the head of the grave. This is now an important Masonic symbol, which does not appear to originate from the Bible.

The third group located the murderers hidden in a cave, on their way to Joppa (see section on Joppa). There is a simple reason for their decision to make for that city. As the nearest port to Jerusalem, Joppa offered the quickest escape out of the country. They were taken back to King Solomon and sentenced to death.

Hiram Abif's dead body was recovered (in Masonic terms 'raised') from the makeshift grave, and various signs and words are derived from this incident. Once back in Jerusalem, the body was re-buried 'as near to the Sanctum Sanctorum as the Israelitish law would permit' as the Traditional History of the Third Degree relates. This means that he would have been buried somewhere on Mount Moriah.

It should be noted that unlike Jesus, Hiram Abif was not resurrected. The Third Degree in Craft Masonry and the Royal Master degree in the Order of Royal and Select Masters are a study of death and not resurrection. With the death of Hiram Abif, the sacred word was lost and, according to the ritual, King Solomon adopted 'substituted secrets' until 'time or circumstances should restore the genuine'. The 'time' for this is during the Exaltation to the Royal Arch.

In the Craft, Hiram Abif is represented by the Junior Warden and in consequence, the Junior Warden's chair has the most elaborate carving, using the form of the Corinthian column. Of the three pillars supporting a lodge, he is said to represent 'beauty' because of his 'curious and masterly workmanship' at the temple (these quotes are from the First Degree Tracing Board). During the Most Excellent Master degree, the Junior Warden's chair is left empty and is shrouded in black to mourn his death. In various Masonic degrees, Hiram Abif is referred to as the 'Third Grand Master', but in the Order of Royal and Select Masters, he is given the title 'Principal Conductor of the Work'. When a Craft Grand Lodge is opened, the Deputy Grand Master represents him.

OFFICERS OF KING SOLOMON

Timeline	960 BC
Biblical reference	I Kings • Chapter 1 v19 (Captain of the Host) • Chapter 4 v5–6 (Zabud and Ahishar) II Kings

Biblical reference continued	• Chapter 25 (Captain of the Guard)
Masonic reference	Allied Masonic Degrees • Grand Tilers of Solomon Royal and Select Masters • Select Master

During various Masonic ceremonies, candidates and officers assume the role of a character from the Bible. This is especially the case in the degrees of the Order of Royal and Select Masters. In the Select Master Degree, a story is related about an incursion into a secret vault by Zabud, a friend of King Solomon. Ahishar, who is supposed to be guarding the vault, is sentenced to death for sleeping at his post and Zabud replaces him as one of the 27 'Select Masters'. In reality, the mason playing the part of Ahishar is sent out of the lodge room and discreetly re-enters at an appropriate moment.

In addition to Adoniram (see below), Zabud and Ahishar have fleeting mentions in the Book of Kings. Zabud (son of the Prophet Nathan) is shown as priest and advisor to and friend of the king, whilst Ahishar is a 'steward' responsible for 'everything in the palace'. It is unclear why Zabud and Ahishar were selected for their respective roles in the Select Master story, but Ahishar's title of 'Steward' in the Bible explains why in this degree the Steward is the equivalent of the Inner Guard, who keeps out intruders. In the other Orders, the Steward is an assistant at formal Masonic dinner (Festive Board), who serves the wine and looks after guests.

The character of 'Joabert', the 'King's favourite' and principal secretary to King Solomon appears in the Grand Tilers degree. Joabert does not appear to be based on a Biblical character, but the story is very similar to the legend related in the Select Master ritual. The Grand Tilers ritual also has an officer acting as 'Captain of the Host'. This is a Biblical phrase, used throughout the Books of Samuel, Kings and Chronicles. In modern versions of the Bible it is translated as 'commander of the army'. In the ritual, it is a rather lower position, being the head guard of the secret vault. In a similar manner, an important officer in Royal and Select Masters councils is the 'Captain of the Guard'. He is presented as a member of King Solomon's staff, but in the Bible, the rank appears to refer to a Babylonian General, an enemy of Israel.

ADONIRAM

Timeline	1000–920 BC
Biblical reference	II Samuel • Chapter 20 v24 (In charge of David's slaves) I Kings • Chapter 4 v6 (In charge of Solomon's slaves) • Chapter 5 v13–14 (In charge of levy in Lebanon) • Chapter 12 v18 (Death by stoning) II Chronicles • Chapter 10 v18 (Death by stoning)

Masonic reference	Craft Installation Mark Ceremony of Advancement Royal and Select Masters Select Master Royal Master Red Cross of Constantine Installation of a Knight

Adoniram appears in the Bible in various other guises – Adoram and Hadoram. If this is the same man, he was a long serving servant to the Royal Household, serving three successive kings, David, Solomon and Rehoboam. In the Book of Kings he is shown as in charge of the 'Tribute' (slaves) and the levy (30000 forced Israelite labourers) in Lebanon, who were responsible for obtaining wood for the Temple. This is the role he is stated to have in the Red Cross of Constantine ceremony, where he is given the title 'King Solomon's Intendant of Works on Mount Lebanon'.

In other Masonic rituals he is the understudy to Hiram Abif and also one of the 27 Select Masters who worked on the secret vault. In the Royal Master degree, he is portrayed as a metal worker. During the ceremony he is told the location where the secret word will be deposited, in case any of the three Grand Masters should die – Hiram Abif is slain soon afterwards. At this point, Adoniram takes his place as the senior architect and this is reflected in the Craft Installation ceremony and Mark ritual. He is particularly revered in the Mark degree, as ceremonies are opened and closed in 'the name of Adoniram'. There is no Biblical basis for the account of him being the replacement for Hiram Abif.

Despite his distinguished service, Adoniram came to an unpleasant end. He was appointed as a tax collector for the unpopular successor to King Solomon, Rehoboam. Adoniram was stoned to death by the Israelites, no doubt in response to the high levels of taxation demanded by the new king. The king had accompanied his servant to collect the revenue, but fled back to Jerusalem in his chariot, leaving Adoniram to his fate. The reign of Rehoboam is further explained in the section on the Division of Israel.

ORGANISATION OF THE TEMPLE WORKFORCE

Timeline	960 BC
Biblical reference	I Kings • Chapter 5 v13–18 (Organisation of workmen) • Chapter 5 v18 (Stone Squarers) II Kings • Chapter 12 v11–15 (Masons paid for repairs) • Chapter 22 v4–7 (Masons trusted with money) II Chronicles

Biblical reference *continued*	• Chapter 2 v17 (Use of foreigners as labour) • Chapter 2 v18 (Organisation of work force) • Chapter 24 v12 (Masons paid for repairs) Revelation • Chapter 13 v9 ('If any man have an ear')
Masonic reference	Craft • Second Degree • Third Degree – Traditional History • Installation Ceremony Royal Ark Mariner • Tracing Board Allied Masonic Degrees • Grand Tilers of Solomon Mark • Ceremony of Advancement • Lecture on the Degree Royal and Select Masters • Select Master • Most Excellent Master

The building of the Temple was an enormous undertaking over seven years. There were many trades employed – not just stonemasons. Carpenters, metal smiths, embroiderers, dye makers, engravers and more would have been hard at work. There were also labourers to carry the stones and heavy items, together with sailors to transport materials by sea from the Lebanese ports of Tyre, Sidon and Gebal to Joppa, the harbour serving Jerusalem.

The organisation of the workforce is noted in the Lecture on the Mark Degree, with additional information on the craftsmen included in the Second and Third Degrees of Craft ritual. The Mark lecture contains detailed information and states that there were 110,000 workmen, divided into 80,000 operatives (employed in the quarries or building the temple) and a levy of 30,000 in the forests of Lebanon. The levy was responsible for felling cedar trees and groups of 10,000 worked for one month and then had two months leave. As we have seen, these forced labourers were under the charge of Adoniram.

King Solomon conducted a census and identified 153,600 foreigners in his land. Chronicles states that 70,000 of these were used to carry burdens. In any case, there were a vast number of workers, between 100,000 and 200,000 to be organised, fed and accommodated.

The senior command structure at the Temple is outlined in the lecture on the Second Degree Tracing Board, which notes that three Grand Masters 'bore sway' at the building of the Temple, namely Solomon, King of Israel, Hiram King of Tyre and Hiram Abif. In the Royal and Select degrees, Hiram Abif is called the 'Principal Conductor of the Work'. The middle management consisted of 300 senior overseers. These are that 'superior class of Overseer', who are described in the Third Degree Traditional History. It is from this group, who are also described as *Menatschim* (also spelled *Menatschin*) or 'Prefects' that Hiram Abif's murderers came from. In the Mark Lecture the next management tier is 3300 junior overseers. The Book of Chronicles simply describes 3600 overseers (no junior or senior ranks).

The explanation of the Second Degree Tracing Board states that Entered Apprentices received a weekly allowance of 'corn, wine and oil', whilst the Fellowcrafts received their wages in 'specie' (coins). The first coins appeared in Asia Minor around 650 BC, 100 years before, so this may be historically correct, but has no Biblical source. According to the Second Degree, these wages were paid in the Middle Chamber of the Temple, a location described in the Bible. It must, however, have been a large chamber to take thousands of workmen. It is also unclear where they were paid before this part of the Temple was completed.

The lecture on the Tracing Board further notes that the workmen received their wages 'Without scruple or diffidence. Without scruple, well knowing they were justly entitled to them and without diffidence from the great reliance they placed on the integrity of their employers in those days.' This idea may be taken from the Biblical accounts of the repairs to the Temple during the reigns of two kings of Judah, Joash and Josiah. In both accounts it is stated that the masons and other workmen do not have to account for money entrusted to them as they have acted 'faithfully'.

In the Mark ceremony various punishments are described, using a large axe, for those who tried to obtain dishonestly the wages due to a superior class. The penalties are described as originating in Sidon, but there appears to be no Biblical or historical verification of this claim. There is a quote in the ritual from Revelation, 'If any man have an ear, let him hear.' Its only relevance to the Mark degree is that it mentions an 'ear', which together with the right hand, was one of the items to be severed from the guilty man.

As noted above (see King Hiram), the Israelites were tent dwellers and had few skills in building, particularly major constructions, such as palaces or temples. The Bible outlines the assistance given to King Solomon by Hiram King of Tyre. The Royal Ark Mariner Tracing Board contains a reference to 'skilled craftsmen from Sidonia'. These may have been 'Giblites' from Gebal in Lebanon (north of Sidon). This could be the source of the word *Giblum,* meaning 'Stone Squarers'. The Select Master degree also notes that 22 skilled craftsmen from Gebal (Byblos) were employed on constructing the secret vault, under the Temple. According to the ritual they worked between 9pm and midnight. A similar story appears in the Grand Tilers degree, but neither appears to have any Biblical basis. According to Masonic legend, a further rank was 'Most Excellent Master'. In the degree of the same name, this title is said to have been conferred on the 'most skilful workmen' as a 'special order of merit'.

6

KING SOLOMON'S TEMPLE

THE FIRST TEMPLE

Timeline	957–950 BC – 480 years after the Exodus and 600 years before Alexander the Great
Biblical reference	I Kings • Chapter 6 v1 (Date of building) • Chapter 6 v2 (Size) • Chapter 6 v7 (Stone pre-prepared for building) • Chapter 6 and 7 (Description of Temple) • Chapter 6 v8 (Middle Chamber and winding staircase) • Chapter 7 v5 (All doors and posts square) • Chapter 7 v13–51 (Hiram Abif's work) • Chapter 7 v48–50 (Contents) • Chapter 9 v11–13 (Towns given to King Hiram) I Chronicles • Chapter 22 v14 (Cost of Temple) II Chronicles • Chapter 3 v1 (Location) • Chapter 3 v3–4 (Size with extended height) • Chapter 6 v1 (God lives in 'thick darkness') Ezekiel • Chapter 47 v1 (Vision of river near the Temple) John • Chapter 10 v23 (Jesus walked in Solomon's porch) Hebrews • Chapter 9 v1–12 (Description of Holy of Holies)

Masonic reference	Craft • All degrees Royal Ark Mariner • Tracing Board Mark • All ceremonies Royal and Select Masters • All degrees Holy Royal Arch • Historical Lecture • Questions before Toasts Rose Croix • Ceremony of Perfection Red Cross of Constantine • Knight of St John the Evangelist

The story of the building of King Solomon's Temple is a major feature in a large number of Masonic Degrees. On the Logic Ritual version of the Third Degree Tracing Board, a short account of the building is shown in Hebrew. The construction of the temple also fills five chapters of I Kings and six of II Chronicles and details of the Temple appear in the Books of Ezekiel and Jeremiah.

The Temple was built on Mount Moriah in Jerusalem, for the reasons previously stated – it was the location of Abraham's attempted sacrifice of Isaac and the threshing floor where David prayed to God and stopped the pestilence reaching Jerusalem. It was not the best location, as it was a Hog's Back, which had to be flattened into a platform for the Temple and other buildings.

It should be noted that it was not a temple in which the masses worshipped. Rather it was built as a House of God, a place to house the Ark of the Covenant. As a result, it was not a massive structure, being similar in size to a Parish church. This view of a temple as a house for a God is not unusual; the Sumerians built ziggurats for this purpose.

According to the Biblical accounts it lay east to west and was about 90 feet long, 30 feet wide and 45 feet high – 30m by 10m by 9m (although Chronicles describes the height as 180 feet or 60m). Ezekiel recorded that the stone walls were up to 10 feet thick, tapering towards the top. The Book of Kings shows that all doors and posts were 'square' – this is the first mention of this important Masonic word in the Bible.

Whilst its size may not be impressive by modern standards, its decoration certainly was of the highest standard. The external walls made from highly polished limestone, which glistened in the sunlight. Inside, no stone was visible as the walls were covered with expensive cedar wood panels and curtains made of the finest linen and expertly dyed in shades of purple.

Like other sacred sites in this region, particularly Phoenicia, King Solomon's Temple was divided into three main parts, the *Debir* or Most Holy Place, the *Hekal* or Holy Place and the *Ulam,* or porch. The Most Holy Place (referred to in Masonic Ritual as the 'Sanctum Sanctorum' in the Third Degree) was situated at the rear and housed the Ark of the Covenant. This area was an exact cube, measuring around 35 feet in all dimensions. In a council of Select Masters there are said to be 27 members. This may be linked to the concept of a cube (3 x 3 x 3 = 27).

In the Most Holy Place, God lived in 'thick darkness' according to II Chronicles and the Bible is opened at this description in the Rose Croix ceremony. According to the Third Degree ceremony there was a small 'dormer' window. Knight and Lomas (2003) claim that this was aligned to allow in the light of Venus, the morning star, every 40 years. It is suggested that this resulted in the appearance of the *Shekinah* (see Ark of the Covenant).

The duties of the High Priest in the Holy of Holies are related as part of the explanation of the Third Degree Tracing Board. This appears to be taken from the Letter to the Hebrews, which observes that this area could only be entered by '…the high priest alone once every year' and only after '…divers washings, and carnal ordinances'.

In addition to the three main sections, there were various chambers and store rooms for the priests. The Middle Chamber described in the Book of Kings, which is reached by the winding staircase, features in Masonic Ritual. This is the place where the Fellow Crafts went to receive their wages, according to the explanation of the Second Degree Tracing Board.

In the Royal and Select Masters degrees of Select Master, Royal Master and Most Excellent Master, the Bible must be opened displaying I Kings, Chapter 7. This contains a detailed description of the temple. Verses 48–50 are quoted during the Royal Master degree:

> And Solomon made all the vessels that pertained unto the house of the Lord; the altar of gold, and the table of gold whereupon the shewbread was; and the candle-sticks of pure gold, five on the right side and five on the left, before the oracle; with the flowers and the lamps and the tongs of gold; and the bowls and the snuffers, and the basins and the spoons, and the censers of pure gold; and the hinges of gold, both for the doors of the inner house, the Most Holy Place, and for the doors of the house, to wit, of the Temple.

It can be seen that the contents are very similar to those of the Tabernacle built in the wilderness. The 'flowers' are translated in the Douay-Rheims Catholic Bibles as 'flowers like lilies'. The flowers were therefore ornamental items, unlike the tongs, spoons, bowls and snuffers, which were equipment used with candles.

Outside, the building was surrounded by a paved courtyard and a wall made of stone and cedar beams. The courtyard contained the area for sacrifices and the 'Brazen Sea', a huge basin (9 feet high and 50 feet in diameter), which held up to 16,000 gallons of water, this water being used to cleanse the High Priest.

The Temple was constructed over seven years and was not unique, being of Phoenician design. This is not surprising, given that Hiram, King of Tyre, a Phoenician, supplied the craftsmen. All stone was pre-prepared at the quarry and so no tools could be heard at the Temple site.

According to the Book of Chronicles, the cost of the construction work and decoration was 100,000 gold talents and one million silver talents – approximately £120 million in modern currency. King Hiram also received 20 towns in Galilee, on the northern borders of Israel, but he was not happy with them and returned them to Solomon.

According to the Holy Royal Arch, the temple is the 'Second or Sacred Lodge' and the Knight of St John the Evangelist degree describes King Solomon's Temple as emblematically representing the Christian Church. In the Gospel of St John, Jesus is said to have walked in Solomon's porch. King Solomon's Temple had been destroyed, rebuilt and further renovated by the time of Christ. It therefore must have been an entrance named after the king, rather than being a reference to Jesus being at the First Temple.

THE PLANS

Timeline	960 BC
Biblical reference	II Chronicles • Chapter 3 v11 (Plans in 'writing')
Masonic reference	Mark • Ceremony of Advancement

Eighteenth-century engravings often depict the classical vision of Hiram Abif showing the plans for the Temple to King Solomon on large sheets of paper. It is unclear, however, what form these plans would have actually taken. It is unlikely that such large pieces of papyrus or paper would have been available at that time. Nothing is noted in the Bible on the matter and it is unlikely that the plans were carved in stone – for the simple reason that none have been found. Furthermore, no seals have been discovered from the time of the building of the Temple. The Bible is clear that King Hiram 'answered in writing' when Solomon requested his assistance with the building of the Temple.

It would appear that later plans for renovation work were carved in stone. A blackened stone was found during renovations by Muslim authorities on Temple Mount. The sandstone tablet contains an inscription, written in ancient Phoenician, in which a king tells priests to take 'holy money... to buy quarry stones and timber and copper and labour to carry out the duty with the faith'. If the work is completed well, it adds, 'the Lord will protect his people with blessing.' (The problem of fake treasures emerging in the Middle East should always be borne in mind.)

In the Mark Ceremony of Advancement, the plans for the Temple play a very important part, with the candidate having his worked checked by three Overseers. These Overseers have plans of the various stones required for the building of the Temple. In the Degree, one of the plans is lost and the craftsman played by the candidate prepares the keystone for the arch. This is initially rejected and thrown amongst the rubbish. Hiram Abif (played by the Master) intervenes, reprimands the Overseers for losing part of his plans and the keystone is recovered. This story is Masonic legend, which does not feature in the Biblical account of the Temple.

THE WOOD

Timeline	957 BC
Biblical reference	I Kings • Chapter 5 v6 (Skill of Sidonians with timber) • Chapter 5 v9 (Transported on floats) II Chronicles • Chapter 2 v16 (Cedars from Lebanon) Ezra • Chapter 3 v7 (Cedars used in re-building of Temple)
Masonic reference	Mark • Ceremony of Advancement

Masonic reference *continued*	• Lecture on the Degree Tracing Board

From the earliest times, cedar trees were considered valuable. There were few methods of joining planks securely, so the long tree trunks were ideal for ships' masts and bows. Ancient ship building is described in the Royal Ark Mariner degree, where Noah drives in pins to hold wood together. Cedar wood is also very long lasting; the wood resists insects and decay. For example, the planks used for the roof of the Temple of Apollo in Greece survived for over 1000 years. The cedar tree is so important to the Lebanese that it is the centre piece of their national flag. Even the country's rugby team is named 'The Cedars'.

Due to the mountainous terrain, the felled trees were moved to the coast using water chutes, similar to those used in Norway and Canada. As can be seen in the section on the workforce, 30,000 men were employed in the forests of the Lebanon. Once at the port, they were ferried along the Mediterranean Sea using rafts, or 'floats' as the Bible describes them. This is an important part of the Mark Degree and is recorded in Chronicles. Once at the port of Joppa, 200 miles south of Tyre, the wood was transported to Jerusalem (some 30 miles uphill) using camel trains.

Cedar was again used when the Temple was rebuilt after the Jews returned from their Babylonian exile.

JOPPA, THE PORT SERVING JERUSALEM

Timeline	Prehistory to the present
Biblical reference	II Chronicles • Chapter 2 v16 (Cedar transported to Joppa) Ezra • Chapter 3 v7 (Cedar to repair temple) Jonah • Chapter 1 v3 (Jonah sails from Joppa) Acts • Chapter 9 v36 – 11 v13 (Disciples in Joppa)
Masonic reference	Craft – Third Degree Traditional History Mark • Ceremony of Advancement • Tracing Board (see section on this Order)

The ancient port of Joppa is now 'Jaffa' of oranges fame and is a district of Tel Aviv in Israel. It is a notoriously steep harbour and it was very difficult to unload goods. There was a need for a strong grip to pull men and materials up to the shore. The 'token' or 'secret handshake' used in the Mark Degree is based on this theme. It is an ancient port, so old that legend claims that it was named after Noah's son, Japheth.

Joppa features in various Biblical and Masonic stories:

• The Mark Degree describes the transportation of timber to the port and notes that the degree may have been founded there by King Solomon. The account of materials being taken to the port for use at the temple, in the Book of Chronicles, is the first reference to the city in the Bible.

• Hiram Abif's murderers, as related in the Third Degree Traditional History, make for this port, doubtless, to flee to another country and escape justice. This story is not mentioned in the Bible.

• When Cyrus granted funds to repair the temple, cedar wood was again transported from Sidonia to Joppa (see section on Cyrus).

• Jonah attempted to flee from God from the port, but ended up being swallowed by a whale. This may be the origin of the Masonic story of the attempted escape of the villains in the Third Degree, who were heading for Joppa.

• In the New Testament, Simon Peter and other Disciples visit the city.

• The Knights Templar protected pilgrims on the road between Joppa and Jerusalem (see section of this order).

THE STONE

Timeline	957 BC
Biblical reference	Exodus • Chapter 20 v25 (Metal tools on stone forbidden) Deuteronomy • Chapter 27 v5 (Metal tools on stone forbidden) I Kings • Chapter 6 v7–10 (Tools not used at Temple) Psalms • Psalm 118 v22 (Headstone rejected) Isaiah • Chapter 28 v16 (Foundation stone) Ezekiel • Chapter 44 v1–5 ('Mark well') Revelation • Chapter 2 v17 (Stone with new name)
Masonic reference	Craft • First Degree

Masonic reference continued	Royal Ark Mariner • Tracing Board Mark • Ceremony of Advancement • Installation • Tracing Board • Lecture on the Degree Royal and Select Masters • Most Excellent Master Rose Croix • Ceremony of Perfection Knights Templar

The stone used for the Temple was specially selected for its appearance. It was a form of crystalline limestone, which sparkles when polished. The Jewish historian, Josephus (for information on this man see Destruction of the Third Temple), described the Temple as 'glistening in the sun like a mound of snow'. This form of limestone contains traces of sea shells and fossils, a possible link to when the area was subjected to the Great Flood (a link to the Royal Ark Mariner degree). The sunbeam striking the Temple has special significance in the installation ceremony of a new master in a Mark Master Masons' lodge.

The Bible contains many references to iron polluting stone and the use of such tools was forbidden where the stone was to be used for a sacred building or item, such as an altar. Freemasons will recall that during the ceremony of initiation, they were not permitted to be in possession of any 'money or metallic substances'; this is possibly connected to this Biblical prohibition on the use of iron.

The stone was possibly cut using wooden wedges, which were soaked with water. When they expanded, the stone was broken away from the quarry face. These quarries were two miles from the Temple, not at Zeredatha as stated in the Mark Ritual. This is an area of clay ground used for casting bronze (see below). During the ceremony, the candidate, together with the two Deacons, is symbolically sent to the quarry to prepare stone for the building of the Holy Temple. When they re-enter the lodge, they are wearing long workmen's aprons and carrying squared stones and the keystone for the 'sacred arch' of the temple. The keystone is initially rejected (see Plans for Temple).

Furthermore, the Temple had to be built in sacred silence, so stone was cut and prepared at the quarries and transported to the building site for fitting in its proper place. The lecture on the Royal Ark Mariner Tracing Board notes the numbering system used in this method.

At the time of King Solomon and throughout the Bible, stone and other items are measured in 'cubits'. This is a measure of the human arm, from the elbow to the tip of the middle finger. This is usually around 18 inches, but this may vary. The word 'cubitum' is the Roman word for elbow, which is relevant given the sign used in the Second Degree, when 'cubits' are prominent.

In Craft Masonry, each lodge has two stone cubes, known as 'Ashlars', a rough, unpolished one on the Junior Warden's pedestal and the Perfect Ashlar on the Senior Warden's pedestal. Similar stones appear on the Mark Tracing Board. According to the lecture on the First Degree Tracing Board, the Rough Ashlar represents man in his 'infant or primitive state'. The Perfect Ashlar is emblematic of the older mason, who has spent his life well. There appears to be no Biblical connection.

The Mark Degree utilises the various shapes of stone required at the building – square and oblong ashlars and, most importantly, the keystone for the sacred arch of the Temple. This keystone forms the jewel worn by Mark Masons. The placing of the keystone in the principal arch also prominently features in the Most Excellent Master degree.

During the ceremony of Advancement and the explanation of the Mark Tracing Board, Psalm 118 is quoted: 'The stone which the builders refused is become the headstone of the corner.' In the Mark Degree this is translated into Latin as *Lapis reprobatus caput anguli* and is shown on the tracing board in Hebrew. This part of the Psalm was also quoted by Jesus in three of the Gospels; Matthew, Mark and Luke, and it features in several other places in the New Testament. Jesus was referring to himself in parable form, as he had been rejected by the Pharisees, a tightly knit religious group of that time.

Each Mark Mason has to choose a 'mark', which is based on the symbols cut into stones by operative masons to designate their work. Examples of these marks can be seen in many medieval cathedrals and even the Houses of Parliament in London. The phrase 'Mark well' is used in the ritual and this is taken from a story in Ezekiel, where he has a vision of the new Temple to be built at Jerusalem by Zerubbabel. Parts of Ezekiel (see section on this prophet) are quoted in the ceremony.

Later in the Mark Degree, the Book of Revelation is quoted: 'To him that overcometh will I give to eat of the hidden manna, and I will give him a white stone, and in the stone a new name written, which no man knoweth saving he that receiveth it.' This appears to have been added to the ritual simply because of the reference to stone. The same quote is used in the Knights Templar degree.

The vault and arch is an important part of the Royal Arch ritual. Indeed, the layout of a Chapter room is supposed to represent a Catenarian Arch. This form of arch can be demonstrated as follows – if a rope is suspended by its two ends, the curve into which it falls is called a catenarian curve.

The construction of underground vaults required a high degree of skill, particularly in ancient times. The secret vault under the Temple was, according to the Select Master degree, approached by a series of nine arches. A vault requires a keystone, as does an arch. The earliest vaults were constructed by the Sumerians under ziggurats in Babylonia. The secret vault under Mount Moriah (or the Temple) in Masonic ritual is either built by Enoch (Royal Ark Mariner Tracing Board) or Solomon (Select Master). There are no references in the King James Bible to these legends.

In the Rose Croix degree, a prophecy of Isaiah is quoted. This relates to a 'foundation stone, a tried stone, a precious corner stone, a sure foundation'. This was believed by the evangelists (Matthew, Mark, Luke and John) to be a reference to Jesus, the long-hoped-for Jewish Messiah in their view.

DYES AND LINEN

Timeline	950 BC
Biblical reference	II Chronicles • Chapter 2 v14 (Hiram Abif expert in linen and dyes) • Chapter 3 v14 (Design of veil) Matthew • Chapter 27 v51 (Veil ripped when Jesus dies) Mark • Chapter 15 v38 (Veil ripped)

Biblical reference continued	Luke • Chapter 23 v45 (Veil ripped)
Masonic reference	Craft • Third Degree Royal Ark Mariner • Tracing Board Mark • Ceremony of Advancement Excellent Master (Scotland/Bristol) Royal Arch Chapter • Symbolic lecture Holy Royal Arch Knights Templar Priests • Excellent Mason and Master of the Veils Red Cross of Constantine • Knight of the Holy Sepulchre

The Apron and Sash worn by Holy Royal Arch companions. (By kind permission of Excellent Companion Richard Wileman, Second Provincial Grand Principal of Surrey)

As mentioned previously, no stone could be seen in the interior of the Temple, as the walls were covered with cedar wood or fine linen. This cloth was in various shades of red, blue and purple and was dyed by experts from Sidonia. The dye used was Tyrian Purple, which is also known as 'Royal' or 'Imperial Purple'. From very ancient times, possibly up to 4000 years ago, this has been obtained using mucus from the Murex sea snail, which is found on the coast near Tyre. A Greek legend claimed that the dye was first discovered by Hercules, as a result of his dog's mouth turning purple after chewing on the snails. The Bible, as quoted in the Mark Degree ceremony, shows that Hiram Abif was an expert in 'purple and blue', a clear reference to the dyeing technique. His father was from Tyre, the source of the snails.

The entrance to the various areas of the Temple were covered with red, blue and purple veils and the 'Passing of the Veils' is part of the Excellent Master degree, practised in Scotland (which has separate ruling bodies for Masonic degrees) and the Bristol area in England, which has several unique versions of Masonic degrees. These veils are represented on the Royal Ark Mariner Tracing Board and the temple veils were, no doubt, copies of those used in the tabernacle.

In the Royal Arch Chapter Symbolical lecture, it is stated that the sash worn by Companions is made up of the two colours with which the veil of the Temple was interwoven. These can also be seen on the apron of the order. Few companions of the Holy Royal Arch will realise that the colours are from the mucus of sea snails!

Crimson is the colour of the robe of the officer acting as Zerubbabel in a Royal Arch Chapter. The other two Principals wear robes of purple and blue – all three colours are derived from Murex dye.

In the New Testament, three of the Gospels describe how the veil of the Temple was ripped in two when Jesus died on the cross. This incident forms part of the Knight of the Holy Sepulchre, an Appendant Order of the Red Cross of Constantine. The 'Excellent Mason and Master of the Veils' is a degree conferred during the Knights Templar Priests ceremony.

A further Masonic allusion to a veil is during the Third Degree ceremony, the subject of which is human death. In the ritual, whilst contemplating the 'darkness of death', the Master refers to 'that mysterious veil which the eye of human reason cannot penetrate, unless assisted by that Light which is from above'. The 'Light' referred to is God's word, contained in the Volume of the Sacred Law.

BRONZE AND GOLD

Timeline	957 BC
Biblical reference	Genesis • Chapter 4 v22 ('Brass' first mentioned) Deuteronomy • Chapter 8 v7–9 (Metal ores) I Kings • Chapter 7 v46 (Clay ground used for casting) • Chapter 7 v48–50 (Gold items for the temple) II Chronicles • Chapter 4 v17 (Clay ground used for casting)

Masonic reference	Craft • Second Degree Tracing Board • Questions before Raising Mark • Ceremony of Advancement • Tracing Board • Lecture on Degree Royal and Select Masters • Royal Master

The first mention of brass is in the Book of Genesis in relation to Tubalcain, who, as shown above, features in Masonic ritual. The early books of the Bible are set in the Late Bronze/Early Iron Age and the metal used to make the pillars and other items for the temple is bronze. As has been stated, the use of the word 'brass' throughout the Bible is a mistranslation.

Bronze is an alloy formed by mixing copper with tin. Copper ore was abundant in the Holy Land; and in Deuteronomy, the Lord promises Moses a 'good land' whose 'stones are iron and out of whose hills thou mayest dig brass'. In highland areas of the Promised Land were green stones, formed of malachite, a high yielding copper ore.

The copper used at the Temple may also have been mined near the Red Sea port of Ezion Geber (now called Eilat) and one possible translation of 'Ezion Geber' is 'Holy Vessel casting'. Tin was not so readily available and it had to be obtained from Cornwall, Spain or France. Phoenician merchants, under King Hiram, already sailed the established trade routes to exploit these sources. The wreck of such a ship, with a cargo of tin, was found in the mouth of the River Erme in Dorset, southern England. The ship was dated to 1000 years before the reign of Solomon.

In ancient times, Bronze was prepared in clay furnaces, which used goat skin bellows to raise the temperature of the charcoal fire to 1200 degrees Fahrenheit (650°C). The metal was cast in a clay crucible and then poured into moulds.

Masonic Ritual builds on the accounts in the Book of Chronicles and Hiram Abif is shown as the superintendent of the casting of bronze objects in the 'clay ground between Succoth and Zeredathah' (The Book of Kings names the latter place as 'Zarthan' and Masonic ritual uses several different spellings). Senior Freemasons will have heard these words many times, but few will be aware of their location. In the Royal Master degree, the 'Conductor of the Council' (the Deacon) states to the candidate (acting as Adoniram), that they should leave the Temple and return to the clay ground between Succoth and Zeredatha, as if it is only a short distance away. It is, in fact, some 40 miles from Jerusalem and the return journey involves climbing 2000 feet; a journey of two days in ancient times. It should be noted that Succoth was established many centuries earlier by Jacob (see above) and had been an Egyptian fort.

The map in the section on Jephtha below shows the location of the clay ground. It is on the east side of the River Jordan, where the River Jabbok flows into it. Given its distance from the Temple, there had to be very good reasons for using this area. The main advantage was the plastic and cohesive quality of the clay, which ensured excellent casting. In addition to the two enormous pillars (see below), numerous holy vessels were cast. The largest was the 'Brazen Sea', an enormous water holder used for absolution of priests (see section on King Solomon's Temple).

THE PILLARS: BOAZ AND JACHIN

Timeline	950 BC
Biblical reference	Ruth • Chapter 2 (Ruth meets Boaz) • Chapter 4 v21–22 (Great Grandfather of David) I Kings • Chapter 7 v15–22 (Description of Pillars) • Chapter 7 v41–42 (Chapiters) • Chapter 7 v46 (Casting ground) II Kings • Chapter 25 v13 (Pillars taken to Babylon) I Chronicles • Chapter 9 v10 (Priest called Jachin) II Chronicles • Chapter 3 v15–17 (Size and names) • Chapter 4 v12–13 (Chapiters) • Chapter 4 v17 (Casting ground) Jeremiah • Chapter 52 v17 (Destruction) • Chapter 52 v21 (Thickness of brass)
Masonic reference	Craft • First Degree • Second Degree – Tracing Board • Third Degree Royal and Select Masters • Most Excellent Master

The pillars placed outside King Solomon's Temple are one of the most used symbols in Craft Freemasonry and feature heavily in both the First and Second Degrees, with the candidate for 'Raising' to the Third Degree being tested on their emblematic meanings and 'conjoined signification'. A number of Masonic lodges have copies of the pillars at the entrance and the pillars are further represented by two columns – one on each of the Wardens' pedestals.

The description of the pillars, 'Boaz' on the left and 'Jachin' on the right, as used in the ritual, is a composite taken from the Books of Kings, Chronicles and Jeremiah. All three books of the Bible show them as being made of 'brass' fitted with chapiters, but as we have seen they were really constructed from bronze. Kings and Chronicles note that each was decorated with 200 carved pomegranates. Pomegranates are a symbol of plenty in many cultures, including Greece and Persia, as well as in Masonic ritual.

There is some discrepancy about the height with the Second Book of Chronicles giving 'two pillars of thirty and five cubits high' – this being the height used in Masonic ritual ('seventeen cubits and a half each').The First Book of Kings gives them as being half a cubit taller.Whichever measurement is taken, they were approximately 27 feet (or 9m) high.The books of Chronicles were a comprehensive rewriting, with numbers and measurements changed to emphasise the importance of the Temple.

Chronicles states the circumference, 12 cubits (18 feet/6m) and Kings gives us details of the lily-work and network, as used on the chapiters. Jeremiah contains the reference to the thickness of the bronze being 'four fingers' or a 'hand's breadth' as the Ritual states.There is no mention of them being formed hollow, but given the weight of bronze and distance from the casting ground (see above), this is most likely.The weight of hollow pillars would be around 135 tonnes and so they were likely to have been cast in rings and joined together on site.Therefore, whilst the ritual tells us they were formed hollow 'the better to serve as archives to Freemasonry', the true reason for them being hollow was to enable them to be transported from the casting area.There is evidence, however, that the Ancient Egyptians did place sacred scrolls in the walls of their temples. It would, therefore, not be unusual for the Israelites to follow this practice, especially as Moses would have brought many aspects of Egyptian culture into the Israelite religion. In the Masonic legend and Biblical account of King Josiah (see Division of Israel), scrolls are found at various periods when the Temple is renovated or rebuilt.

Masonic ritual states that there were two spheres at the top of the chapiters, decorated with maps of the celestial and terrestrial globes.This is Masonic symbolism, as the real pillars had no such adornment. It was not until 400 years later that the Greeks suggested that the world may be round, rather than flat.

In reality, at the top were two bowls (or *goolots* in Hebrew), which were used to burn oil.This gave a pillar of cloud by day and fire by night – hence the symbolism of the pillars that guided Moses and the Israelites out of Egypt to the Promised Land.This symbolism does not appear have a Biblical basis. British soldiers serving in Palestine corrupted the word *Goolots* into 'gooleys', testicles.After the author's talks in numerous Masonic lodges, this seems to be the one fact that many Masons remember!

The word 'Network' in relation to the pillars is mentioned twice in the Ritual, network being on the Chapiters and then the pillars were 'considered complete when the network or canopy was thrown over them'.The meaning of this latter 'network' is unclear.

In Masonic Lodges, the pillars on the Master, Senior and Junior Wardens' chairs are representations of the Greek orders of architecture Ionic, Doric and Corinthian respectively.The Second Degree Tracing Board adds two Roman Orders,Tuscan and Composite to make the 'Five Noble Orders'.The latter two are not represented in the lodge.What is sure is that the pillars at the Temple were of none of these designs.The oldest is Ionic, which first appeared around the seventh century BC and was not in general use until the fifth century BC, some 500 years after the building of the first Temple.The Doric Order features in the Most Excellent Master degree, but there appears to be no obvious reason for its use.

The pillars were broken down and carried to Babylon after Nebuchadnezzar conquered Israel (see Destruction of Jerusalem).They are not mentioned again in the Bible but a recent dig at the site of the Temple resulted in the discovery of a thumb-sized pomegranate. Around the shoulder of the pomegranate is an engraved inscription in early Hebrew characters, which reads: *qodes kohanim l-beyt yahweh*. 'Sacred donation for the priests of (in) the House of Yahweh'. There is, however, a major issue with fraudulent artefacts in the Middle East and all such finds are to be treated with scepticism.

In Masonic ritual, the pillars Boaz and Jachin are named respectively after one of the great grandfathers of David and the Assistant High Priest at the dedication of the Temple (see sections on Boaz and Jachin).There appears to be no Biblical evidence to support the pillars being named after these men.

THE DEDICATION OF THE TEMPLE
AND JACHIN THE HIGH PRIEST

Timeline	950 BC
Biblical reference	Leviticus • Chapter 2 v13 (Use of salt in offerings) I Kings • Chapter 7 v21 (Pillar called 'Jachin') • Chapter 8 v22 (Solomon's dedication prayer) • Chapter 8 v63 (Temple dedicated) • Chapter 8 v64 (Offerings made) I Chronicles • Chapter 6 v31–32 (Temple musicians) • Chapter 9 v10 (Priest called Jachin) II Chronicles • Chapter 3 v17 (Pillar called Jachin) • Chapter 6 v12–42 (Solomon's dedication) • Chapter 7 v1–7 (Offerings made) • Chapter 7 v5 (Temple dedicated) Ezra • Chapter 6 v9 (Wheat, salt, wine and oil)
Masonic reference	Craft • First Degree Tracing Board • Second Degree Royal and Select Masters • Most Excellent Master Various Degrees • Consecration of Lodges

The Temple was dedicated by King Solomon and there is a detailed description of his prayers and offerings in the Books of Kings and Chronicles. The consecration of the building, together with the 'thanksgivings, oblations, burnt sacrifices and costly offerings' is mentioned during the explanation of the First Degree Tracing Board. The Second Degree lecture is then concerned with the completion of the Temple. The Most Excellent Master degree, however, is the only degree that deals exclusively with the dedication. The lecture during this ceremony recalls the important role that music played at the consecration and these musicians are noted in I Chronicles.

The name 'Jachin' features prominently in Craft ritual and in a Grand Lodge he is represented by the Senior Grand Warden. There are a number of men called 'Jachin' in the Bible, in the Books of Genesis, Exodus, Numbers, Chronicles and Nehemiah. The latter two books refer to the man as a priest. Chronicles contains an account of the building and dedication of the Temple, but the Jachin listed is a returnee from the exile in Babylon many centuries later.

The Bible states that King Solomon performed the dedication ceremony and it is unlikely that any priest called 'Jachin' was present, whether as 'High Priest' or 'Assistant High Priest' as he is variously called in Masonic ritual. The book 'The Freemason at Work' (Carr 1992) states that the linking of the priest called Jachin and the pillar of the same name is due to 'excessive zeal' by the ritual compilers.

The ceremony to consecrate a new lodge is not based on the dedication of the First Temple. It involves the use of corn (symbol of plenty), wine (joy), olive oil (peace) and salt (fidelity and friendship). From the time of Moses, as shown in Leviticus, God demanded that salt was added to offerings made to Him. Corn, wine, oil and salt appear together in Ezra, where King Darius of Persia gave an order that the priests from Jerusalem must be given these items for use as sacrifices. This relates to the dedication of the Second Temple.

THE QUEEN OF SHEBA

Timeline	950 BC
Biblical reference	I Kings • Chapter 10 v1–13 (Visits Solomon) II Chronicles • Chapter 9 v1–12 (Visits Solomon) Job • Chapter 1 v15 (Sabean raiders) Luke • Chapter 11 v31 (Jesus noted the visit of the Queen)
Masonic reference	Craft • Installation Ceremony (Taylor's Ritual)

The Queen of Sheba visited King Solomon to test his wisdom and to see the Temple. She left him with gold and other gifts and returned to her homeland. Her royal visit is featured in the Installation ceremony of at least one form of Masonic ritual, known as 'Taylor's'. This is when the new Master is installed into the 'Chair of King Solomon' by his predecessor, together with other Past Masters.

Jesus informed a crowd in Jerusalem that on Judgement Day, the Queen of Sheba will decide their guilt or innocence, as she travelled far to learn wisdom from Solomon.

The location of Sheba is still unclear. Various theories have located it in modern-day Yemen in Arabia or Ethiopia in East Africa. It may be the land of the Sabeans, which is noted in the Book of Job (see section on Raiders from the East). According to legend, Haile Selassie, the last Ethiopian emperor, who is revered by Rastafarians, was descended from Menelik – the son of Solomon and the Queen of Sheba.

7

AFTER SOLOMON
AND INTO EXILE

A TIME OF PROPHETS

Timeline	938 BC – Death of Solomon 930 BC – Israel and Judah divide 900 BC – Time of Prophet Elijah 770 BC – Reign of King Uzziah 734 BC – Israel falls to the Assyrians 640–609 BC – Reign of Josiah in Judah 586 BC – Judah falls to the Babylonians
Biblical reference	I Kings • Chapter 11 v43 (Rehoboam made king) II Kings • Chapter 1 (Elijah and King Ahaziah) • Chapter 2 v23–25 (Revenge of the bald Elisha) • Chapter 14 v21 (Uzziah/Azariah made king) • Chapter 22 v10–12 (Book of Law found) II Chronicles • Chapter 9 v31 (Rehoboam made king) • Chapter 26 v1 (Uzziah made king) • Chapter 34 v14–21 (Book of Law found) • Chapter 36 v19 (Use of fire in sieges) Ezra • Chapter 4 v2 (King of Assyria was Esar-haddon) Tobit • Chapter 12 v12 ('…bury the dead') Isaiah • Chapter 1 v16–17 (Cleansing and putting away evil)

Biblical reference continued	• Chapter 2 v3 (All nations will obey God) • Chapter 2 v5 ('Walk in the light of the Lord') • Chapter 8 v1 (Maher-shalal-hash-baz) • Chapter 21 v12 (God's message to Edom) • Chapter 26 v4 (Trust in the Lord) • Chapter 30 v24 (Shovel as a tool) • Chapter 36 v12 (Vulgar Assyrian threats) • Chapter 44 v6 (God is the first and the last) • Chapter 44 v7 ('Ancient people') • Chapter 44 v13 (Measuring rule and compass) • Chapter 53 (Prophecy of Christ) • Chapter 54 v8–10 (God's promise as it was to Noah) • Chapter 54 v17 ('No weapon that is formed against thee may prosper' • Chapter 60 v19 ('An everlasting light') • Chapter 61 v5–6 (Promise to Israel) Hosea • Chapter 1 v6–9 (Ammi and Ru-hamah) • Chapter 2 (God's relationship with Israel) Amos • Chapter 7 v7–9 (Plumb line) • Chapter 9 (Prophesies fall of Israel) Micah • Chapter 6 v8 ('...do justly, and to love mercy') Matthew • Chapter 1 v8–9 (Uzziah/Ozias, in line of Jesus)
Masonic reference	Craft • Working Tools in all three degrees Royal Ark Mariner Degree • Ceremony of Elevation • Tracing Board Allied Masonic Degrees • Red Cross of Babylon Order of the Secret Monitor • Scarlet Cord – All Grades Mark • Ceremony of Advancement Royal and Select Masters • Super Excellent Master

Masonic reference continued	Holy Royal Arch • Ceremony of Exaltation • Installation of Joshua Rose Croix • Ceremony of Perfection Holy Royal Arch Knights Templar Priests • Installation of Knights Templar Priest • Installation of High Priest Red Cross of Constantine • Installation of Knight • Knight of the Holy Sepulchre Knights Templar
Historical context	776 BC – First Olympic Games held in Greece 612 BC – Assyrian capital, Ninevah, destroyed 605 BC – Assyrian Empire disappears

The kingdom of Israel, united by David fell apart after Solomon's son, Rehoboam, became king around 979 BC. Due to his policy of heavy taxation, ten of the tribes revolted and formed the northern kingdom of Israel, with Samaria as their capital. These northern Israelites were to become the hated idol-worshipping Samaritans. This left Rehoboam as king of Judah, based on Jerusalem in the south. During this period of Jewish history, a number of the greatest prophets preached God's word, amongst them Elijah, Isaiah, Hosea and Amos. All feature in Masonic ritual.

The well known prophet Elijah makes a very low key appearance in Masonic ritual and is never actually mentioned in a lodge. When the Super Excellent Master degree is opened, the Royal and Select Masters ritual book states that the Bible must be opened at II Kings, Chapter 1. This is the story of Elijah and King Ahaziah of the northern kingdom of Israel. The king was badly injured in a fall and rather than pray to the Lord, he asked the priests of a false god, Baal, if his injury was fatal. This angered God and Elijah informed the king he would die and later destroyed two companies of soldiers sent by the king to capture him. Here God sent fire from heaven to defeat the army. It is unclear why this part of the Bible must be on display as the degree relates to the story of Zedekiah, which features over 20 chapters later.

When Elijah was taken up to heaven in a fiery chariot, he was succeeded by his follower, Elisha. The latter does not feature in Masonic ritual, but given that Freemasons are usually middle aged (or older) it is useful to note that Elisha was bald. When some boys made fun of his lack of hair, he cursed them and two bears appeared and killed them. Bald Freemasons may find some comfort in this odd Biblical story!

From around 770 BC, the southern kingdom of Judah was ruled by Uzziah (also called Azariah or Ozias), who reigned for over 50 years. He was a wise ruler, but his pride led to his downfall. For usurping the priests and making his own sacrifices, God punished him by giving him leprosy. His name is used as part of the Red Cross of Constantine degree, a Christian Order. Nothing further is explained about him in the ceremony, but he was selected as he appears in the genealogy of Jesus in the Gospel of St Matthew and the four pillars of the degree spell out 'IHSV' (see section on Constantine for explanation), with Uzziah representing the 'V' (this letter being the ancient

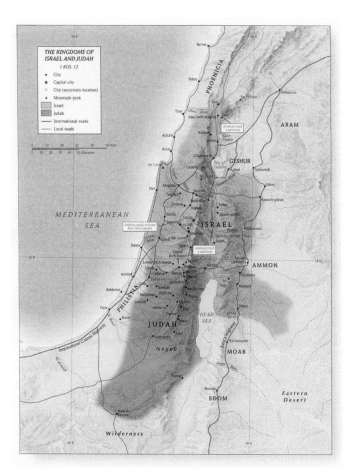

The Divided Kingdom.

form of 'U'). For the sake of completeness, I = Immanuel (see section on Herod's Temple and Early Life of Jesus), H = Hiram, the widow's son and S = Shiloh (see Ark of the Covenant).

During the rule of Uzziah, the Prophet Hosea lived in the northern kingdom and at God's command he married a prostitute. God compares his unfaithful wife with the unfaithful manner in which the Israelites have turned to the false god, Baal. God named Hosea's children *Lo-Ammi* meaning 'not my people' and *Lo-Ruhamah* meaning 'no more mercy'. In the Second Chapter of Hosea, *Ammi* and *Ruhamah* are used without the negative prefix and these words have significance in the Holy Royal Arch Chapter ritual (see also sections on St Peter and St Paul). The life of Hosea also features during the installation of the 'High Priest' or Master of a Tabernacle of Knights Templar Priests, when God promised to return Israel's vineyards and bring His people from the 'Valley of Sorrows' (see Joshua and Rahab) through a 'door of hope'. Then Israel will stop worshipping the false god, Baal and will call the Lord *Ishi* (meaning 'my husband').

Isaiah appeared in the latter part of Uzziah's reign and continued to act as a prophet for over 40 years until around 700 BC, when Hezekiah ruled Judah. His prophesies are often used to foretell the coming of Christ (see section on Jesus and the Third Temple) and he is, by far, the most quoted prophet in the New Testament. Chapter 54 contains God's promises to Israel and sections are read out during the Royal Ark Mariner ceremony of Advancement and reiterated when the Tracing Board of the degree is explained. 'For the mountains shall depart, and the hills be removed; but my kindness shall not depart from thee, neither shall the covenant of my peace be removed, saith the Lord that hath mercy on thee.'

This is linked to the Royal Ark Mariner degree as God states that His promise has the same validity as His promise to Noah that waters would no more cover the earth. Isaiah's words also appear in the Installation ceremony of the officer 'Joshua' in a Royal Arch Chapter. The words are not attributed to Isaiah, but the ritual uses much of Chapter 1 v16–17: 'Wash you, make you clean; put away the evil of your doings from before mine eyes; cease to do evil; Learn to do well; seek judgment, Relieve the oppressed.'

Considering the Masonic importance of Hiram Abif, the widow's son, it is odd that the verses are not completed, as in the Bible it continues 'judge the fatherless, plead for the widow.' Another confusing use of the prophecies of Isaiah is in the Scarlet Cord. All three grades paraphrase words from God's message to the city of Edom: 'The watchman said, The morning cometh, and also the night: if ye will inquire, inquire ye: return, come.' The reason for the inclusion for this verse is unclear.

The Chapter installation ceremony of Joshua also includes a prayer which refers to the mercies shown to 'Thy ancient people'. This is taken from a section of Isaiah where God stated that he has chosen the Children of Israel. He makes clear that He is the only God and, in a reference similar to that used in Revelation (see section), the Lord stated 'I am the first and I am the last.'

Isaiah's second son holds the record for the longest name in the Bible: *Maher-shalal-hash-baz*, which translates as 'Hurry to spoil! He has made haste to the plunder!' or 'Hurrying to the spoil he has made haste to the plunder'. God instructed Isaiah to use this name to foretell of the impending Assyrian invasion of Damascus and Samaria, the capital of the northern kingdom of Israel. The name *Maher-shalal-hash-baz* is recalled during the Knights Templar ceremony. Assyria was a major power at this time and they occupied the land to the north (including modern-day Turkey). The northern kingdom fell to them in 720 BC and the people were taken into exile in Assyria. The Book of Ezra names the conquering king as Esar-haddon (but uses 'Assur' rather than Assyria). This detail is read out during the Red Cross of Babylon ceremony. The Assyrians were notoriously cruel conquerors. In the Book of Isaiah, they make a threat to the soldiers of Jerusalem that they will make them 'eat their own dung and drink their own piss' – the translators of the Bible were not afraid to use vulgar language.

Isaiah did, however, prophesy that Jerusalem would be great in the future and that all nations, not just Jews, would obey the Lord. Such is the importance of this reference is that it is used twice during the Knights Templar Priest ceremony. A second reference from Chapter 2, which contains the expression 'walk in the light' (see also St John) and a further one from Chapter 60 (another vision of the future greatest of Jerusalem), 'the Lord shall be unto thee an everlasting light' appear to have been placed in the ritual as lamps feature in the ceremony.

The Knights Templar Priest ceremony uses at least two further sections from Isaiah. Chapter 60 is a promise to Israel that they will be seen as the servants of God. Chapter 26 is a song of praise to God and the ritual uses one of the verses, 'Trust ye in the Lord for ever: for in the Lord Jehovah is everlasting strength.' 'Jehovah' is an important part of the Chapter ritual and therefore links with this ceremony, the full title of the order being 'Holy Royal Arch Knights Templar Priest'. It should be noted that the Book of Isaiah covers hundreds of years and it may be that there were several men called 'Isaiah'.

The exile in Assyria is the setting of the Book of Tobit, which is found only in Roman Catholic versions of the Bible. Tobit sent his son, Tobias from the Assyrian capital, Nineveh, to collect money from the land of Media (the land of the Medes in modern day in Iran). During his many adventures, including being attacked by a giant fish, Tobias was protected by the angel Raphael. Raphael is used as the name of one of the officers in the Rose Croix ceremony. The Book of Tobit also provides the last of the seven 'Corporal Works of Mercy' – 'Go, bury the dead,' which feature in the Knight of the Holy Sepulchre ritual (see Ministry of Jesus).

In the Biblical account of this period, the minor Prophet Micah warned the Israelites to 'do justly, and to love mercy', and this appears to be the origin of the phrase in the Mark Degree to 'do justice, love mercy'. Around the same time, the prophet Amos prophesied the fall of Israel. This is of interest to Freemasons as he had a vision of God 'with a plumb line in his hand' to establish how crooked the Israelites had become. In the same manner, the plumb line or 'Plumb Rule' as it is described in Masonic ritual is a symbol of 'Uprightness of life and actions' and it features throughout various degrees:

• Badge of office of the Junior Warden in Craft Freemasonry (worn on collar and displayed on the pedestal)
• First Degree Tracing Board
• Second Degree – one of the Working Tools
• Third Degree – one of the tools used to murder Hiram Abif
• Royal Ark Mariner Tracing Board – badge of office of Junior Warden and a hand holding a plumb line.

A number of the other 'Working Tools' used to symbolise moral values in Masonic ritual appear in the Bible. The 'maul' is mentioned in Proverbs, whilst the axe, prominent in the Mark and Royal Ark Mariner degrees is used throughout the Bible. Isaiah notes that the carpenter 'stretcheth out his rule' (the 24 inch gauge) and uses a compass. In the Royal Arch degree, the shovel, pickaxe (see St Paul) and crowbar are used in the ceremony to symbolically clear the ground for the rebuilding of the Second Temple. Shovels generally appear in the Bible as a ceremonial implement for use at the Temple. It is only in Isaiah where a shovel appears as a working tool. The square, level, mallet, chisel, pick and crowbar do not appear in the Bible.

Strangely, the finding of the Book of Law (Deuteronomy) and the repairs to the Temple organised by King Josiah around 600 BC are not included in English Masonic ritual. The account of the finding of the Book of Law may, however, have influenced the Royal Arch ceremony and in some versions of Chapter ritual outside of England, Josiah replaces Joshua as one of the principal officers.

Less than 150 years after the fall of the Northern Kingdom, the Babylonians conquered much of the then known world, including Assyria and Judah, with Jerusalem taken by them in 587 BC. We now move to the setting of the start of Chapter ritual.

JERUSALEM FALLS TO THE BABYLONIANS

Timeline	601–597 BC
Biblical reference	II Kings • Chapter 23 v36 (Jehoiakim made king) • Chapter 24 v1–4 (Nebuchadnezzar invades Judah) • Chapter 24 v7 (Egypt powerless) • Chapter 24 v10–11 (Siege of Jerusalem) • Chapter 24 v13 (Holy Vessels taken) • Chapter 24 v14–16 (Important Jews taken into exile) • Chapter 24 v17–18 (Zedekiah made king) II Chronicles • Chapter 36 (Fall of Jerusalem) Isaiah • Chapter 13 v19 (Babylon, the glory of kingdoms)

Biblical reference continued	Jeremiah • Chapter 5 (Wickedness of Judah) • Chapter 24 v1 (King Jehoiakim taken prisoner) • Chapter 25 v11–12 (Prophecy – 70 years in Babylon) • Chapter 29 v10 (Return to Israel after 70 years) Daniel • Chapter 1 v1–2 (Fall of Jerusalem) • Chapter 9 v2 (Exile would last 70 years) Micah • Chapter 4 v10 (Prophecy of exile and return) Habakkuk • Chapter 1 v6 (God will use Babylonians to punish)
Masonic reference	Royal and Select Master • Super Excellent Master Holy Royal Arch

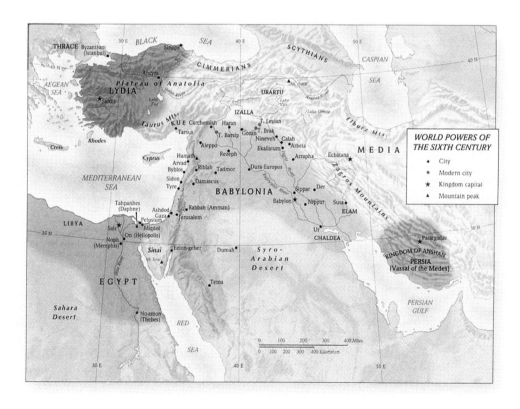

The Babylonian Empire – controlling most of the Fertile Crescent.

By now the great power was Babylon, whose people are often referred to as the Chaldeans. Babylon is described by Isaiah as 'the glory of kingdoms, the beauty of the Chaldees' excellency'. Situated within the Fertile Crescent, the city was the centre of the known world and was protected by huge walls, guarded by 250 watchtowers.

During the reign of the King Jehoiakim (some rituals use the spelling 'Jehoiachim'), the Babylonians, under Nebuchadnezzar II, invaded Judah and made it a vassal state. The Bible shows these invasions as punishments for wickedness and these had been foretold by the prophets Jeremiah, Habakkuk and Micah. Jeremiah's prophecy of the Israelites being exiled in Babylon for 70 years, which is repeated in the Book of Daniel, features in the Royal Arch ritual. Ten thousand of the important Israelites, including Jehoiakim, were taken prisoner, together with 7000 soldiers and 1000 craftsmen, and forced to live in exile in Babylon. This was nearly 500 miles from Jerusalem. The exiles included the Prophet Ezekiel, who had many bizarre visions (see section on Ezekiel). All the Holy Vessels originally cast by Hiram Abif for King Solomon's Temple were also seized and taken to Babylon, but the Ark of the Covenant may have been hidden in a cave by Jeremiah (see Ark of Covenant above).

The removal of entire populations was commonplace at this time and was practised by the Babylonian, Assyrian and Persian empires. Deportees would be resettled in an unfamiliar region making revolt unlikely and after a few generations the people would lose their identity and become assimilated into the empire. Some of the educated classes would be selected to serve the new rulers and this was the case with Daniel, who was one of four young Israelites chosen to learn the Babylonian language and serve Nebuchadnezzar.

The Babylonians were able to place a vassal king on the throne of Israel, but this led to further rebellion and the destruction of Jerusalem. This is the basis of the Super Excellent Master degree.

THE DESTRUCTION OF JERUSALEM: BIBLICAL WARFARE (PART IV)

Timeline	586 BC
Biblical reference	II Kings • Chapter 24 v17–18 (Zedekiah made king) • Chapter 24 v20 (Rebellion against Babylon) • Chapter 25 v1–3 (Siege and famine) • Chapter 25 v4–6 (Zedekiah flees, but is captured) • Chapter 25 v7 (Bound in fetters of brass) • Chapter 25 v8–9 (Temple destroyed by fire) • Chapter 25 v11 (Only poor left in Jerusalem) • Chapter 25 v13 (Pillars broken) • Chapter 25 v18 (Three keepers of the Temple) • Chapter 25 v22 (Gedaliah appointed governor) • Chapter 25 v25 (Gedaliah assassinated) Psalms • Psalm 137 v1 (Exile 'by the rivers of Babylon') Isaiah • Chapter 51 v17 (Dregs of the Cup of Fury)

Biblical reference continued	Jeremiah • Chapter 7 v33 (Fowls and beasts of the earth) • Chapter 15 v3 (Fowls and beasts of the earth) • Chapter 16 v4 (Fowls and beasts of the earth) • Chapter 19 v7 (Fowls and beasts of the earth) • Chapter 27 v1 (Zedekiah made king) • Chapter 29 v2 (Important people taken into exile) • Chapter 34 v20 (Fowls and beasts of the earth) • Chapter 39 (Fall of Jerusalem) • Chapter 40 v1–4 (Nebuzaradan frees Jeremiah) • Chapter 40 v6 (Jeremiah stays with Gedaliah) • Chapter 41 v2 (Ammonites kill Gedaliah) • Chapter 50 v5 (Prophecy of return from exile) • Chapter 52 (Zedekiah and his punishment) Lamentations • Chapter 1 (Destruction of Jerusalem) • Chapter 4 v1 (Babylonians enter the Holy of Holies) • Chapter 4 v20 (King captured by Babylonians) Ezekiel • Chapter 17 v11–21 (Zedekiah's fate foretold) • Chapter 17 v17 (Babylon's use of siege devices) • Chapter 21 v3–4 (Babylon used as God's sword)
Masonic reference	Royal and Select Master • Super Excellent Master Holy Royal Arch • Ceremony of Exaltation Societas Rosicruciana in Anglia • Fifth Grade 'Adeptus Minor'
Historical context	612 BC – Collapse of Assyrian Empire

Following the first Babylonian siege of Jerusalem, Mattaniah, the uncle of the deposed ruler, was made vassal king. His name was changed to Zedekiah, which according to the Masonic ritual means 'Justice of Jehovah' or literally 'Yahweh is might', in case he forgot his loyalty. The Bible relates that, despite counsel from the Prophet Jeremiah, Zedekiah rebelled. This forms the basis of the Super Excellent Master degree. In an attempt to free the country from Babylonian rule, he made an alliance with Egypt, which had been a major power for many centuries, but by this time its influence was waning – a political situation which is clearly described in the Bible in the penultimate chapter of II Kings and in Ezekiel. The alliance triggered an attack by the Babylonian overlords.

Jerusalem was besieged for eighteen months and a famine spread. The Book of Kings explains that there was no bread to eat. In more poetic language, Isaiah states that Jerusalem had angered God so much that its inhabitants had drunk 'the dregs' of the 'cup of His fury'. Jeremiah is believed to have composed the Book of Lamentations and this describes the destruction of the

Slaughter of the Sons of Zedekiah before their Father (1866) by Gustave Doré.

city and the capture of Zedekiah in a 'pit' or trap. The once great Jerusalem is likened to a 'widow' and a 'tributary' (slave). As with the story of David and Goliath, Jeremiah states that bodies will be devoured by the 'fowls of the heaven' and 'beasts of the earth'. This is quoted on five occasions in the Book of Jeremiah and is similar to the 'physical penalty' formerly included in the Second Degree obligation.

The Babylonians were experts at siege tactics, particularly the use of fire and ramparts; this is noted in the Bible and the 'conflagration of the former Temple' is mentioned in the Holy Royal Arch ceremony. As the attack on Jerusalem was reaching its climax and Nebuchadnezzar's general, Nebuzaradan, was about to enter the city, Zedekiah and his officers 'basely fled' (this quotation is from Holy Royal Arch ritual) by night to the Plains of Jericho, to the north west of Jerusalem. He was captured and had to witness his sons being executed at Riblah, an ancient town to the north of Israel, where Nebuchadnezzar had his headquarters. Zedekiah was then blinded and taken to Babylon bound in what the Bible and Super Excellent Master degree describe as 'fetters of brass' (large bronze chains).

According to the Book of Mormon, which is the sacred text of the Church of Latter Day Saints, one of Zedekiah's sons escaped. This son, Mulek, sailed to America and established a new civilization.

The Babylonians, under Nebuzaradan, destroyed Jerusalem, breaking down the pillars at the Temple, so important in Masonic ritual. The remaining treasures were plundered and all but the poorest people were sent to Babylon. The Holy Royal Arch ritual describes them as 'those left behind by the Babylonian general for the purpose of tilling the land'. The Super Excellent Master degree and Book of Jeremiah note that the royal family, priests and craftsmen were all taken into exile. The Israelites had now gone full circle – returning to near Ur, where Abraham had begun his epic journey many centuries before.

This is the time when the 'Sacred Word', so important to Masons, was lost and has to be found in the Holy Royal Arch ceremony. The Book of Lamentations describes how 'the stones of the sanctuary are poured out in the top of every street' meaning that the Babylonians had entered the Holy of Holies, where only the High Priest had been allowed to enter. Despite all this destruction, General Nebuzaradan did release Jeremiah, who had been thrown into prison (and down a well) for warning the Israelites of God's anger and the impending destruction of Jerusalem as punishment for their sins. For a short time, Jeremiah lived with Gedaliah, who was later appointed governor of Judah, by the new Babylonian masters.

In the Super Excellent Master degree there are 'Three Keepers of the Temple'. These positions are taken from the Biblical account and the Master of a Council of Super Excellent Masters takes the role of Gedaliah. According to the Bible, Gedaliah was assassinated soon after by the Ammonites. The Ammonites are continually engaged in conflict with the Israelites throughout the Bible and in some Masonic ritual most notably against Jephtha, many centuries earlier. King David had also defeated them.

Zedekiah was the last king of Judah and this fact is an important part of the Super Excellent Master degree. The Israelites were now in exile – 'By the rivers of Babylon' and were to remain there for 70 years. This is lamented in Psalm 137, with Jerusalem described as 'Zion'. Their time in Babylon was, however, far better than their life as slaves in Egypt many centuries before. Whilst some had been harshly dealt with for their rebellion, some were selected for duties in the Royal Household and others set up in business. The king deposed after the initial invasion, Jehoiachin, was freed and was allowed to live as befitted his status.

Jeremiah foresaw that Babylon would fall and that the Israelites would return to Jerusalem from exile, where they would enter into an everlasting agreement with God. The second part of this verse from Jeremiah is quoted during the Fifth Grade of Societas Rosicruciana in Anglia: 'They shall ask the way to Zion with their faces thitherward, saying, Come, and let us join ourselves to the Lord in a perpetual covenant that shall not be forgotten.'

EZEKIEL

Timeline	593–573 BC
Biblical reference	Leviticus • Chapter 25 v8–13 (Jubilee) Ezekiel • Chapter 1 (Vision of cloud and creatures) • Chapter 4 (Destruction of Jerusalem foretold) • Chapter 9 v4–6 ('Taw' mark on forehead) • Chapter 17 v11–21 (Zedekiah's broken vow) • Chapter 17 v17 (Babylon's use of siege devices) • Chapter 40 v22–26 (Seven steps to the Temple) • Chapter 44 v1–5 (East Gate and 'Mark well') • Chapter 47 v1 (River on south side of temple)
Masonic reference	Craft • Second Degree Tracing Board • Third Degree Mark • Ceremony of Advancement Royal and Select Masters • Super Excellent Master degree Holy Royal Arch • Ceremony of Exaltation • Mystical Lecture

Ezekiel's Vision (1518) by Raphael. Note the four faces of God: man, lion, ox and eagle.

Ezekiel was a priest and prophet taken into exile by Nebuchadnezzar after the fall of Jerusalem. Whilst living in Babylon, he had a series of bizarre visions of God, the first of which sounds like the arrival of a cloud-like UFO. This 'cloud' contained four creatures, which each had four faces – man, lion, ox and eagle (the same four are shown on the banners at the front of a Holy Royal Arch chapter room). Ezekiel also prophesied the later destruction of Jerusalem by the Babylonians and the fate of Zedekiah. The latter is noted in the Super Excellent Master degree, where the broken vow and punishment of Zedekiah are used to emphasise the importance of being faithful and honourable at all times.

Destruction and death were continually God's punishment for the failings of the Israelites. In one vision, which is quoted in Chapter ritual, Ezekiel is told to 'Go, through the midst of Jerusalem, and set a mark upon the foreheads of the men that sigh and cry for all the abominations that be done in the midst thereof.' This mark was the 'Taw', the last letter of the Hebrew alphabet. Those without, young or old, male or female, were to be slain without mercy. Taus are used on the apron in place of rosettes once a Mason has been Master of his lodge

Ezekiel also had visions of the Temple, which had to be rebuilt and of interest to Freemasons is the reference to the Temple having seven steps. In the Master Mason degree and the Holy Royal Arch, the candidate approaches the pedestal with seven physical (and symbolic) steps and the Royal Ark Mariner Degree has seven signs. On the Second Degree Tracing Board, the Temple has seven steps, which allude to King Solomon taking 'seven years and upwards' to complete the building. These seven steps are also said to allude to the Seven Liberal Arts and Sciences, namely: grammar, rhetoric, logic, arithmetic, geometry, music and astronomy (see St Thomas Aquinas). Seven appears as a symbolic number in the Bible. For example, it took seven days to create the world, God sent a message on a seven sided stone (see section on Haggai and Zechariah) and there are seven churches and seven seals in Revelation. The Law of Moses stated that after seven times seven years (49 years) there was a 'Jubilee' to celebrate the 50th year, according to God's command.

Ezekiel also saw a river on the south side of the Temple (modern translations of the Bible make this clearer than the King James Version, for example the Youth Bible New Century Version). Given that the Temple is located on a hill, this is impossible. The Second Degree Tracing Board, however, shows such a river. Hence the Temple shown thereon is not just King Solomon's Temple (as most Freemasons believe) – it is an amalgamation of that temple and Ezekiel's vision of a later building – see image of Tracing Board in section on The First Temple.

When God speaks to Ezekiel He uses the phrase 'Mark well', which is important to the Mark Degree (see Stone for the temple). Ezekiel also saw a vision of the East Gate of the Temple, which is the position of the Master Overseer in the same degree.

BELSHAZZAR'S FEAST

Timeline	539 BC
Biblical reference	Jeremiah • Chapter 50–51 (Prophesy of the fall of Babylon) Daniel • Chapter 5 (Writing on the Wall) Habakkuk • Chapter 2 v16 (Prophesy of the fall of Babylon)
Masonic reference	Craft • Second Degree Tracing Board (Holy Vessels)
Historical occurrences at that time	539 BC – Cyrus the Great forms Persian Empire

Whilst not featuring directly in Masonic ritual, the story of Belshazzar's feast and the 'writing on the wall' links together the time between the sacking of the Temple by the Babylonians under Nebuchadnezzar and the return of the Jews from exile. Additionally, this incident is quoted frequently, and was famously used by the British Prime Minister and Freemason, Sir Winston Churchill.

The fall of Babylon had been predicted by the prophets Jeremiah and Habakkuk and the story of the feast marks the end of that empire. As ruler of Babylon, Belshazzar ordered that the holy vessels, originally cast by Hiram Abif in the clay ground between Succoth and Zeredathah and stolen from the Temple, be brought to his table. This is the first mention of the vessels since the destruction of Jerusalem. He then foolishly toasted false gods with the vessels and a hand appeared and wrote upon the wall four words, *Mene, Mene, Tekel, Upharsin*.

Belshazzar's Feast (1635) by Rembrandt.

None of his magicians or priests could explain the meaning and eventually, Daniel, a Jew in exile, was called for to explain them as he had previously explained the meaning of dreams. Daniel, who later survived the lions' den, interpreted the words as follows:

- '*Mene Mene*' – God has numbered your kingdom and finished it.
- '*Tekel*' – 'Thou art weighed in the balance and art found wanting'. '*Tekel*' is similar to 'Shekel' a unit of currency and weight in ancient times.
- '*Upharsin*' – Your kingdom is divided and given to Medes and Persians

Churchill quoted the phrase 'Thou art weighed in the balance and found wanting' to describe Britain and France, who signed the Munich agreement in 1938, giving the Sudetenland from Czechoslovakia to Germany. This left the Czechs, who had no say in the agreement, without border defences and the policy of appeasement failed utterly with Hitler invading the country. Churchill had joined Studholme Lodge in 1901.

The last word, *Upharsin,* is very significant as it relates to the conquest of Babylon by the Persian king, Cyrus the Great (see next section). The rule of Cyrus brought the release of the Jews and this Biblical story is the start of the Holy Royal Arch ritual. It should be noted that the Book of Daniel describes the kingdom as taken over by Darius the Mede, but scholars believe that it was Cyrus, as at the time the Medes were ruled by the Persians. The Book of Ezra shows the correct sequence of the rulers featured in Masonic ritual – Nebuchadnezzar, Cyrus and later Darius (see sections on these rulers). Despite these discrepancies, there is no doubt that Belshazzar existed as he is mentioned on the Nabonidus Cylinder, a Babylonian text from the fifth century BC. Copies of this document are held in museums in London and Berlin.

CYRUS THE GREAT

Timeline	539–530 BC
Biblical reference	II Chronicles • Chapter 36 v22–23 (Declaration by Cyrus) Ezra • Chapter 1 v1–2 (Declaration by Cyrus) • Chapter 3 v7 (Funds Temple repairs) • Chapter 5 v14 (Holy treasures returned) Psalms • Psalm 83 v18 (Jehovah the Most High) Isaiah • Chapter 45 v1 (Cyrus anointed by God)
Biblical reference continued	Daniel • Chapter 6 v28 (Daniel in Babylon at time of Cyrus)
Masonic reference	Holy Royal Arch • Ceremony of Exaltation Rose Croix • 15th degree (Knight of the Sword, or of the East)

The conquest of Babylon by the Persians was a very significant event for the Jews in exile and is celebrated in Royal Arch Chapter ritual. Cyrus is also recalled during the Rose Croix ceremony, where the 15th degree (Knight of the Sword or of the East) and the 16th degree (Prince of Jerusalem) refer to the assistance of Cyrus and later Darius in the rebuilding of the temple.

In 539 BC, traditionally described as 70 years after the Jews had been taken from Jerusalem, Persian troops under Cyrus entered Babylon. They met no resistance. To celebrate his victory, Cyrus took the title of 'King of Babylon, King of Sumer and Akkad, King of the four corners of the world'. Given that his kingdom covered the vast majority of the then known world, it was not an unreasonable claim.

In the first year of his rule, Cyrus made a declaration, which is quoted in the Royal Arch chapter ritual: 'Thus saith Cyrus king of Persia, The Lord God of heaven hath given me all the kingdoms of the earth; and he hath charged me to build him an house at Jerusalem, which is in Judah.' This version is taken from Ezra, but a similar version appears at the end of II Chronicles.

Cyrus the Great, King of the 'Four Corners of the World'.

The author with the 'Cyrus Cylinder' at the British Museum in London.

The Jews were released from Babylon and the holy treasures taken from Jerusalem by Nebuchadnezzar were returned to them. Cyrus even paid for craftsmen and materials to re-build the Temple, including replacing cedar wood from Sidonia. Not all the Israelites returned and Daniel, who was taken into exile by Nebuchadnezzar, is shown in the Bible as serving Cyrus and Darius (see section on Darius and Daniel).

For some time there was doubt as to why any ancient king would release slaves or be tolerant to different religions. In 1879, however, the 'Cyrus Cylinder' was discovered in the Marduk Temple in Babylon. In Babylonian cuneiform, inscribed on a clay cylinder, there is a declaration promoting religious tolerance and freedom. It also describes how temples have been restored and displaced people allowed to return home. This artefact has been described as the world's first charter of human rights and a copy of the cylinder is on display at the Headquarters of the United Nations in New York. The original is in the British Museum in London.

The Cylinder appears to confirm the Biblical and Masonic accounts concerning Cyrus' magnanimity in allowing the Jews to return to the 'Promised Land'. From a political viewpoint, Cyrus must have been aware of the usefulness of a friendly state based in Jerusalem and controlling the strategically important land routes connecting many parts of his empire.

In Isaiah, God is said to have held Cyrus' right hand and subdued his enemies. Hence, the Israelites believed that Cyrus' victory over the Babylonians was as a result of the king acting under divine guidance; God had directed a foreign king in a place faraway from their homeland. This was a turning point in the Jewish religion as Jehovah was now seen as the God of the world, not just Israel. This is reflected in Psalm 83, where God is called the 'most high over all the earth'. Likewise, in Masonic ritual, He is referred to as the 'Most High' in the Craft Third Degree prayer and in the Royal Arch ritual.

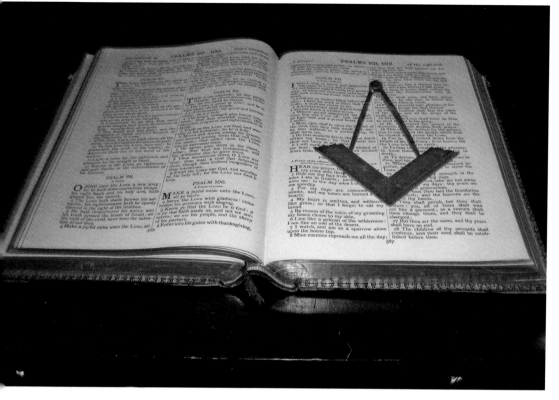

e Bible with square and compasses, as used in Masonic lodges.

lon lodge Archbishop Tenison 5163.

Cain and Abel by Pietro Novelli.

Godfrey of Bouillon depicted as one of the Nine Worthies in a fresco by Giacomo Jaquerio, *c.*1420. The Coat of Arms of the 'Kingdom of Jerusalem' is emblazoned on his tunic.

The Sistine Chapel fresco showing the Great Flood by Michelangelo.

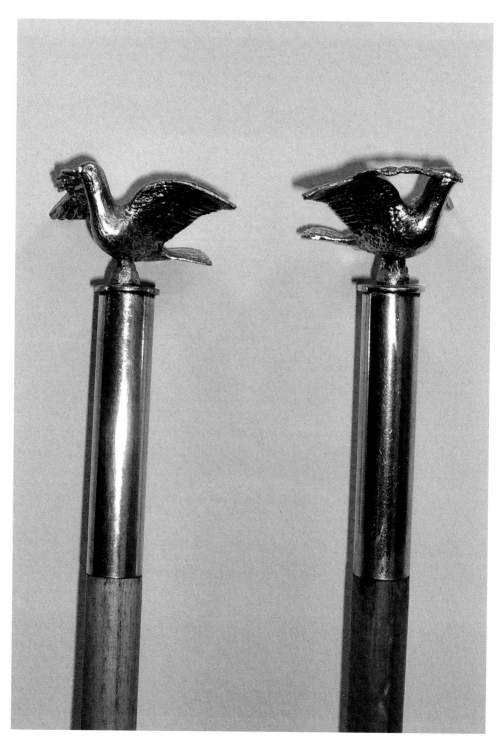

Deacons' wands surmounted by doves, as used in many Masonic Orders.

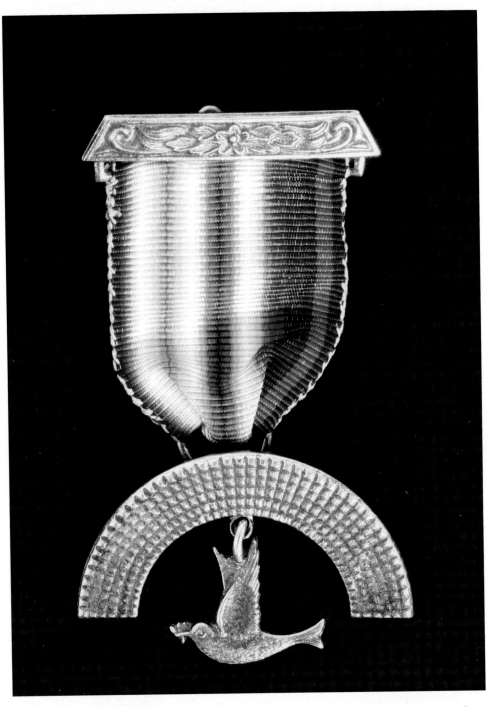

The Jewel of a Royal Ark Mariner, worn in RAM lodges – a rainbow, dove and olive branch. Note the colours of the rainbow on the ribbon from the Biblical account.

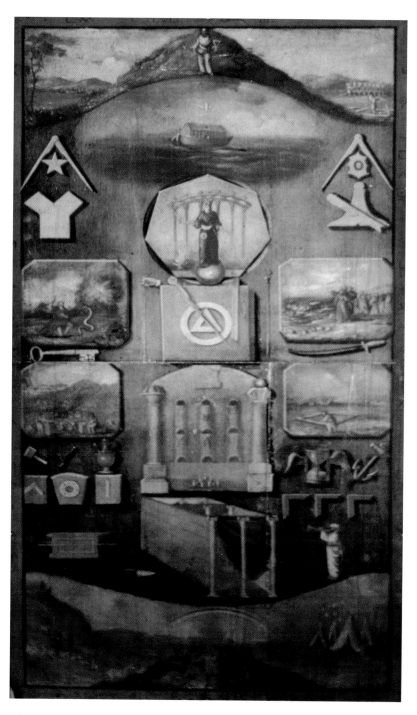

The Royal Ark Mariner Tracing Board. The Ark is top centre with Noah standing above and Mount Ararat is bottom left. Noah at the altar with his sons is bottom centre and tents are bottom right. The two pillars and nine arches described in the section on Enoch can be seen lower centre.

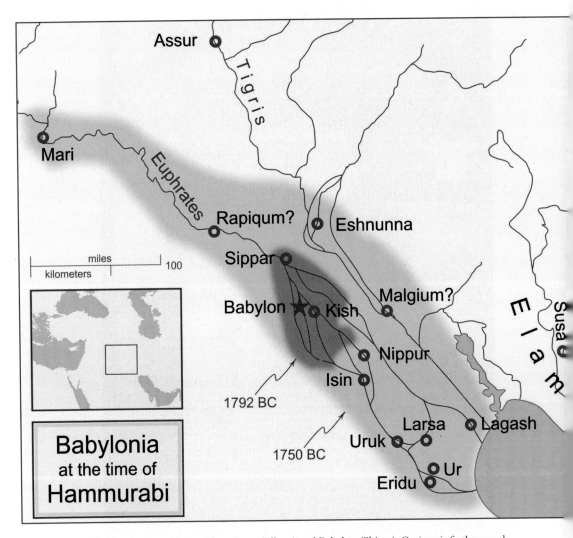

The area controlled by the Four Kings – Elam, Larsa (Ellasar) and Babylon (Shinar). Gutium is farther north.

Tracing Board with ladder at the top.

The Crossing of the Red Sea (1515) by Bernardino Luini.

Modern copy of the lamp stand known as a 'Menorah' in Hebrew – this stands in Jerusalem and is copied from the image on the Arch of Titus.

The author as Thrice Illustrious Master of Warlingham Council of Royal and Select Masters. Note the half size model of Ark of the Covenant in the foreground.

Detail from *The Return of Jephtha* (1700–1725) by Giovanni Antonio Pellegrini.

The Star of David as part of the Chapter Jewel.

The stairs leading to the Middle Chamber of the Temple as shown on the Second Degree Tracing Board; they are noted in the Book of Kings. There was no river near the real Temple, but that depicted may be based on one of Ezekiel's visions.

The Perfect and Rough Ashlars used by Frederick Lodge of Unity 452 – the former from the quarries of King Solomon and the latter from the Pyramid at Giza.

The author at the Wailing or Western Wall, the remains of the Second Temple.

The breast jewels worn by a member of an Allied Masonic Degrees council. Note the gridiron of St Lawrence on the left.

The Church of the Holy Sepulchre in Jerusalem.

Banner of the Tribe of Judah as used in a Royal Arch Chapter.

The 'superb cupola' of the Church of the Holy Sepulchre, as described in the Red Cross of Constantine appendant Orders.

The Hereford Mappa Mundi (1300) drawn in the T and O style, attributed to Richard of Haldingham and Lafford. Jerusalem is in the centre with Europe shown on the left. The map would have to be rotated clockwise to give a conventional modern view of the world.

A Masonic version of the Bible.

8

THE SECOND TEMPLE

ZERUBBABEL AND THE SECOND TEMPLE

Timeline	539 BC (Return from exile)
	516 BC (Temple rebuilt)
Biblical reference	I Chronicles
	• Chapter 3 v19 (Descended from King David)
	Ezra
	• Chapter 1 v5 (Tribes of Judah and Benjamin)
	• Chapter 2 (List of people returning with Zerubbabel)
	• Chapter 3 (Rebuilding of Temple)
	• Chapter 4 (Samaritans cannot assist in rebuilding)
	Nehemiah
	• Chapter 7 v7 (List of people returning)
	• Chapter 12 v1 (Priests returning)
	• Chapter 12 v47 (Payment to Temple singers)
	Haggai
	• Chapter 1–2 (Haggai tells Zerubbabel God's word)
	• Chapter 2 v20 (Zerubbabel is God's signet ring)
	Zechariah
	• Chapter 4 v4–10 (Succeeds by God's spirit)
	Matthew
	• Chapter 1 v13 (Zerubbabel in line of Jesus)
	Luke
	• Chapter 3 v27 (Zerubbabel in line of Jesus)

| Masonic reference | Allied Masonic Degrees
• Red Cross of Babylon

Royal and Select Master
• Royal Master

Holy Royal Arch
• Ceremony of Exaltation
• Historical Lecture
• Questions Before Toasts

Holy Royal Arch Knights Templar Priests

Red Cross of Constantine
• Knight of the Holy Sepulchre

Knights Templar |
| Historical context | 521 BC – Persian Empire under Darius I stretches from Nile to Indus |

The final part of the Masonic 'Solomonic' epic is the Holy Royal Arch, where members meet in a Chapter. This is often the same lodge room, but it is set out very differently, with the three Principals seated at the front, rather than as a Master and two Wardens in a Craft Lodge. In the latter, the three officers sit apart, in the east, west and south of the room. In England, the Royal Arch is governed by the same body as the Craft, the United Grand Lodge. In Scotland and other parts of the world it is a completely separate body. The Holy Royal Arch is described in the Mystical Lecture, given at the end of the ceremony of Exaltation, as the 'climax of Freemasonry'.

In the Royal Arch ritual, the three principal officers are called Zerubbabel, Haggai and Joshua (who are also recalled in the lecture on the Royal Master degree). The most senior post is referred to as the 'MEZ' or 'Most Excellent Zerubbabel'. These three characters form part of the Biblical account of the return from Babylon to Jerusalem after being freed by King Cyrus. Zerubbabel features in numerous books of the Bible, including Zechariah, the penultimate book of the Old Testament.

Zerubbabel means 'One sown in Babylon' or 'One exiled in Babylon' and either version would be an accurate description of him. He was descended from the line of King David and later features in the New Testament in the line of Jesus, although the two lists differ. He was the grandson of King Jehoiachim, who had been replaced as king by Zedekiah (see above). His line of descent is unclear as he is shown as having two fathers, Shealtiel and Pedaiah. This could simply be an error in the text or Shealtiel may have been the head of the household and Pedaiah, his brother, could have been the biological father of Zerubbabel. Masonically, Shealtiel is considered to be his father. In some versions of the Bible, he is referred to as 'Zorobabel' or as 'Sheshbazzar' which appears to be a Persian version of his name.

In 539 BC, Zerubbabel led the first group of 42,360 Jews and over 8000 servants back to Jerusalem; but enormous changes had now taken place. The Israelites were now known as 'Jews' and were more of a religious sect than a nation. The Book of Ezra observes that the Jews consisted of just two tribes – Judah and Benjamin, with the Levite priests (these two tribal names are significant in the Red Cross of Babylon ceremony). The people had left Babylon, the centre of the world and returned to Jerusalem, a city laid to waste 70 years before.

Zerubbabel was advised by Haggai the Prophet and Joshua, the son of the High Priest. He was also assisted by the Prophet, Zechariah and during some versions of Chapter ritual sections of the

Chapter 4 of the Book of Zechariah are quoted. Here the prophet is told by God that Zerubbabel will succeed by His spirit and not military might. God also promised that Zerubbabel would complete the rebuilding of the temple.

In Masonic terms, the name 'Zerubbabel' holds an exalted position, being the senior officer in what is viewed by many Masons as the most important degree in Freemasonry. The candidate in the Red Cross of Babylon degree also bears the name of Zerubbabel (see Darius below).

As has been noted, according to the ritual in the Knight of the Holy Sepulchre, an Appendant Order of the Red Cross of Constantine, the founders of Freemasonry were Zerubbabel, Moses and Solomon. To join the Red Cross of Constantine, a Mason must already belong to a Chapter, so it is not surprising that Zerubbabel is given such status.

The Temple was completed about 516 BC and dedicated the following year. According to Holy Royal Arch ritual, this is the 'Third or Grand and Royal Lodge'. Many of the treasures from the original Temple were restored, but the Ark of the Covenant and its contents, the Ten Commandments, Pot of Manna and Aaron's Rod, had been lost forever.

In the Masonic story related in a Royal Arch Chapter, three 'sojourners' return and assist in the renovation of the Temple. There they find the 'secret word' and this links the Degree to the stories related in the Royal Master degree (secret word hidden), Third Degree (secret word lost as a result of death of Hiram Abif) and the Second Degree ('Archives of Freemasonry' concealed in pillars). This story does not appear in the Bible, but appears to be based on several different incidents, including a fourth-century legend of the discovery of a vault under the Temple (see section on The Development of Christian Theology). The ritual may also be based on the Biblical account of the finding of the Book of Law during the repairs to the Temple organised by King Josiah and excavations later made at the Temple site by the Knights Templar (see later section).

JOSHUA OR JESHUA: THE SON OF JOSEDECH THE HIGH PRIEST

Timeline	539 BC
Biblical reference	Ezra • Chapter 2 v2 (Returns to Jerusalem with Zerubbabel) • Chapter 3 v2 (Altar built) • Chapter 3 v8 (Start of rebuild of Temple) • Chapter 5 v2 (Rebuilding the Temple) Nehemiah • Chapter 7 v7 (Returns with Zerubbabel) Ezekiel • Chapter 43 v1−12 (Priests in charge of the Temple) Haggai • Chapter 1 (Joshua son of the High Priest) Zechariah • Chapter 3 v1−5 (Vision of Joshua in white mitre) • Chapter 3 v9 (Stone with seven sides) • Chapter 6 v13 (King and High Priest to rule together)

Masonic reference	Allied Masonic Degrees • Red Cross of Babylon Royal and Select Masters • Royal Master Holy Royal Arch • Ceremony of Exaltation • Historical Lecture • Questions Before Toasts Holy Royal Arch Knights Templar Priests • Installation of a Knight Templar Priest

A possible cause of confusion is a second major character called 'Joshua' in the Bible and Masonic ritual. To add further complications, he is referred to as 'Jeshua' in the Book of Ezra and in some versions of the Holy Royal Arch ceremony. He was the son of the High Priest (Josedech in the ritual or Jozadak in Ezra), who was descended from Aaron. Joshua was likely to have been born in Babylon, as he returned to Jerusalem with Zerubbabel. Together, they built the altar and re-laid the Temple foundations. The prophet Haggai advised both men on God's wish to have the Temple restored.

At the time of Zerubbabel, Israel was ruled by a governor and a High Priest. This is not unique. In more recent times, the Holy Roman Empire was ruled jointly by the Emperor and the Pope. There was, however, a change in the control of the Second Temple. In the time of Solomon, the king had been in charge of the temple. The new temple was not to be contaminated by political power and was in the hands of the priests alone. This is made clear in the Book of Ezekiel.

In the Book of Zechariah, this prophet has a vision of Joshua in filthy clothes in the presence of Satan. An angel re-clothed him in clean clothes and placed a white mitre (later translations call it a turban) on his head to symbolically cleansing Joshua from sin. Satan then disappears from the narrative and God placed a seven-sided stone in front of Joshua. The Lord promised to carve a message on to the stone (the message is not stated). Such a stone is displayed prominently on the Royal Ark Mariner Tracing Board (see image of Tracing Board in the colour section), but its presence is not explained. The story of the clean mitre is quoted in the Knights Templar Priest ceremony.

In Royal Arch Chapter Ritual, Companion 'Joshua' is the Third Principal. He holds a sceptre topped with a symbol of the High Priest's mitre (see Aaron). A section of the Book of Ezra is read out during the Red Cross of Babylon ceremony and Joshua is noted as being involved in the rebuilding of the temple.

HAGGAI AND ZECHARIAH

Timeline	539–516 BC
Biblical reference	Ezra • Chapter 5 v1 (Prophets – Haggai and Zechariah) • Chapter 6 v14 (Involvement in temple rebuilding) Haggai • Chapter 1 (Informs Zerubbabel of God's command)

Biblical reference continued	• Chapter 2 (God's commands for the new temple) • Chapter 2 v18 (Foundation of the temple) Zechariah • Chapter 2 v1 (Man with a measuring line) • Chapter 4 v9 (Zerubbabel and temple foundations) • Chapter 8 v9 (Temple foundations) • Chapter 9 v9–10 (Prophesy of Christ)
Masonic reference	Royal Ark Mariner • Tracing Board Allied Masonic Degrees • Red Cross of Babylon Royal and Select Masters • Royal Master Holy Royal Arch • Ceremony of Exaltation • Historical Lecture • Questions Before Toasts

In a Royal Arch Chapter the Second Principal is denominated 'Excellent Companion Haggai'. Little is known about the life of this prophet and the Book of Haggai is very short, with only two chapters. He is likely to have been born during the exile in Babylon but returned with Zerubbabel and worked with Joshua re-building the new Temple.

The Book of Haggai describes how God passed His commands through Haggai to Zerubbabel and Joshua. At the start of the book, God is described as being angry that the Jews have focused more on building their own houses than they have on His Temple. To stir them into action, God threatened to start a drought near the time of the harvest, after which the Book of Haggai describes the clearing of the old stones and laying of the foundations for the new temple. Zechariah also refers to the foundations. This is a link to the Chapter ritual, where the 'Three Sojourners' are employed on this part of the work.

The restoration work on the Temple had been stopped for eighteen years by problems created by the Samaritans (see Darius and Daniel below). Haggai and another prophet, Zechariah (the son of Iddo according to the Book of Ezra), assisted in getting the work resumed, with the Temple being completed in four years. A section of the Book of Ezra is read out during the Red Cross of Babylon ceremony, which names Haggai and Zechariah as the prophets who advised at the rebuilding.

The Book of Zechariah is believed by Christians to contain a foretelling of Christ – a 'Prince of Peace', who will enter Jerusalem riding on a donkey. It also contains a reference to a 'man with a measuring line in his hand', which could be linked to the Working Tools in either the First Degree (24" measuring gauge) or the Third Degree (the skirret for marking out ground). The straight line produced by the skirret represents to Freemasons the 'straight and undeviating line of conduct laid down for our guidance in the Volume of the Sacred Law'.

DARIUS AND DANIEL

Timeline	522 BC–486 BC Reign of Darius
Biblical reference	Ezra • Chapter 4 v5 (Samaritans frustrate re-building) • Chapter 4 v5–7 (Persian rulers) • Chapter 4 v12–16 (Accusations made against Jews) • Chapter 4 v21–24 (Work suspended by decree) • Chapter 5 v1 (Haggai encourages rebuilding) • Chapter 5 v3 (Governor Tatnai and Shethar-boznai) • Chapter 5 v6–17 (Letter sent to Darius) • Chapter 6 v1–11 (Darius finds Cyrus's decree) • Chapter 6 v12 (Authorises rebuilding) • Chapter 6 v15–16 (Temple completed and dedicated) I Esdras (also known as 3 Ezra) • Chapter 3–4 (Which is the stronger – wine, the king or women?) • Chapter 4 v13 (Zorobabel/Zerubbabel) • Chapter 4 v35 ('Great is Truth') • Chapter 4 v47 (Darius authorises Zerubbabel to return to Jerusalem) Esther • Chapter 7 v10 (Haman suffers Persian execution) Daniel • Chapter 2 v5 (Offender's home made into dunghill) • Chapter 6 (Daniel in the lions' den) • Chapter 6 v1–2 (Darius selects Daniel as a Governor) • Chapter 6 v28 (Darius and Cyrus) • Chapter 9 v1 (Darius was son of Xerxes) • Chapter 11 v4 ('Four winds of heaven') • Chapter 12 v2–3 (Resurrection of the dead) Haggai • Chapter 1 v1–2 (Rebuild in Darius's reign) Luke Chapter 10 v25–37 (The Good Samaritan)
Masonic reference	Craft • Third Degree Allied Masonic Degrees • Red Cross of Babylon Royal and Select Masters • Ritual Book explanation of degree Rose Croix • 16th degree (Prince of Jerusalem)

Historical context	510 BC – Roman Republic founded
	490 BC – Battle of Marathon
	480 BC – Battle of Salamis

Darius ruled the Persian Empire some ten years after Cyrus, extending it eastwards into India and westwards into Greece. He centralised the empire's administration and developed the legal system. He also continued Cyrus's policy of benevolence towards non-Persian faiths. There is some confusion in the chronology of the reigns of the various kings of this period when the Biblical and historical accounts are compared, with the sequence of the reigns of Darius, Cyrus and Artaxerxes being confused. The Book of Ezra shows them in the correct historical order, but Daniel, Chapter 6, seems to state that Darius was before Cyrus and Chapter 9 shows Darius as the son of Xerxes (in Hebrew 'Ahasuerus'), whilst Darius was, in fact, the father of Xerxes.

Whoever was the ruler at that time, the construction of the Second Temple was fraught with difficulties. Whilst Cyrus had given permission to rebuild, the neighbouring Samaritans caused problems for the Jews. The Samaritans were the descendants of the ten breakaway tribes who had formed the northern state of Israel after the death of King Solomon. The Samaritans had offered to help but this was declined by Zerubbabel and Joshua, as they were viewed as idol worshippers.

The Samaritans wrote to the new Persian king, Artaxerxes (465–424 BC), and alleged that if the Jews were permitted to rebuild the walls and temple at Jerusalem this would result in future problems for the Persian Empire. They went on to claim that the inhabitants would refuse to pay taxes and a check in the ancient records would confirm that this had occurred on previous occasions. As a result of the Samaritans' efforts, work was suspended on the Temple until the rule of King Darius.

With the encouragement of the prophets, including Haggai, Zerubbabel appealed to the new king and Darius ordered a search of the records for details of Cyrus's decree. This was found in the Babylonian palace at Achmetha (or Ecbatane in some Bibles) – modern day Hamadan in Iran – and royal authority was granted to rebuild. Darius also ordered the regional governor to provide offerings, including wheat, salt, corn, wine and oil for use at the Temple.

In the First Book of Esdras (also known as the Third Book of Ezra), Zerubbabel is a guard in the king's household, who took part in a debate with two other guards as to what has the most power over men. The other guards suggested wine or the king. Zerubbabel won the debate with his argument that women are the strongest (a woman gives birth to a king), but truth is even greater. This so impressed Darius that he allowed Zerubbabel to return to Jerusalem and rebuild the Temple. The First Book of Esdras (Greek for 'Ezra') is considered as apocryphal and is not included in Roman Catholic or Protestant versions of the Bible but it does form part of the Bible used by the Eastern Orthodox Church. (The apochryphal Second Book of Esdras was, interestingly, a great motivation to Columbus, apparently telling him the earth was round and that the distance westward from Europe to Asia, or 'India', was very short.)

According to Haggai, work on the Second Temple was started in the second year of Darius's reign and it was completed in 516 BC, the sixth year of his rule. The reign of Darius was successful, with an increase in population and trade links established across the Mediterranean. As well as allowing the rebuilding of the Temple at Jerusalem, he authorised the construction of temples in Egypt and his name can still be seen on these buildings.

In Masonic terms, this story is retold in the Red Cross of Babylon degree, part of the Allied Masonic Degrees. This degree was once known as the 'Red Cross of Daniel' and King Darius is featured in the Book of Daniel (indeed it was Darius who threw Daniel into the lions' den for failing to worship him, but freed him after an angel stopped the beasts from devouring Daniel). Daniel had originally been taken to Babylon by the forces of Nebuchadnezzar (see section on Fall of Jerusalem) and served various rulers during the exile, also see section on Belshazzar's Feast.

A Council of the Red Cross of Babylon is opened 'in the name of the Mighty Darius' and during the ceremony large sections of the Book of Ezra are quoted. The degree is in two parts – Jewish court and Babylonish court and requires a significant number of officers to perform the ceremony. The degree features two very obscure Biblical characters, Tatnai (or Tattenai), a Persian governor and his deputy, Shethar-boznai. Tatnai controlled the area 'Beyond the River', which meant west of the Euphrates. The readings from the Book of Ezra include the names of more minor Biblical characters, including Kadmiel and the sons of Henadad and Asaph, who had duties at the rebuilding of the Temple.

The main Jewish character in the ceremony, Zerubbabel, is also the First Principal in a Royal Arch Chapter. The offerings used feature during the ceremony of the dedication of a new lodge. According to the Royal and Select Masters ritual book, which offers a summary of this degree, Darius helped Zerubbabel because they had been soldiers together. This is incorrect – it can be seen above that the Book of Esdras states that Darius was the king and Zerubbabel was one of his guards. Darius is mentioned during when the 15th and 16th degrees are conferred (in name only) on a Rose Croix candidate.

The hatred of the Samaritans by the Jews stemmed from this period. This is the reason, 500 years later, that Jesus used the story of the good Samaritan to answer the Jewish lawyer's question, 'Who is my neighbour?' By choosing a hated enemy as the hero of the parable, Jesus was making clear that all mankind are 'neighbours'.

This is linked to The Charge recited to newly initiated Freemasons at their first lodge meeting. The duties to 'God, your neighbour and yourself' are clearly explained. A 'neighbour' must be treated as the Mason would expect to be treated himself.

The Book of Daniel contains the clearest reference in the Old Testament to the resurrection of the dead, with eternal life for the righteous and damnation for the wicked: 'many of them that sleep in the dust of the earth shall awake, some to everlasting life, and some to shame and everlasting contempt.'

The next verse appears to be the basis of the prayer in the Third Degree. This is made all the more likely as the subject of this ceremony is the mortality of man. 'And they that be wise shall shine as the brightness of the firmament; and they that turn many to righteousness as the stars for ever and ever.' The Masonic prayer ends with the phrase, 'to shine as the stars for ever and ever'. Furthermore, the Third Degree punishment states that the Master Mason who unlawfully discloses the secrets of the degree will have 'his bowels burned to ashes and those ashes wafted across the face of the earth and water by the four cardinal winds of heaven'. The 'four winds of heaven' appear in Daniel's vision of the empires that will rule the world after Persia.

Whilst Masonic oaths contain horrible symbolic punishments, the Persians were particularly ruthless in practice. 'Hanging' in Persia meant being impaled on a sharp stake and being displayed in public. This was the fate of Haman, a Persian official, who planned to kill all the Jews in the reign of Xerxes. The Babylonians also displayed little pity (as we saw with the fate of Zedekiah) and Nebuchadnezzar threatened that he would turn the homes of those who failed him into a 'dunghill'. These two punishments were combined in the legend related in the old Mark ritual from the eighteenth century, which was recently revived for demonstrations as a result of the work of the Masonic expert, the Reverend Neville Barker-Cryer (who wrote the foreword for this book).

EZRA THE SCRIBE

Timeline	460 BC
Biblical reference	Ezra • Chapter 1 (Cyrus's decree)

Biblical reference continued	• Chapter 7 v13–28 (Decree authorising Ezra's work) Nehemiah • Chapter 9 v5–37 (Summary of history) • Chapter 12 v26 (Lived a generation after Joshua)
Masonic reference	Craft • Second Degree Holy Royal Arch Officer of the Lodge 'Scribe Ezra'
Historical context	Age of Greek classical culture, including: Hippocrates (470–406 BC) – medicine Socrates (469–399 BC) – philosophy

Ezra is a major post-Exile figure in Jewish history, who led 5000 more Jews from Babylon to Israel. He was born in Babylon to a descendant of Aaron, Seraiah the High Priest, who was taken into exile when Jerusalem was destroyed at the time of Zedekiah.

Ezra is venerated as a 'Scribe' in the Bible and in Jewish tradition. In a Holy Royal Arch, the officer known as 'Scribe Ezra' or 'Scribe E' performs the duties of secretary, recording the business of the chapter. In a Chapter, Ezra is involved in the ceremony together with officers playing the roles of Zerubbabel, Haggai and Joshua. This is at variance with the Biblical setting, where Ezra was active at least a generation later. He is shown in the Book of Nehemiah as living 'in the days of Joiakim the son of Joshua' and there are at least 80 years between Zerubbabel and Ezra.

Ezra was commissioned by King Artaxerxes of Persia (465–424 BC) to return to Jerusalem to re-organise religious and civil affairs. This decree is included in the Book of Ezra. On his arrival in the city, he personally dictated 24 books of the Old Testament, which would otherwise have been lost during the exile. Whilst the Bible appears to credit Moses with establishing the council of 72 elders, Jewish history credits Ezra with establishing the Great Assembly of prophets and scholars. This was the forerunner of the Grand Sanhedrin, which is noted in Chapter ritual.

Ezra read out loud the Law of Moses to the Israelites. The priests then praised the Lord and their prayer included a summary of the lives of Abraham and Moses. The pillars of fire and cloud, as recalled during the explanation of the Second Degree Tracing Board, are included in the speech.

The relationship of Ezra (priest) with Nehemiah (secular governor) is very similar to the relationship of Joshua and Zerubbabel a generation earlier. It should be noted that the Books of Ezra and Nehemiah were originally one book. Ezra's tomb is said to be in Basra in modern-day Iraq.

NEHEMIAH AND MALACHI

Timeline	444 BC (Nehemiah arrived in Jerusalem) 413 BC (Nehemiah died) 420 BC (Malachi prophesied)
Biblical reference	Ezra • Chapter 2 v2 (Returns with Zerubbabel) Nehemiah

Biblical reference continued	• Chapter 1 v11 (Nehemiah's prayer) • Chapter 2 v1–10 (Sent to Jerusalem by Persian King) • Chapter 4 v16–18 (Builders armed at all times) • Chapter 6 v15–16 (City walls rebuilt) • Chapter 7 v1–3 (Appoints guards at city gates) • Chapter 8 (Ezra and Nehemiah) • Chapter 10 v1 (Governor of Jerusalem) Malachi • Chapter 4 v2 ('Sun of righteousness')
Masonic reference	Royal Order of Scotland Royal and Select Masters • Select Master Holy Royal Arch • Officer of the Lodge 'Scribe Nehemiah' • Historical Lecture Red Cross of Constantine • Enthronement of Sovereign
Historical context	431–404 BC – Peloponnesian War between Sparta and Athens

In a Royal Arch Chapter, an officer is known as 'Scribe Nehemiah'. His duties include a similar role to that of 'Inner Guard' in a Craft Lodge; that is to say the Brother responsible for guarding the door from the inside. The Biblical Nehemiah was responsible for rebuilding the walls of Jerusalem. This, no doubt, is the reason for 'Companion Nehemiah' being in charge of Chapter security.

Whilst Nehemiah may be present at the same time as Zerubbabel, Haggai and Joshua in a Chapter, it would appear that he lived around 100 years after the return from Babylon. It is therefore very unlikely that he could have had any contact with them. The Bible does show him as returning to Jerusalem with Zerubbabel, but if this was the case, he would have lived to be nearly 150 years old.

During Nehemiah's life the Persian Empire remained the dominant power and Judea was a small province under its charge. He held a senior position within the empire, being a Royal Cup Bearer to King Artaxerxes at the Palace of Shushan, which is in modern Iran. The cup bearer was responsible for tasting the monarch's wine to ensure that it had not been poisoned. Nehemiah appears to have been in favour with his king, who granted him a long period of leave to enable him to work on the restoration of Jerusalem.

On his arrival in the city, Nehemiah conducted a secret night-time survey and after formulating a plan, quickly organised the work; the Bible records that the walls of Jerusalem was renovated in less than two months. The craftsmen, however, were in constant fear of attack, and had to work with a trowel in one hand and a sword in the other. This is noted in the Historical Lecture of a Royal Arch Chapter and the trowel is an important emblem of the Order of Royal and Select Masters, where it sits with the square and compasses on top of the open Bible. The sword and trowel are the 'implements' of a Select Master and in the Royal Order of Scotland, the candidate holds a sword in his right hand and a trowel in his left when taking his obligation. The trowel is also shown on the Royal Ark Mariner Tracing Board.

During the Installation ceremony of the officer known as 'Joshua' in a Royal Arch Chapter, a section from the Book of Nehemiah is used as a prayer. Much of Chapter 1, verse 11 is paraphrased and the prayer used is, 'O Lord, we beseech Thee, let now Thine ear be attentive to the prayer of Thy servants who fear thy name: and prosper, we pray Thee, Thy servant this day, and grant him mercy in Thy sight.'

Nehemiah was the Persian-appointed Governor of Judea until his death. It was around the time of Nehemiah that Malachi was a prophet. His words feature in the Red Cross of Constantine ritual, when the Sovereign (Master) is 'enthroned' and told that 'the Son of Righteousness has risen with healing in His wings.' Here lies an important difference with the King James'Version, which has the same words, but with an important difference. It is 'Sun of Righteousness' – note the spelling of 'Sun'. John Wesley, the eighteenth-century Christian theologian and co-founder of the Methodist Church, observed in his Bible Commentary that this 'Sun' is a foretelling of Christ. In the King James' Version of the Bible, Malachi is the last book in the Old Testament, but as we shall see, other editions take the story further towards the birth of Christ.

EUCLID AND PYTHAGORAS

Timeline	580–490 BC (Pythagoras)
	300 BC (Euclid)
Biblical reference	I Maccabees
	• Chapter 13 v28 (Pyramids)
Masonic reference	Craft
	• First Degree Tracing Board
	• Installation Ceremony
	Royal Ark Mariner
	• Tracing Board
	Red Cross of Constantine
	• Knight of St John the Evangelist
	Order of Athelstan
	Societas Rosicruciana in Anglia
	• First Grade 'Zelator'
	Fifth Grade 'Adeptus Minor'
Historical context	525 BC – Cambyses, son of Cyrus, conquered Egypt
	490 BC – Greeks defeat Persians at Marathon
	480 BC – Greeks defeat Persians at Salamis
	323 BC – Death of Alexander the Great

Neither Euclid nor Pythagoras are Biblical characters, but they feature in Masonic ritual and the latter may well have been in Babylon when some Jews were still to return from exile. During the Order of Athelstan, Euclid is described as an 'early Egyptian Geometrician'. He lived around 300 BC and the 47th proposition of the First Book of Euclid is represented by the collar jewel worn by

Past Master's collar jewel, with 47th proposition of the First Book of Euclid. A similar design can be seen on the Royal Ark Mariner Tracing Board.

the Past Master of a Craft Lodge. This is presented during the Board of Installed Masters as part of the Installation Ceremony.

On the Royal Ark Mariner Tracing Board, the same mathematical diagram is described as the Pythagorean Theorem. Pythagoras was born on the Greek Island of Samos. His father was a Phoenician from Tyre, who had studied in Sidon. As a result, he would have had little difficulty communicating with the Israelites, who had long been in an alliance with the Sidonians.

He is recalled in the preamble of the First Degree Tracing Board. This piece of ritual begins by describing how the Egyptian Magi or Priests concealed their secrets and then states: 'Pythagoras seems to have established his system on a similar plan…' At first sight, there does not appear to be any link between Freemasonry or Biblical stories with the famous mathematician and the First Degree Tracing Board could simply be discounted as an eighteenth-century embellishment, but there is evidence that he could have been in Babylon with the Jews.

When Cyrus conquered the Babylonish Empire in 539 BC, his son, Cambyses, was appointed ruler of the city of Babylon. When Cyrus died, Cambyses became sole ruler of the empire. As part of the expansion of the empire, he invaded Egypt and there he made Pythagoras his prisoner. Pythagoras was held in Babylon for twelve years but used this opportunity to study the mysteries of the east. This is the time when the Jews would still have been in the city and the two may have influenced each other. The 'Three Sojourners' in the Chapter ritual provide evidence of Jews leaving Babylon much later than the initial returnees.

It is therefore relevant that in a Royal Arch Chapter, the 'Five Regular Platonic Bodies' are on display and feature in the Symbolical Lecture, delivered by Excellent Companion Haggai. They are said to represent the 'four elements and the sphere of the universe', as first described by Pythagoras.

In the Red Cross of Constantine, pyramids are used to denote the durability of the Christian faith and human mortality. There is an obscure reference to pyramids in the Book of Maccabees (see next section) and this is the only mention of them in any version of the Bible. Pythagoras also features in the first and fifth grades of SRIA, which discusses the links between religion, geometry and the ancient sciences.

THE DESECRATION OF THE SECOND TEMPLE AND THE MACCABEAN REVOLT

Timeline	169 BC
Biblical reference	I Maccabees • Chapter 1 v1 (Alexander the Great) • Chapter 1 v20–24 (Temple desecrated) • Chapter 1 v44–50 (Greek religion forced on Jews) • Chapter 7 v39 (Nicanor camped at Bethoron) • Chapter 9 v54 (Alcimus tried to change the temple) • Chapter 9 v55 (High Priest suffering from palsy) II Maccabees • Chapter 5 v11–14 (Slaughter in Jerusalem) • Chapter 6 v1–11 (Greek religion forced on Jews) • Chapter 15 v14–15 (Jeremiah appears in a vision)
Masonic reference	Order of the Secret Monitor • Scarlet Cord 3rd Grade Holy Royal Arch
Historical context	218 BC – Hannibal invades Italy 146 BC – Greece under Roman domination

Once again, a great empire seized the strategically important Holy Land. From 332 BC to 186 BC, Jerusalem was a Greek province. The Persian Empire fell to Alexander the Great, with the last Persian king, Darius III, killed in 331 BC. After Alexander's early death, power in the region passed to one of his generals, Seleucus. This resulted in the Seleucid Empire, which ruled over Babylon and much of the Near East. From 215 to 164 BC; the empire was ruled by Antiochus IV.

During this time, a process of Hellenisation (spreading of Greek culture) took place in Israel. This was readily accepted by some Jews, whilst others viewed it as treachery. A major area of dispute between the two factions was the appointment of the High Priest and Antiochus appointed a Greek-leaning Jew to the position. When Antiochus was fighting in Egypt, a false rumour was spread that he had been killed, at which the Israelites seized the moment, took charge of their capital city and forced the Greek-appointed High Priest to flee Jerusalem.

To reassert his power, Antiochus marched north and re-captured Jerusalem, where his reprisal was brutal. The Temple was desecrated, with pigs being killed on the altar and the priests made to eat the burnt pork. According to II Maccabees, 40,000 Jews were slaughtered and the same number sold into slavery. Much of the Temple treasure was stolen by the Greeks and to prevent further problems, in 167 BC Antiochus decided to enforce the Hellenisation of the area and outlawed the Jewish religion. He even installed a statue of the Greek god Zeus in the Temple in Jerusalem.

The resistance to this attempt to destroy Jewish culture and religion was led by Judah Maccabee (Maccabee may mean 'Hammer') and the story of the revolt is related in the First and Second Books of Maccabees. These were not included in the current King James Bible, but can be found in Roman Catholic and Eastern Orthodox versions. These books are viewed by Jews and Protestants as historically correct but not part of scripture. The Scarlet Cord ritual includes part of the story of the Maccabean revolt, particularly the story of the High Priest, Alcinus (or Alcimus), who was a supporter of the Greek rulers and the Seleucid commander, Nicador.

Judah Maccabee is celebrated as a great Jewish soldier, both in the Bible and in the Scarlet Cord ritual. He was a very clever commander; at first he realised that he had insufficient forces to meet the might of the Greek Seleucid forces in open battle and therefore utilised guerrilla tactics to harass his enemy. By 166 BC, his army had expanded and he was able to defeat General Nicador at the Battle of Emmaus (see sections on Apostles after Crucifixion and Knights Templar for further references to this village). This victory was the start of the liberation of Judea, with Jerusalem re-taken within two years. The Temple was then purified and re-dedicated.

Unfortunately, the Jewish victory did not bring peace and the pro-Greek and anti-Greek factions continued to seek power. The appointment of Alcimus (called Alcinus in the Scarlet Cord) was a pivotal moment. Despite being a descendant of Aaron, the first High Priest, Alcimus was a supporter of Hellenisation and he displayed his ruthlessness by executing 60 priests. Alcimus was then forced out by the Maccabeans and he fled to Syria to seek Seleucid assistance to restore his position.

A large Greek army under Nicador was subsequently despatched in 161 BC to re-take Jerusalem and camped to the north of the capital at Bethoron (modern day Beit Horon). A vision of Prophet Jeremiah holding a golden sword inspired the Jewish army to victory at the Battle of Adasa, where Nicador was killed and his head and right hand were cut off and displayed in Jerusalem in triumph. Nicador's camp at Bethoron and the vision are all included in the Scarlet Cord ceremony.

The war, however, continued and the Greeks again besieged Jerusalem and at the Battle of Elasa, six miles from the city, Judah Maccabee was killed. Alcimus was re-installed as High Priest but his victory was short-lived. He attempted to change the layout of the Temple and gave orders to pull down the inner wall of the sanctuary, destroying in the process, as the Bible describes it, 'the works of the prophets'. He was then stricken down with palsy, which rendered him unable to speak and died in great agony, which was considered to be a divine punishment. Alcimus also features in the Scarlet Cord, where he is described as 'the false High Priest'.

The revolt inspired by Judah Maccabee continued and his brothers, Jonathan and Simeon, continued the fight and established an independent Jewish state under the Hasmonean dynasty. This was to rule for over 100 years, until the power of Rome was asserted in the region.

THE NEW TESTAMENT AND FREEMASONRY

HEROD'S TEMPLE AND THE EARLY LIFE OF JESUS

Timeline	4 BC–29 BC
Biblical reference	Song of Solomon • Chapter 2 v1 (Rose of Sharon) Isaiah • Chapter 7 v14 (Prophecy of Immanuel) • Chapter 8 v8 (Prophecy of Immanuel) • Chapter 9 v6 (Prophecy of Prince of Peace) • Chapter 50 v6 (Prophecy of Christ) • Chapter 53 v5 (Prophecy of Christ) Matthew • Chapter 1 v1–17 (Genealogy of Jesus) • Chapter 1 v23 (Jesus is Emmanuel) • Chapter 2 v1–12 (Wise men or Magi) • Chapter 2 v16 (Herod massacres the infants) • Chapter 4 v5 (Devil tempts Jesus on the temple) Luke • Chapter 2 v14 ('Glory to God in the highest') • Chapter 2 v22–24 (Boy Jesus at the temple) • Chapter 2 v41–50 (Boy Jesus found at the temple) • Chapter 4 v9 (Devil tempts Jesus on the temple) John • Chapter 1 v1–5 (The word was God) • Chapter 1 v29 (Jesus is the Lamb of God) • Chapter 1 v45–46 (Good from Nazareth) • Chapter 2 v13–16 (Money lenders turned out)

Biblical reference continued	• Chapter 2 v20 (Temple took 46 years to build) • Chapter 10 v11 (Jesus is the Good Shepherd) • Chapter 14 v6 ('The Way, the Truth and the Life') II Peter • Chapter 1 v19 ('Day star') Revelation • Chapter 17 v14 ('Lord of lords' 'King of kings') • Chapter 22 v16 (Jesus is bright and morning star)
Masonic reference	Royal Ark Mariner • Ceremony of Elevation • Tracing Board Allied Masonic Degrees • Knight of Constantinople Royal and Select Masters • Royal Master • Most Excellent Master Rose Croix • Ceremony of Perfection Holy Royal Arch Knights Templar Priests • Knight of the Three Kings Red Cross of Constantine • Installation of a Knight • Order of the Holy Sepulchre • Order of St John the Evangelist Knights Templar Societas Rosicruciana in Anglia • First Grade 'Zelator' • Third Grade 'Practicus' • Fifth Grade 'Adeptus Major' Eighth Grade 'Magister'
Historical context	27 BC – Collapse of Roman Republic and rise of Empire 43 AD – Roman invasion of Britain

We now turn to the New Testament, the scripture sacred to followers of the Christian faith. A number of Masonic degrees are exclusively Christian and these include Rose Croix, Red Cross of Constantine and Knights Templar. All contain many references to important events in the life of Christ. Evidence of the removal of Christian references from Craft masonry can be seen in a quotation from the Gospel of St John. After healing a blind man, Jesus said, 'for the night cometh,

A model of Herod's Temple where Jesus turned out the money lenders.

when no man can work.' This quotation is used in several ceremonies, including during the explanation of the Royal Ark Mariner Tracing board, as part of the closing prayer in the Knight of Constantinople and during the Royal Master degree. In the Royal Ark Mariner degree the quotation is preceded by the words 'Be careful to perform your allotted task while it is yet day.' The same words are used in the Third Degree ceremony but the words used by Jesus are not included and may have been removed during the eighteenth century when Craft masonry was opened to men of all faiths.

At the time of Christ, another great empire controlled the Near East; from 63 BC to 135 AD Judea was a Roman province and when Jesus was born the area was governed by a Roman-appointed Jewish king, Herod. Around 19 BC King Herod rebuilt and expanded the Temple complex. According to the Jewish historian, Josephus, Herod added 60 cubits to the height of the structure, so that it matched the magnificence of King Solomon's Temple. This building is still referred to as the Second Temple, as sacrifices continued on the site throughout the renovation, which the Gospel of John records as taking 46 years.

Herod's Temple was the one where Jesus was found by his parents, was tempted by the devil and where the money lenders were turned out. This new Temple did not appear to improve the relationship between God and Israel, which was at a low ebb at this time. Again according to Josephus, the oracular Urim and Thummim, recalled in Chapter ritual, had ceased to shine at least 200 years before.

Despite his efforts to improve the Temple, Herod is infamous in the New Testament for his attempts to kill baby Jesus by massacring all the male infants in Bethlehem. The announcement used by the angels when Christ was born, as recorded in the Gospel of St Luke, is used as part of the opening ceremony in the Royal Ark Mariner degree and the closing of a Royal Arch Chapter: 'Glory to God in the highest, and on earth peace, good will towards men.'

Christians believe that the coming of Jesus was foretold in the scriptures, particularly by Isaiah; and the Rose Croix ritual contains many of the prophecies of Christ from the Old Testament, in particular, the whole of Chapter 53 is quoted during the ceremony. In the Knights Templar ceremony, part of Chapter 50 is read out. It appears to be a foretelling of the fate of Christ: 'I gave my back to the smiters, and my cheeks to them that plucked off the hair: I hid not my face from shame and spitting.'

Jesus is further linked to the Old Testament by the Gospels of Matthew and Luke, which relate His genealogy. Luke traces Jesus back to Adam, with Matthew commencing at Abraham. Jacob, Boaz, David and Zerubbabel feature in both lists, but Matthew's line of descent includes King Solomon and King Uzziah. The latter features in the Red Cross of Constantine ceremony. In the Book of Matthew, there are 27 generations from David to Jesus. (There are also 27 books in the New Testament). This may be a further link to the idea of a perfect cube (or in Masonry the Perfect Ashlar), $3 \times 3 \times 3 = 27$, as described in the section on the First Temple, where the Holy of Holies is such a shape.

Jesus' earthly father was Joseph, a carpenter and Jesus is traditionally shown as following that profession prior to his ministry (see next section). It is interesting to note that the Greek word used in Matthew is 'teklon' meaning a 'builder' and so they may have been stonemasons.

The 'Magi', or wise men, who brought gifts to the baby Jesus are recalled during the explanation of the First Degree Tracing Board and during the Rose Croix ceremony. They travelled from the east and the Tracing Board ritual further notes that 'learning originated in the east and thence spread its benign influence to the west.' There is an unworked Knights Templar Priest ceremony, the Knight of the Three Kings. It should be noted that the Bible does not state the number of kings who visited Christ; it is surmised owing to the number of gifts – three – gold, frankincense and myrrh.

Throughout the Red Cross of Constantine ceremony references are made to the 'Lamb of God' and this is linked to the Book of Revelation and the prophecy of Isaiah, who refers to a 'lamb to the slaughter' in the section known as the 'Suffering Servant'. Confusingly, this is one of the many different titles used to describe Jesus in the Bible and in Masonic ceremonies, as can be seen below.

Title or Reference to Jesus	Masonic Reference
Bright Morning Star	Craft – Third Degree/Knight Templar
Day Star of Mercy	Red Cross of Constantine
Divine Master	Societas Rosicruciana in Anglia 6th Grade
Emmanuel	Rose Croix/Knight Templar/Red Cross of Constantine/Knights Templar Priest
Galilean	Red Cross of Constantine
Great High Priest of our Faith	Red Cross of Constantine
IHSHVH Jehoshuah or Jesus	Societas Rosicruciana in Anglia 8th Grade
Immanuel	Red Cross of Constantine
INRI	Societas Rosicruciana in Anglia
Jesus Agnus Dei – Holy Jesus	Red Cross of Constantine
Jesus Nazarenus Rex Judæorum (INRI)	Societas Rosicruciana in Anglia 3rd Grade
King of kings	Red Cross of Constantine/Knights Templar Priest

King of Righteousness	Knights Templar Priest
Lamb of God	Red Cross of Constantine
Lily of the Valley	Rose Croix/Red Cross of Constantine
Lord of lords	Red Cross of Constantine/Knights Templar Priest
Master	Red Cross of Constantine
Messiah	Red Cross of Constantine
Pastor	Rose Croix
Prophet, Priest and King	Knights Templar Priest
Rabboni ('Master')	Royal and Select Master – Most Excellent Master
Redeemer	Rose Croix
Root of David	Knights Templar Priest
Rose of Sharon	Rose Croix/Red Cross of Constantine / Societas Rosicruciana in Anglia 1st Grade
Shepherd	Rose Croix
Sovereign Ruler and Master	Red Cross of Constantine
The Way, the Truth and the Life	Rose Croix
The Word	Red Cross of Constantine

The 'Rose of Sharon' is part of the love song in the Song of Solomon, but it is unclear which flower the Biblical quote refers to. The red rose symbolises the Passion of Christ and additionally in the Rose Croix is an emblem of secrecy and silence. The ceiling of the United Grand Lodge of England is decorated with roses to remind all those involved in ceremonies of the need for silence and secrecy. In Rose Croix ritual the pelican is used as a symbol of Christ and it is shown on the collar (see image of the collar in the section on Moses). In medieval times the pelican was believed to feed its own blood to its young when no other food was available. Images of this 'vulning' or self-wounding were used to symbolise Jesus shedding His blood to save mankind. The Rose Croix 18th degree includes the conferring of the title 'Knight of the Pelican and Eagle' on the candidate. (For explanation of the word 'Rabboni' and its link to Christ, see p.163.)

THE MINISTRY OF JESUS

Timeline	29–33 AD
Biblical reference	Psalms • Psalm 78 v2 (Stories containing secrets) Isaiah • Chapter 58 v6–7 (Origin of Works of Mercy)

Biblical reference continued	**Matthew** • Chapter 4 v17–22 (Four disciples chosen at Galilee) • Chapter 5 v1–11 (Beatitudes) • Chapter 5 v24 ('Be reconciled to thy brother') • Chapter 6 v5–8 (How to pray) • Chapter 6 v9–13 (Lord's Prayer) • Chapter 7 v12 (Do unto others as you would have them do unto you') • Chapter 10 v1–4 (List of Apostles) • Chapter 13 v10–17 (Parables and secrets of heaven) • Chapter 13 v35 (Jesus and parables) • Chapter 16 v21 (Jesus predicts His own death) • Chapter 16 v24 (Following Jesus) • Chapter 17 v1–9 (Transfiguration) • Chapter 20 v1–16 (Parable of the Vineyard Workers) • Chapter 20 v12 ('Heat and burden of the day') • Chapter 22 v12 ('How camest thou hither?') • Chapter 23 v12 (Reward for being humble) • Chapter 25 v21 ('…thou good and faithful servant') • Chapter 25 v31–46 (Corporal Acts of Mercy) **Mark** • Chapter 3 v13–19 (List of Apostles) • Chapter 4 v10–12 (Parables and secrets of heaven) • Chapter 9 v2–13 (Transfiguration) • Chapter 9 v30–32 (Jesus predicts His own death) • Chapter 16 v16 (Those who believe in Jesus will be saved) **Luke** • Chapter 3 v23 (Jesus' age when baptised) • Chapter 6 v12–16 (List of Apostles) • Chapter 6 v31 (Do unto others as you would have them do unto you') • Chapter 7 v11–17 (Jesus raises a widow's son) • Chapter 9 v28–36 (Transfiguration) • Chapter 10 v25–37 (The Good Samaritan) • Chapter 11 v1–4 (Lord's Prayer) • Chapter 14 v15–24 (Parable of the Great Feast) • Chapter 18 v14 (Reward for being humble) **John** • Chapter 1 v43–51 (Philip and Nathanael) • Chapter 8 v1–11 (Cast the first stone) • Chapter 8 v12 (Jesus is the light of the world) • Chapter 9 v4 ('night cometh when no man can work') • Chapter 11 (Jesus raises Lazarus) **Romans** • Chapter 10 v9 (Salvation by faith in resurrection) **Galatians**

Biblical reference continued	• Chapter 2 v16 (Salvation by faith in Christ) James • Chapter 2 v14–26 (Faith is nothing without action)
Masonic reference	Craft • First Degree Royal Ark Mariner • Ceremony of Elevation • Tracing Board Allied Masonic Degrees • St Lawrence the Martyr • Knight of Constantinople Mark • Opening Prayer • Tracing Board Holy Royal Arch • Ceremony of Exaltation Rose Croix • Ceremony of Perfection Holy Royal Arch Knights Templar Priests • Knight of Bethany • Installation of a Knight Templar Priest Red Cross of Constantine • Installation of Knight • Knight of the Holy Sepulchre Knights Templar

Jesus' ministry began when he was about 30 years old, with his baptism in the River Jordan by St John the Baptist (see section on St John). This was followed by 40 days and nights in the wilderness, where He was tempted by the devil. Christ then selected twelve disciples or Apostles to assist him and a number appear in the Masonic Christian degrees. Surprisingly, there is no definitive list of the twelve as the gospels contain slightly different names. The following is a composite list taken from the gospels, including their background, if described in the Bible:

1 Peter originally called 'Simon' but renamed by Jesus. A fisherman on Lake Galilee (see section on Peter)
2 Andrew, brother of Peter, also a fisherman
3 James ('James the Greater'), son of Zebedee and brother of John, a fisherman
4 John, a fisherman (see section on St John above)
5 Philip

6 Bartholomew (the Gospel of John names him as 'Nathanael')
7 Matthew, the tax collector
8 Thomas, also called 'Didymus' both names meaning 'The Twin'
9 Thaddeus, possibly also known as Jude
10 James ('James the Less'), son of Alphaeus
11 Simon the Zealot (or Simeon)
12 Judas Iscariot

The story of Philip recruiting his fellow Apostle, Nathanael, is read out during the Rose Croix ceremony. When Philip said, 'We have found him of whom Moses in the law, and the prophets did write, Jesus of Nazareth.' Nathanael answered 'Can there any good thing come out of Nazareth?' Philip relied, 'Come and see.'

It should be noted that Mark and Luke, the Gospel writers, were not members of the Twelve Apostles. Jesus explained the consequences of following Him, and this is quoted during the Red Cross of Constantine degree. During the ceremony, two Bibles are opened at Matthew, Chapter 16 v24, 'Then said Jesus unto his disciples, If any man will come after me, let him deny himself, and take up his cross, and follow me.'

Soon after His ministry began, Jesus gave the Sermon on the Mount (the exact location is unknown, although traditionally is said to be on the north shore of the Sea of Galilee). This message came to be known as the 'Beatitudes', from the Latin 'beatus', meaning 'blessed'. Verse 8 (pure in heart) can be found in Masonic ritual as it features in the Knights Templar Priest ceremony. According to Matthew (Luke has a different list), the Beatitudes are:

Blessed are the poor in spirit: for theirs is the kingdom of heaven.
Blessed are they that mourn: for they shall be comforted.
Blessed are the meek: for they shall inherit the earth.
Blessed are they which do hunger and thirst after righteousness: for they shall be filled.
Blessed are the merciful: for they shall obtain mercy.
Blessed are the pure in heart: for they shall see God.
Blessed are the peacemakers: for they shall be called the children of God.
Blessed are they which are persecuted for righteousness' sake: for theirs is the kingdom of heaven.
Blessed are ye, when men shall revile you, and persecute you, and shall say all manner of evil against you falsely, for my sake.

Jesus taught love for others and one of His most important messages appears in the Royal Ark Mariner ceremony – 'do unto others as you would that they should do unto you.' Whilst this is a New Testament quotation, which appears in a degree open to men of all faiths, the verse goes onto state that this is the 'law of the prophets'. Thus it is applicable to Judaism and Islam, with the sentiment being repeated in many other religions. The phrase 'be reconciled with your brother' in the same ceremony is a modern translation of part of Matthew (which uses 'thy brother'). It appears in the Bible where Jesus is teaching about anger and making peace with enemies.

The Lord's Prayer is recorded in the Gospels of Matthew and Luke. It is included during the Knights Templar and Knights Templar Priest ceremonies. Jesus taught his disciples to use this prayer and advised them to pray in private as follows:

Our Father, which art in Heaven, Hallowed be Thy name. Thy kingdom come. Thy will be done, in earth as it is in heaven. Give us this day our daily bread. And forgive us our trespasses. As we forgive them that trespass against us. And lead us not into temptation; But deliver us from evil: For Thine is the kingdom, the power and the glory, for ever and ever. Amen

Throughout His ministry, Jesus often taught his message through the use of Parables or short stories. In relation to Masonic secrets and the ceremonies that contain much symbolism, it is interesting to note that Jesus informed His disciples that He used parables to teach the masses. Only the disciples had been chosen to know the 'mysteries of the kingdom of God'. Later in Matthew, Jesus quotes from Psalm 78, which relates to using stories with secrets or 'dark sayings'.

Possibly the most famous parable is of the good Samaritan and the background to this story has already been explained in section on Darius and Daniel. Suffice to say, that the treatment of one's neighbour is an important section of The Charge to the newly made Freemason. In England, the New Masonic Samaritan Fund is one of the charities under the United Grand Lodge of England and is concerned with medical treatment.

During the explanation of the Tracing Board in the Mark Degree, there is a welcome from Matthew, 'Well done, thou good and faithful servant, enter thou into the joy of thy Lord.' This quotation is from Jesus' Parable of the Talents, where three servants are entrusted with their Master's gold. The full story is not used in the ritual, but it may also be the basis of part of the Opening Prayer in the same degree, which states 'When He shall come to reckon with us, we may obtain our reward.' Following on from this story is Jesus' parable of the 'Sheeps and Goats', from whence is derived six of the seven 'Corporal Works of Mercy'. These form part of Roman Catholic theology and are included in the Knight of the Holy Sepulchre ceremony as follows:

1   Go, feed the hungry
2   Give drink to the thirsty
3   Clothe the naked with a garment
4   Visit and ransom the captives
5   Harbour the harbourless, give the widows and orphans where to lay their heads
6   Visit and relieve the sick
7   Go, bury the dead.

The acts are not numbered in Matthew and four of them may be based on Isaiah, Chapter 58, where God related the actions that please Him. The seventh is from the Book of Tobit (see section on the Division of Israel). The Parable explains that when Jesus returns to earth, the nations will be divided into 'sheep' on his right side and 'goats' on his left. The 'goats' will suffer eternal damnation for their failure to live by the Acts of Mercy.

Freemasons are taught that the 'Grand Principles of the Order' are 'brotherly love, relief and truth'. 'Relief' means charity and doing good works and whether Christians find salvation through good deeds or faith in Christ alone has been a matter of debate for centuries. The great German theologian, Martin Luther, argued that it was faith, not works, that resulted in salvation. The Bible's message does not appear to be so clear. Jesus noted six of the seven Corporal Acts of Mercy that were required for admission to heaven, but He also stated that faith in Him alone would be sufficient (see Gospel of Mark). St Paul (see section on Paul) believed faith was the major factor, but he does seem to accept that good 'works' are important (Romans Chapter 2 v7 – which is used in the Mark Degree closing prayer). Jesus' brother, James, however, argued that faith without action was 'dead'. James emphasised the deeds of Abraham and Rahab – both of which appear in Masonic ritual as we have seen.

Whether it is faith or works which is the most important, the Parable of the Workers in the Vineyard has a simple message – however late you turn to God it is not too late. In this story, Jesus related how men hired at the end of the day were paid the same as those hired at the very beginning. It contains a reference to various times of the day, including the 'sixth hour'. This is the time when the workmen in the Mark degree cease labour and parade to collect their wages. This is an important part of that ceremony. The Parable also includes the expression 'the heat and burden of the day', which is included in the explanation of the First Degree Tracing Board, although not in the context of workmen. Masonically, it is used to show that a Freemason should look after his parents in their old age.

Throughout his ministry, Jesus was in conflict with the Scribes and the Pharisees (religious leaders) and they often sought to test his judgement. It was for this reason that they brought a woman before Him and accused her of adultery. They asked Jesus why she should not be stoned to death, in accordance with the law of Moses. This is when He uttered the famous phrase: 'He that is without sin among you, let him first cast a stone.'

The crowd dispersed and Jesus said 'I am the light of the world: he that followeth me shall not walk in darkness, but shall have the light of life.' This quotation is used, with other references to light, in the Knights Templar Priest ceremony.

In the Gospels of Matthew and Luke, Jesus makes several allusions to behaviour at meals, including the Parable of the Great Feast (or the Marriage Feast). Twice Jesus advises that 'the poor, and the maimed, and the halt, and the blind' should be invited – unlike relatives, such people cannot return the invite, but it will result in the host being blessed. This description of the 'poor' and the 'halt' are used in the St Lawrence the Martyr degree. Masons may well wish to note the advice given by Jesus in relation to where to sit at dinner. The Festive Board often has a table plan, with the senior Masons sat on the 'top table', where places are actively sought. Jesus advises that guests should sit in a lowly seat – it is far better to be asked to move up, rather than be embarrassed by initially sitting in too lofty a place, only to be asked to move down the table. The lecture on the Knights of Constantinople degree ends with Jesus' words: 'whosoever exalteth himself shall be abased; and he that humbleth himself shall be exalted.' These words are so important that they feature three times in the Gospels: twice in Luke and once in Matthew. The virtue of being humble is also in Holy Royal Arch, where the Principals praise the Sojourners for their 'humility and docility'. In the Grand Tilers of King Solomon, the phrase 'How camest thou hither?' from Matthew's version of the parable is used. This means that of the five ceremonies in the Allied Masonic Degrees, three use words from the Parable of the Great Feast.

Near the end of His ministry, Jesus was 'transfigured' and appeared with Moses and Elijah. This was witnessed by three apostles, Peter, James and John. The Bible does not describe the exact location, but it is traditionally taken to be Mount Tabor, which appears in Masonic ritual (see section on Holy Mountains). Around the time of the transfiguration, Jesus predicted his own death and resurrection.

In his short ministry of just three years, Jesus performed many miracles, but only two are referred to in Masonic ceremonies. The Knights Templar Priest ceremony includes the conferring of the degree of 'Knight of Bethany'. It was at Bethany that Jesus raised Lazarus from the dead. The healing of the blind man features in the ritual in the quotation shown above, 'the night cometh when no man can work.' These words feature in at least three different degrees – Royal Ark Mariner, Knight of Constantinople and Royal Master. It should be noted that, whilst not expressly mentioned in Masonic ritual, Jesus raised a widow's son from the dead in the city of Nain, near Galilee. As we have seen, the Third Degree is concerned with the 'raising' of a 'widow's son' – Hiram Abif.

St John: The Patron Saint of Freemasons

Timeline	4 BC – John the Baptist born around this date 30 AD – Jesus baptised 100 AD – 1 John written around this time
Biblical reference	Matthew • Chapter 3 v13–17 (Jesus baptised) • Chapter 11 v7 (John the Baptist not a 'reed shaken by the wind')

Biblical reference continued	• Chapter 14 v1–12 (John the Baptist is beheaded) Mark • Chapter 6 v14–29 (John the Baptist beheaded) Luke • Chapter 1 v5–25 (Birth of John the Baptist foretold) • Chapter 1 v57–80 (Birth of John the Baptist) • Chapter 7 v24 (John the Baptist not a 'reed shaken by the wind') John • Chapter 1 v1–5 (The Word was God) • Chapter 1 v19–22 ('Who art thou?') • Chapter 4 v23 ('the hour cometh') • Chapter 13 v23 (Disciple whom Jesus loved) • Chapter 14 v2 (In my Father's house are many mansions') • Chapter 20 v1–9 (Jesus' tomb is empty) I John • Chapter 1 v7 ('Walk in the light') • Chapter 3 v16–17 (Compassion and the love of God) • Chapter 4 v7 ('Let us love one another') Revelation • Chapter 1 v9 (Revelation written on Patmos)
Masonic reference	Craft • First Degree Tracing Board • Third Degree Tracing Board Royal Ark Mariner • Ceremony of Elevation Allied Masonic Degrees • St Lawrence the Martyr Royal and Select Masters • Super Excellent Master Holy Royal Arch Knights Templar Priests • Knight of Patmos or Philippi • Installation of a Knight Templar Priest Rose Croix • Ceremony of Perfection Red Cross of Constantine • Knight of St John the Evangelist • Installation of Viceroy

Masonic reference continued	Order of Athelstan Knights Templar • Knight Templar • Order of St Paul • Knight of Malta Societas Rosicruciana in Anglia • First Grade 'Zelator' • Sixth Grade 'Adeptus Major'

St John is the Patron Saint of Freemasons, but it is unclear why John was chosen as St Thomas was already the Patron Saint of architecture and building. To add to the confusion it is uncertain whether 'St John' is John the Baptist or John the Evangelist. Whichever John is the Patron Saint, the feast days of both saints appear to have been important to early Freemasons. The Premier Grand Lodge was formed in England in 1717 on 24 June (Feast of St John the Baptist) and festival meetings were also held on 27 December (Feast of John the Evangelist).

According to the Bible, John the Baptist was an older cousin of Jesus and, as the Knights Templar degree describes him, 'the forerunner of Christ'. His ministry began before that of Jesus and the Jewish leaders sent messengers to him in the desert to ask 'Who art thou?' as they wanted to know if he was the promised Messiah. John replied that he was only preparing the way for such a man. (To add to the confusion, John the Evangelist related this event about his namesake, John the Baptist).

The phrase 'Who art thou?' is used when a candidate requests permission to enter a Commandery of Knights of St John the Evangelist. As the words can be attributed to St John (albeit the wrong one as the degree is named after John the Evangelist), they replace the standard Masonic question 'Whom have you there?'

John the Baptist's message never changed and he feared no one. To emphasise John's uncompromising stance, Jesus asked the people, 'What did you go out into the wilderness to see? A reed shaken by the wind?' Reeds are used in the Bible as a symbol of weakness and this may be the origin of the section in the Royal Ark Mariner degree, which warns that 'should his step deviate from the straight line his fate will be that of the bulrush swayed to and fro by every breath.'

True to form, John the Baptist was later arrested for criticising the marriage of King Herod to Herodias, who had been married to his brother. At a great feast, the daughter of Herodias pleased Herod with her dancing and was offered anything she desired. She requested the 'head of John the Baptist'. John was then killed on the orders of the king and the head was presented to his niece on a plate.

The other St John, John the Evangelist, was originally a fisherman who worked on Lake Galilee. Together with Simon Peter, Andrew and James, he was chosen as a disciple by Jesus. This John is often referred to in the Bible as the 'disciple whom Jesus loved' and he is believed to be the 'other disciple' in the Gospel of John, who visited the tomb. Furthermore, St John was the first to believe that Christ had truly risen from the dead. The Knights Templar ritual describes him as 'the Beloved Apostle of Our Lord, who finished by his learning what St. John the Baptist had commenced by his zeal.'

The first five verses of the Gospel of St John are recited by a candidate in the Knight of St John the Evangelist ceremony. They also appear in the first grade 'Zelator' of Societas Rosicruciana in Anglia, with the first verse included in Rose Croix. This passage is used to support the doctrine of the Holy Trinity and is further discussed in the section on the Development of Christian Theology.

In the beginning was the Word, and the Word was with God, and the Word was God. The same was in the beginning with God. All things were made by him; and without him was not any thing made that was made. In him was life; and the life was the light of men. And the light shineth in darkness; and the darkness comprehended it not.

In Masonic ritual, the two Saint Johns can be linked to the 'point within a circle' displayed on the First and Third Degree Tracing Boards. This centre point is described during the explanation of the First Degree Tracing Board and the opening ceremony for the Third Degree as 'a point within a circle from which the Brethren cannot err.' On the First Degree version the circle is bounded by 'two grand parallel lines' and this is recalled during the Super Excellent Master ceremony. In English ritual, which has had much of the Christian content removed, these lines are said to represent Moses and Solomon. In some American rituals (and in the recently formed Order of Athelstan – see below) the lines continue to symbolise John the Baptist and John the Evangelist, with Christ in the centre.

In the degree of St Lawrence the Martyr, the candidate is said to represent a 'Brother of St John', in reference to him being the Patron Saint. Oddly, a Mason does not have to be a Christian to join this order. This ritual is believed to have been written during the eighteenth century and this reference to the saint appears to have been missed when Christian references were removed. Another ancient ritual demonstrating a hidden link with St John is the Royal Ark Mariner degree, which quotes from the First Epistle General of John (I John). This is believed to be a letter written to the early churches by John the Evangelist when he lived in Ephesus. The Senior Warden, explaining how a Royal Ark Mariner should assist a brother suddenly changes from the vernacular into the language of the King James Bible and states the following, which is not attributed to the Bible: 'For whoso seeth his brother have need, and shutteth up his compassion from him, how dwelleth the love of God in him?'

The Virgin and Child Enthroned between St John the Baptist and St John the Evangelist (1484) by Sandro Botticelli.

The preceding verse 'perceive we the love of God, because he laid down his life for us: and we ought to lay down our lives for the brethren', is used in the Knights Templar Priest ceremony. The use of the word 'brethren' has obvious Masonic links. The same ritual quotes from the first Chapter of the letter, using the phrase (originally from Isaiah) 'walk in the light', when it is explained that God forgives our sins. This contains an important tenet of Christianity: 'The blood of Jesus Christ his Son cleanseth us from all sin.'

The Royal Ark Mariner prayer refers to the 'mansions of everlasting rest', which may have been based on Jesus' famous words from the Gospel of St John (which also appear in the sixth grade of SRIA): 'In my Father's house are many mansions.' The Freemasons' Patron Saint is further celebrated in the Red Cross of Constantine Appendant Order of a 'Knight of St John the Evangelist' (see section on Crusades) and sections of his gospel are found in the ritual. At the conclusion of the 'Legend' section of this ceremony, the Gospel of John is quoted: 'The hour cometh, and now is, when the true worshippers shall worship the Father in spirit and in truth.'

Furthermore, when the installation ceremony of the Viceroy in this Order is conducted, part of the First Epistle of St John is used in the closing ceremony: 'Let us love one another.' The Jewel of the Knight of St John the Evangelist features the eagle, the emblem of St John, which alludes to the height he rose to in the first chapter of his Gospel. John the Evangelist was the only Apostle not to be martyred and he lived to an old age. There is some debate as to whether he died in Ephesus, in modern-day Turkey or on the island of Patmos, where the Book of Revelation was written (see section on Revelation). The degree of 'Knight of Patmos' is one of the unworked rituals included in the Knights Templar Priest degrees.

In the Knights Templar degrees, John is celebrated in the 'Ancient and Masonic Order of St. John of Jerusalem, Palestine, Rhodes and Malta'. This ceremony relates the history of the Hospitaller Knights of St John and their various bases in the Holy Land and on Mediterranean islands (see section on Knights Templar).

ST PETER

Timeline	Around 30–64 AD
Biblical reference	Matthew • Chapter 4 v17–22 (Peter chosen at Galilee) • Chapter 10 v2 (Peter in list of Apostles) • Chapter 16 v18 (Peter is the rock) • Chapter 16 v19 (Peter will be given keys to heaven) • Chapter 26 v69–75 (Peter denied Jesus) Mark • Chapter 3 v16 (Jesus named Simon 'Peter') • Chapter 4 v35–41 (Boat in a storm) Luke • Chapter 6 v14 (Peter in list of Apostles) • Chapter 22 v61 (Peter denied Jesus) John • Chapter 18 v10 (Peter armed with sword) Acts

Biblical reference continued	• Chapter 4 v11 (Peter describes Jesus as the rejected stone) Galatians • Chapter 2 v7 (Peter is the Apostle to the Jews) I Peter • Chapter 2 v4–5 ('Living stone' and 'holy priesthood') • Chapter 2 v7 ('Stone which the builders disallowed') • Chapter 2 v9 'Peculiar people') • Chapter 2 v11–17 ('Love the Brotherhood') • Chapter 4 v10 ('Good stewards') • Chapter 5 v4 ('Crown of glory') • Chapter 5 v14 ('Peace be with you') II Peter • Chapter 3 v10 ('Elements shall melt with fervent heat')
Masonic reference	Craft • Second Degree • Installation of Master Royal Ark Mariner • Ceremony of Elevation Mark • Ceremony of Advancement Holy Royal Arch Knights Templar Priests • Installation of a Knight Templar Priest Red Cross of Constantine • Installation of Viceroy Knights Templar

Simon Peter (or simply Peter) was one of the Apostles chosen at Lake Galilee. He appears to have been a senior member of the Apostles, together with John and James the Elder and in the lists of the Apostles in the Bible, Peter always appears first. Peter's fishing boat or 'barque' features in the Bible and became an early Christian symbol. This, and the story of Jesus calming a storm, may have been the inspiration behind the references to steering the 'barque of this life over the rough seas' in the presentation of the Second Degree Working Tools.

It was Jesus who changed Simon's name to 'Peter', which means 'rock'. Jesus said that Peter was the rock on which he would build His church. He also promised to give Peter the keys of heaven. It should be remembered that the Bible states that Peter was armed with a sword when the High Priest came to arrest Jesus. During this incident, Peter cut off the ear of the one of the High Priest's servants.

However, once Christ had been arrested, Peter famously denied Him 'before the cock crowed three times'. After the crucifixion, Peter, according to St Paul, was the apostle to the Jews, whilst Paul was the apostle for the Gentiles. Two of Peter's letters to the early Christian churches are contained in the New Testament. Part of his first letter to the churches in Asia Minor is extensively quoted in the Knights Templar degree. It urges Christians to obey the laws of their rules and avoid 'fleshly lusts'. It also includes the phrase 'Honour all men. Love the Brotherhood. Fear God. Honour the king.' The Masonic and military connections are readily apparent.

Masonic ritual appears to paraphrase a section of this letter relating to a 'crown of glory that fadeth not away'. During the Installation Ceremony, the new Master is advised to strictly adhere to the Bible, so that he can be rewarded with 'a crown of joy and rejoicing which will never fade away'.

Both of Peter's letters are quoted during the Royal Ark Mariner degree. The ceremony includes a reference to '…as good stewards of the manifold grace of God', which appears in his first letter, but as 'manifold gifts'. Additionally, the ritual includes Peter's promise of a new heaven and earth, when 'the elements shall melt with fervent heat'. The quotation is unattributed and is a further example of sections of the New Testament appearing in degrees which have long been believed to have been de-Christianised.

Another example of hidden Christian references is during the Closing Prayer in the Mark Degree, which includes the phrase 'may we…be built up as living stones into a spiritual house'. This is very similar to a section in Chapter 2 of the Peter's first letter, which refers to Jesus as a 'living stone' and Christians as 'lively stones' who build 'a spiritual house'. The verse then appears to quote Psalm 118 as it mentions the 'stone which the builders disallowed, the same is made the head of the corner.' (Peter describes Jesus with these words in the Book of Acts.) This is a very important reference in the Mark Degree and appears several times in the ceremony.

Chapter 2 is also the origin of several phrases in the prayer during the Installation of a Viceroy in the Red Cross of Constantine. These include 'peculiar people' (God's own people) and 'a Holy Priesthood'. Additionally, verses 5–9 are read out during the Knights Templar Priest ceremony. The last line of Peter's first letter, 'Peace be with you' is used in the same degree. (The same phrase occurs in Paul's letter to the Romans.)

According to tradition, St Peter was the first Pope or Bishop of Rome, where he was later crucified for his Christian beliefs at the time of the Emperor Nero. Peter insisted that he was hung upside down as he was not worthy to die in the same manner as Christ.

THE CRUCIFIXION AND RESURRECTION OF JESUS

Timeline	29–33 AD
Biblical reference	Psalms • Psalm 22 v1 ('My God, why hast thou forsaken me') • Psalm 118 v22 'The stone which was rejected') Isaiah • Chapter 53 v7 ('Lamb to the slaughter') Zechariah • Chapter 12 v10 (Prophecy of Christ's suffering) Matthew • Chapter 5 v33–37 (Do not swear oaths) • Chapter 20 v18–19 (Jesus predicts his fate) • Chapter 21 v33–44 (Parable – Wicked Husbandmen) • Chapter 24 v1–2 (Destruction of the temple foreseen)

Biblical reference *continued*	• Chapter 26 v14–16 (Thirty pieces of silver) • Chapter 26 v36 (Jesus prays at Gethsemane) • Chapter 26 v48 (The kiss of Judas) • Chapter 26 v63 (Jesus put on oath) • Chapter 27 v5 (Judas commits suicide) • Chapter 27 v29 (Crown of thorns) • Chapter 27 v37 ('King of the Jews') • Chapter 27 v33 (Crucified at Golgotha) • Chapter 27 v45–46 (Jesus dies) • Chapter 27 v51 (Veil of the temple ripped in two) • Chapter 27 v57–60 (Joseph of Arimathea) • Chapter 28 v1–6 (Christ is risen) • Chapter 28 v19 (Father, Son and Holy Ghost) Mark • Chapter 10 v33–34 (Jesus predicts his fate) • Chapter 11 v15–17 (Money lenders turned out) • Chapter 12 v1–12 (Parable – Wicked Husbandmen) • Chapter 14 v10–11 (Judas agrees to betray Jesus) • Chapter 14 v32 (Jesus prays at Gethsemane) • Chapter 14 v44–45 (The kiss of Judas) • Chapter 15 v17 (Crown of thorns) • Chapter 15 v22 (Crucified at Golgotha) • Chapter 15 v26 ('King of the Jews') • Chapter 15 v33–41 (Jesus dies) • Chapter 15 v38 (Veil of the temple ripped in two) • Chapter 15 v42–47 (Joseph of Arimathea) • Chapter 16 v1–6 (Tomb empty – He is risen) • Chapter 16 v19 (Jesus at right hand of God) Luke • Chapter 12 v38 ('Third Watch') • Chapter 20 v9–18 (Parable – Wicked Husbandmen) • Chapter 21 v5–6 (Destruction of the temple foreseen) • Chapter 22 v48 (The kiss of Judas) • Chapter 23 v38 ('King of the Jews') • Chapter 23 v44 (Jesus dies) • Chapter 23 v45 (Veil of the temple ripped in two) • Chapter 23 v50–54 (Joseph of Arimathea) • Chapter 24 v1–3 (Empty tomb) • Chapter 24 v51 (Jesus ascends to heaven) John • Chapter 2 v13–16 (Money lenders turned out) • Chapter 19 v2 (Crown of thorns) • Chapter 19 v5 ('Behold the Man!') • Chapter 19 v17 (Crucified at Golgotha) • Chapter 19 v19 ('King of the Jews') • Chapter 19 v34 (Pierced by spear)

Biblical reference continued	• Chapter 19 v38 (Joseph of Arimathea was a secret follower of Jesus) • Chapter 20 v1–2 (Tomb empty) • Chapter 20 v16 (Jesus called 'Rabboni') Hebrews • Chapter 12 v1–2 (Follow Jesus' example) Revelation • Chapter 2 v10 (Crown of life)
Masonic reference	Mark • Ceremony of Advancement • Tracing Board Royal and Select Masters • Most Excellent Master • Super Excellent Master Rose Croix • Ceremony of Perfection Holy Royal Arch Knights Templar Priests • Installation of a Knights Templar Priest Red Cross of Constantine • Installation of a Knight • Knight of the Holy Sepulchre • Knight of St John Evangelist Knights Templar Societas Rosicruciana in Anglia

Some days prior to his death, Jesus informed his disciples in confidence of the fate that awaited Him in Jerusalem – that He would be betrayed and killed, but He would rise again after three days. This section of the Gospels of Matthew and Mark is quoted during the Rose Croix ceremony.

> Behold, we go up to Jerusalem, and the Son of Man shall be betrayed unto the chief priests and unto the scribes, and they shall condemn Him to death, and shall deliver Him to the Gentiles to mock, and to scourge, and to crucify Him, and the third day He shall rise again.

On His arrival in the city, Christ was greeted by large crowds, who had gathered for the Passover Festival. Later He created a disturbance at the temple, by turning out the moneylenders. Jesus told them the temple was a 'house of prayer' but they had turned it into a 'den of thieves'. This reference to a 'house of prayer' may be the reason that during the Second Degree King Solomon's Temple is mistakenly referred to as 'place of divine worship' rather than a place for God to reside on the Ark of the Covenant.

During this time, the leading priests at the temple began to question Jesus' authority. Jesus then told the Parable of the Wicked Husbandmen, where the owner of a vineyard rented his land

At the Garden of Gethsemane. The Jerusalem Cross is on the door, which features on the jewel of the Knight of St John the Evangelist.

to a number of farmers. The landowner later sent servants to collect his profits, but the farmers killed the servants. The owner then sent his son, but the farmers feared that the son would inherit the land and take it away from them, so they murdered him as well. This was clear reference to the relationship between the priests and Jesus, the son of God. An important aspect of the Mark Degree features at the end of the Parable when Jesus quoted from Psalm 118: 'The stone which the builders rejected, the same is become the head of the corner.'

Jesus' prophecy of His own death began to take shape when Judas, one of the Apostles, agreed to betray Him for 30 pieces of silver. This betrayal is noted in a number of Christian degrees, but most particularly during the 'Legend' section of the Installation of a Knight of St John the Evangelist (part of the Red Cross of Constantine). According to the Bible, the High Priests and Scribes wanted to deal with Jesus by stealth, as they feared that the people may riot. As a result, the arrest of Jesus took place at night, with Judas identifying Him by a kiss – a pre-agreed signal. The location of the betrayal was in the Garden of Gethsemane, at the foot of the Mount of Olives, in the east of Jerusalem. 'Gethsemane' is significant in the Knight of St John the Evangelist degree.

Jesus was later tried by Caiaphas, the Jewish High Priest, who put Jesus on oath (the King James' versions uses the verb *adjure* – 'to swear by oath') and asked Him if he was the Son of God. This is interesting in that Jesus had previously advised His followers never to use oaths. The High Priest declared that Jesus was guilty of blasphemy and handed Him over to Pilate the Roman Governor. Pilate presented Jesus to the crowd and declared 'Behold the Man!' or in Latin *Ecco Homo*. The Latin phrase is contained in the Knight of St John the Evangelist degree. Despite Pilate doubting that Jesus had done anything wrong, the crowd demanded that he should be crucified.

Jesus was forced to carry his own cross, but as he so weakened by his ordeal that the Roman soldiers had to force a bystander to assist. This man was called Simon (or Solomon) of Cyrene (a Greek colony on the Libyan coast). Jesus was crucified at Golgotha, which means the 'Place of the Skull' in Hebrew. He was mocked by the Romans and called 'The King of the Jews'. A sign was placed on the cross declaring Him 'I N R I', the initials of the Latin phrase *Jesus Nazarenus Rex Judaeorum* meaning 'Jesus of Nazareth, King of the Jews'. The initials 'I N R I' feature in the Knights Templar and Rose Croix ceremonies. They are also used in the prayers throughout the nine grades of Societas Rosicruciana in Anglia.

Christ was further ridiculed by being made to wear a Crown of Thorns, described in three of the Gospels and which appears as an emblem on the Rose Croix collar. The ritual explaining the symbol uses a quotation from Revelation, 'Be thou faithful unto death and I will give thee a crown of life.'

The Knight of St John the Evangelist degree uses the version of Jesus' death described in the Gospels of Matthew and Mark. Just before he died, Jesus declared in Hebrew '*Eloi, Eloi, lama sabachthani*', which is translated as 'My God, my God, why hast thou forsaken me.' The Aramaic words are used in the ceremony and it is stated in the ritual that the 'Jews did not comprehend'; (according to Mark, they thought Jesus was calling for Elijah). It does seem odd, however, that those present at the crucifixion did not recognise the words as the first verse of Psalm 22.

Ecce Homo (1525–30) by Antonio Allegri da Correggio. Pilate presents Christ to the crowd.

Christ Between the Two Thieves (1635)
by Peter Paul Rubens.

According to the Bible, Jesus died at 'the ninth hour', which is 3pm (the first hour of a Roman day was 6am) on Good Friday. As he died, the veil of the Temple was 'rent in twain' (ripped in two). This is recalled in the Red Cross of Constantine and Rose Croix ceremonies. The account of His burial by Joseph of Arimathea from the Gospel of Mark is read out during the Knight of the Holy Sepulchre ceremony. In Luke, Joseph of Arimathea is described as an 'honourable counsellor' and this is taken to mean a member of the Jewish Sanhedrin. It is also stated that he did not agree with the actions of the other Jewish leaders against Jesus, but the Gospel of John makes it clear that Joseph was a secret disciple of Jesus, who feared his contemporaries. Whilst Luke informs us that Arimathea was a city 'of the Jews' (in Judah), its exact location is unclear and several modern towns have been suggested as the location. Later legends claim that Joseph brought the Crown of Thorns and the Holy Grail to England.

Jesus' resurrection took place on the first hour of the third day (6am on Easter Sunday) and this is recalled in the Rose Croix ceremony. The Knight of the Holy Sepulchre degree continues to use the Gospel of Mark, where three women, Mary Magdalene, His mother, Mary and a follower of Jesus called Salome, found an angel in the tomb. The angel informed them that Jesus had risen.

According to the Gospel of John, Jesus appeared to Mary Magdalene outside his tomb and she called Him *Rabboni*. This word is used in the King James version of the Bible and is translated as 'Master'. Masonically, this word is used in the Order of Royal and Select Masters, where it is used to describe a 'Good Master' or 'Most Excellent Master'. Jesus made several appearances to his followers (see next section), before ascending into heaven to sit at the right hand of God. His ascension into heaven is the basis of one of the signs in the Red Cross of Constantine ceremony of Installation of a Knight.

In Luke, Jesus warned His followers that they should always be ready for his return and gave an example of servants waiting for their master even until the 'third watch' (meaning midnight). This term is used in the Super Excellent Master degree, where workmen are secretly employed at King Solomon's Temple until that time of night.

Jesus lived for 33 years and this may be the origin of the reference to 33 being the 'mysterious number' in the Red Cross of Constantine ceremony. It is also the number of degrees in Rose Croix, where all candidates give their age as 33 and travel a symbolic journey of 33 days.

In Christian Masonic degrees, the candidate has to express a faith in the Trinitarian Faith, that God exists in three persons (Father, Son and Holy Ghost) in one substance. The word 'trinity' does not appear in the Bible, but after His resurrection, Jesus appeared to the disciples on a mountain in Galilee and instructed them to baptise people of all nations 'in the name of the Father, and of the Son, and of the Holy Ghost'. The Trinitarian faith was further developed by St Paul (see section on Paul). Christians are advised in Hebrews to follow Jesus' example and this section is quoted during the Knights Templar Priest ceremony.

THE APOSTLES AFTER THE CRUCIFIXION

Timeline	Around 30 AD
Biblical reference	Luke • Chapter 1 v3 (Most excellent Theophilus) • Chapter 24 v13–35 (Apostles and Emmaus) John • Chapter 20 v24–28 (Doubting Thomas) • Chapter 21 v1–14 (Disciples catch 153 fish) Acts • Chapter 1 v26 (Matthias replaces Judas) • Chapter 2 v11 ('Wonderful works of God') • Chapter 8 v26–40 (First African Christian) • Chapter 23 v26 (Most excellent governor Felix) James • Chapter 4 v11 ('Speak not evil one of another') • Chapter 4 v17 (Failing to do good is a sin) Jude • Chapter 1 v11 (Wickedness of Korah) • Chapter 1 v20–21 (Keep faith awaiting Christ)
Masonic reference	Craft • Second Degree Allied Masonic Degrees • Grand High Priest Mark • Ceremony of Advancement Holy Royal Arch Red Cross of Constantine • Installation of Knight • Installation of Viceroy

Masonic reference *continued*	Holy Royal Arch Knights Templar Priests • Installation of a Knight Templar Priest
	Knights Templar

The story of Thomas, who did not believe that Christ had risen from the dead, is included in the Knights Templar degree. The section of Gospel of St John relating to Thomas is read out, during which Thomas refuses to believe unless he himself can 'see in His hands the print of the nails, and put my finger into the print of the nails, and thrust my hand into His side.' Jesus appeared to 'Doubting Thomas' after eight days and gave him the proof he desired.

Luke describes the journey of two apostles (one named as Cleopas) to Emmaus, on the day of the resurrection of Christ. On the road they are joined by a stranger, who surprises them by seemingly knowing nothing of the crucifixion. Once they arrived at their destination, they persuaded the stranger to stay and at dinner, He broke bread and blessed it. At this point, they recognised Him as Jesus, who disappeared in an instant. The village of Emmaus was fought over during the Maccabean Revolt and features in one of the Masonic Knights Templar ceremonies, set at the time of the First Crusade over 1000 years after Jesus' appearance there (see Knights Templar below).

The Book of Acts describes the conversion of the first African to Christianity. St Philip met a servant of the Ethiopian queen, who was reading the Book of Isaiah. The Apostle preached the Gospel to him and the African was baptised 'and he went on his way rejoicing'. The latter phrase is used in the Mark Degree.

Perfect shapes feature throughout the Bible – this book has described how the altar used by Aaron was a double cube and the Holy of Holies in King Solomon's Temple (see section on First Temple) was a perfect cube. Freemasonry also makes much use of the symbolism of shapes – the square, circle and triangle appear in several degrees. This 'sacred geometry' may be linked to an account of the resurrected Jesus appearing to seven disciples on the shore line of Lake Galilee. The disciples had failed to catch any fish during the night, but at Jesus' command they re-cast their net and caught 153 fish. At first sight it appears odd that the Bible should state such an exact number, rather than 'a lot of fish'. When analysed, however, the number 153 has some unusual properties. It forms an equilateral triangle – place one dot, then two dots underneath and continue to seventeen dots (a total of 153 dots). 153 is also the sum of 100 (a square number, 10 x 10), 28 (a triangular number in the same manner 153) and 25 (a circular number – a number that ends with the same number as itself, i.e. five squared is 25). These links to the number 153 were identified by Evagrius Ponticus, a fourth-century Christian monk.

Two Apostles appointed after the death of Jesus are used in Masonic ceremonies – St Matthias and St Paul (see below). Matthias, a relatively unknown Biblical character, is significant in the Red Cross of Constantine degree. Matthias appears in the Books of Acts, The Bible explains that Matthias was selected by the remaining eleven disciples to replace Judas, who, according to Matthew, hanged himself after betraying Christ (although the Acts states that he died when his bowels burst open). Matthias was therefore the first apostle to be chosen by members of the church and not Jesus.

Soon after Matthias was chosen, the Holy Spirit descended on the disciples and gave them the power to speak in many languages to enable them to spread the Gospel and speak of the 'wonderful works' of the Almighty. This phrase appears several times in Psalms and it is used in the Fellowcraft (Second Degree ceremony).

Matthias preached around the Black Sea coast, but he was a martyr, being beheaded after stoning failed to kill him. In addition to the fact that he was chosen after the crucifixion, Matthias appears to have been used in the Red Cross of Constantine ceremony for two further reasons.

The Miraculous Catch of Fish (1444) by Konrad Witz. Why does the Bible give the exact number 153?

Firstly, he was written about by Bishop Eusebius (see below), who is prominent in the degree and second, because St Helena (also see below), Constantine's mother, took his relics from Jerusalem and divided them between churches in Rome and Trier.

The Epistle of St James appears to have been written after the death of Christ. Its claim that 'works' are more important than faith has been discussed in the section on the Ministry of Jesus. This Epistle contains many instructions to the early Christians and one command, 'speak not evil one of another, brethren' is used during the Red Cross of Constantine ceremony to install the Viceroy. Likewise, the last verse of the same chapter, which states that knowingly failing to do good is a sin, appears in the same ritual, where it is rendered as 'let us always do good to one another.'

A short section of the letter from Jude is read out during the Knights Templar Priest ceremony. Whether this is Thaddeus, the apostle of Jesus, who was also known by this name, is unknown. The quotation exhorts the early Christians to keep faith in Jesus, whilst awaiting His return. During his letter, Jude quotes from the Book of Enoch, which was excluded from the King James' Version of the Bible. It does, however, appear in the Royal Ark Mariner degree in part of the explanation of the Tracing Board (see section on Genealogy of Noah). He also mentions various examples of wickedness from the Old Testament. This includes a reference to 'Core', an alternative spelling of 'Korah', whose failed challenge to the leadership of Moses is recalled during the Grand High Priest ceremony (see section on Moses).

Luke, a Greek surgeon from the city of Antioch, was a follower of St Paul (see below). Luke is believed to have written the Gospel that bears his name. This includes some of the most famous incidents in Jesus' life, including the Parable of the Good Samaritan (see Ministry of Jesus). Luke also wrote the Acts of the Apostles (the longest book in the New Testament) which is an account of the early Christian Church. In both his Gospel and Acts, Luke prefixes names with the title 'most excellent', which is the style of address used for the senior officer in a Holy Royal Arch chapter. According to tradition, Luke died on mainland Greece in 84 AD.

ST PAUL

Timeline	46–57 AD – Missionary journeys of St Paul
Biblical reference	Acts • Chapters 6–7 (Stephen's speech before martyrdom) • Chapter 7 v58 (Saul's first appearance in the Bible) • Chapter 9 v1–19 (Saul's conversion to Christianity) • Chapter 13 v9 (Saul's name changed to Paul) • Chapter 20 v35 ('More blessed to give than receive') • Chapter 28 v1–11 (Paul on Malta) Romans • Chapter 2 v7 ('Patient continuance in well doing') • Chapter 7 v22 (Inward man) • Chapter 9 v25–33 ('Not my people' and 'living God') • Chapter 9 v29 ('Lord of Sabaoth') • Chapter 12 v10 ('Brotherly love') • Chapter 12 v20 (Treatment of enemies) • Chapter 13 v1 (The powers that be) • Chapter 13 v9 ('Love thy neighbour as thyself') • Chapter 13 v10 ('Love is the fulfilling of the law') I Corinthians • Chapter 3 v10 (Paul is a master builder) • Chapter 3 v16–17 (Spirit of God dwells within) • Chapter 11 v26 ('For as often as ye eat this bread') • Chapter 13 v12 ('Through a glass, darkly') • Chapter 13 v13 ('Faith, hope and charity') • Chapter 15 v52 ('The last trump') • Chapter 15 v55 ('Death, where is thy sting?') II Corinthians • Chapter 3 (End of Mosaic Dispensation) • Chapter 4 v16 (Inward man) • Chapter 5 v1 ('House not made with hands') • Chapter 6 v14–16 (Warning about non-believers) • Chapter 13 v14 (Father, Son and Holy Ghost) Galatians • Chapter 6 v10 ('Household of faith') • Chapter 6 v16 ('as many as walk according to this rule, peace be on them')

Biblical reference continued	Ephesians • Chapter 1 v10 (God's plan fulfilled in Christ) • Chapter 2 v19–22 (All one in Christ) • Chapter 3 v14–21 (The Love of Christ) • Chapter 3 v21 ('world without end') • Chapter 4 v3 ('unity of the Spirit') • Chapter 6 v10–17 (The 'Armour of God') • Chapter 6 v17 ('Sword of the Spirit') Philippians • Chapter 1 v1 (Paul's letter to Philippi) • Chapter 2 v14–16 (Work hard without complaint) • Chapter 2 v25 ('Fellow soldier') Colossians • Chapter 2 v5–7 (Continue to have faith in Christ) I Thessalonians • Chapter 2 v2 (Paul attacked in Philippi) • Chapter 2 v19 ('Crown of rejoicing') • Chapter 4 v9 ('Brotherly love') I Timothy • Chapter 1 v17 ('…eternal, immortal, invisible, the only wise God') Hebrews • Chapter 4 v16 ('Throne of grace') • Chapter 7 (Melchizedek and Aaron) • Chapter 9 (Christian faith replaces Law of Moses) • Chapter 9 v15 (Transgressions) • Chapter 10 v7 ('Volume of the book') • Chapter 11 v1 (Faith and hope) • Chapter 11 v4 (Cain and Abel) • Chapter 11 v5 (Enoch was 'translated') • Chapter 11 v7 (Noah and 'righteousness') • Chapter 11 v8–9 (Abraham, Jacob and Isaac) • Chapter 11 v10 (City with foundations) • Chapter 11 v11–21 (Abraham, Jacob and Isaac) • Chapter 11 v23–30 (Moses) • Chapter 11 v31 (Rahab) • Chapter 11 v32 (Jephtha, Samuel and David) • Chapter 11 v37 ('Sawn asunder') • Chapter 11 v38 (Wandered in mountains) • Chapter 12 v23 ('Just men made perfect') • Chapter 13 v1 ('Brotherly love') James • Chapter 5 v4 ('Lord of Sabaoth')

Masonic reference	Craft
	• First Degree
	• First Degree Tracing Board
	• Second Degree
	• Third Degree
	• Installation Ceremony
	Royal Ark Mariner
	• Ceremony of Elevation
	• Tracing Board
	• Installation of Commander
	Allied Masonic Degrees
	• Grand High Priest
	• Red Cross of Babylon
	Mark
	• Ceremony of Advancement
	• Tracing Board
	• Address to the Overseers
	Royal and Select Masters
	• Royal Master
	• Super Excellent Master
	Holy Royal Arch
	• Ceremony of Exaltation
	• Symbolical Lecture
	Holy Royal Arch Knights Templar Priests
	• Knight of Patmos or Philippi
	• Installation of a Knight Templar Priest
	Rose Croix
	• Ceremony of Perfection
	Red Cross of Constantine
	• Installation of a Knight
	• Knight of the Holy Sepulchre
	• Installation of Viceroy
	Knights Templar
	• Knights Templar
	• Order of St Paul
	• Knight of Malta
	Societas Rosicruciana in Anglia
	Sixth Grade 'Adeptus Major'

Paul is the second most prolific contributor to the New Testament (after Luke, the writer of Luke and Acts) and at least seven and possibly up to thirteen letters in the New Testament can be attributed to him. He is arguably the greatest influence in the development of Christianity, preaching the new religion throughout Asia Minor, Greece and Rome, despite never meeting Jesus and appointing himself as an apostle.

He is certainly the most quoted apostle in Freemasonry and as we shall see, his words are used in more ceremonies than any other Biblical character. He describes himself as a spiritual 'Master Builder' and uses the phrase 'brotherly love' (one of the three Grand Principles of Freemasonry) three times. His quotation of Psalm 40 in the letter to Hebrews (although his authorship is now disputed by modern scholars), using the phrase 'Volume of the book' may be the reason that Freemasons refer to the Bible as the 'Volume of the Sacred Law'.

Chapter 11 of Hebrews mentions many of the characters used in Craft Masonry and appears to have guided the ritual writers in the selection of characters used in the ceremonies. Some of the phrases used to describe Old Testament characters – Abel making a better offering than Cain, Enoch being 'translated' and Noah being 'a teacher of righteousness' appear in some versions of the First Degree Tracing Board. Additionally, the reference to 'a city which hath foundations' may have influenced the storyline in Chapter ritual. The same chapter also contains the punishment of being 'sawn asunder' (sawn in half), which is part of the Red Cross of Babylon degree. Chapter 7 of Hebrews is also the basis of an entire ceremony – the Order of Grand High Priest.

Paul was originally called 'Saul' and was a Jew born in modern-day Turkey, who held Roman citizenship. He was originally a persecutor of the early Christians and he first appears in the Bible as a witness to the stoning of the first Christian martyr, Stephen. Prior to his execution, Stephen made a speech in which he summarised the Old Testament. This seems to have influenced the Masonic ritual writers' choice of characters in a similar manner to the Letter to the Hebrews. At this time, however, the Bible states that Saul was pleased with Stephen's punishment, with the next chapter of Acts describing how he began to arrest Christians.

Despite being one of the new religion's greatest enemies, Saul converted to Christianity after being temporarily blinded on the road to Damascus, where he heard the voice of Jesus asking him 'Saul, Saul, why persecutest thou me?' His blindness ended when 'scales' fell from his eyes. This may be the origin of the phrase used in the Royal Master degree – 'there the scales of doubt and darkness will fall from our eyes.' Furthermore, Masons are blindfolded when they enter the lodge for the first time and then restored to light after taking their obligation. The story of St Paul's conversion may have influenced this part of the ceremony.

Later, whilst preaching on the island of Cyprus, Saul was 'filled with the Holy Ghost' and his name was changed to 'Paul'. Throughout his writings he emphasised that belief in Christ had replaced the need to obey the law of Moses, such as the strict dietary code and the requirement for circumcision. The removal of the strict Law of Moses also had a very practical effect – it made it much easier (and less painful) for Gentiles (non-Jews) to join the new religion. An example is Chapter 6 v15–16 of his letter to the church in Galatia, the Roman province, which is now Turkey. (The second sentence, verse v16, is quoted as part of the Royal Ark Mariner ceremony): 'For in Christ Jesus neither circumcision availeth anything, nor uncircumcision, but a new creature. And as many as walk according to this rule, peace be on them, and mercy.'

The Knight of the Holy Sepulchre makes reference to the end of the 'fragmentary forms and types of the Mosaic dispensation' – the requirement to obey the laws relating to religious procedures given to Moses. A 'dispensation' is a form of commission given by God to his chosen servants (e.g. Abraham, Moses and others) to dispense his Holy Will to the people of earth. These rules were 'fragmentary' as His will had been revealed over a period of time to many different prophets. Paul confirmed the change in several of his letters, including II Corinthians, Ephesians

The Conversion of Saul (1542–1545) by Michelangelo.

and Hebrew. He makes clear that the laws of the 'old testament' are abolished and replaced by the requirement to have faith in Jesus, who is the fulfilment of God's plans.

Again in the Royal Ark Mariner ritual, the prayers utilise the words of Paul. When the new Commander is installed, the prayer notes the 'unity of the Spirit in the bond of peace' from Ephesians. The prayer when a new member joins that degree includes the phrase 'knowing that love is the fulfilling of the law.' This is taken from the letter to the Romans, where Paul emphasises that Christians must 'love thy neighbour as thyself'; a lesson which is also included in The Charge in the First Degree ceremony.

In the section on 'The Division of Israel' it was shown how the words *Ammi* and *Ruhamah* were from the Book of Hosea. Paul quotes from this story in Romans (Hosea is shown as *Osee*) when he discussed the relationship between God and the new Christians, irrespective of them being Jews or Gentiles. It appears to be linked to the Holy Royal Arch chapter ritual, as not only does it use the words 'not my people' *(Lo-Ammi),* the next verse speaks of 'the living God' – Chapter ritual uses the phrase 'true and living God'. Paul's letter may have given the ritual writers the idea of using these words at the start of the exaltation ceremony.

This section of Romans also relates how *Esaias* (Isaiah) had spoken of God as the 'Lord of Sabaoth' who destroyed Sodom and Gomorrah. The modern translation of 'Lord of Sabaoth' is 'Lord All-Powerful' but in the past has been given as 'Lord of Hosts' – that is to say, 'Lord of the Armies' or 'military strength'. 'Lord of Sabaoth' is used during the ceremony of installing the Viceroy in a Red Cross of Constantine conclave. (The phrase is also used in the Epistle of St James).

Romans includes the phrase 'by patient continuance in well doing', when Paul promises eternal life for those who continually do good work for the glory of God. The phrase forms part of the Closing Prayer in the Mark Degree. The same letter from Paul also declares that 'the powers that be are ordained by God' and advises that Christians should obey their laws. This may be the basis of the section in The Charge which urges the newly made Freemason to avoid 'any act which may have a tendency to subvert the peace and good order of society'. Paul relates how enemies should be treated in this letter. He states that 'if thine enemy hunger, feed him; if he thirst, give him drink.' These words are paraphrased in the Grand High Priest ritual.

Paul's letter to the church in Ephesus (the fourth largest city in the Roman Empire), further emphasised that the distinction between Jews and Gentiles had ended and all were one in Christ. This is noted in the Knights Templar Priest ceremony. Chapter 6 is quoted in the Knights Templar and Knights Templar Priest ceremonies. This chapter is most fitting for a Masonic military Order as it is addressed to 'my Brethren' and contains much symbolism relating to knights, with references to the 'Armour of God', 'breastplate of righteousness', 'Shield of Faith' and the 'sword of Spirit', together with other allusions to spiritual warfare. The 'sword of the spirit' also appears in two ceremonies of the Red Cross of Constantine as the 'chief defence of our sanctuary' and the phrase 'fellow soldier' (from Philippians) is also used in this knightly Order.

Part of Chapter 3 of Ephesians speaks of the love of Christ and this is quoted during the Knights Templar Priest ceremony. This chapter ends with the expression, 'world without end', which is used to end a prayer in the Red Cross of Constantine. A section of Paul's first letter to Timothy, a Christian leader in the same city, is paraphrased during the Rose Croix ceremony: 'Now to the King, eternal, immortal, invisible, the only wise God, be the Kingdom, the power and the glory for ever and ever.'

The Grand College of Knights Templar Priests controls a degree entitled 'Knight of Patmos or Philippi'. St Paul's Epistle to the Philippians is a letter to the early Christian leaders in the Greek city of Philippi. (See section on St John regarding Patmos). Paul had been attacked by people who opposed his Christian message when he had visited the city, but he was emboldened by his faith and continued to preach the gospel. In the Knights Templar Priest ceremony a section of the letter is quoted. This urges the new Christians in Philippi to work without 'murmurings and disputings' in an evil world, whilst waiting for the return of Jesus.

It can be seen that the ritual is filled with references from Paul – some obscure, some well known. An example of an unfamiliar quotation is 'household of Faith' (from Galatians), which appears in the Installation of a Knight ceremony of the Red Cross of Constantine. In the Book of Acts, Paul reminds the church at Ephesus of Jesus' words, 'It is more blessed to give than to receive.' These are some of the most famous words in the Bible and they feature in the Royal Ark Mariner ceremony of Elevation, when the Junior Warden advises the candidate on how to assist a brother.

In his first letter to the Corinthians, Paul uses the phrase 'faith, hope and charity' (some versions of the Bible translate 'charity' as 'love') and explains that the latter word is the most important (however it is translated). Masonically, these three attributes are linked to the staves of Jacob's ladder, each one representing a moral virtue and they appear in the Rose Croix and Red Cross of Babylon ceremonies and during the explanation of the Tracing Boards in the First Degree and Mark Ritual. The importance of Chapter 11 of Hebrews to Masonic ritual has already been explained and the first verse of this chapter states that 'faith is the substance of things hoped for, the evidence of things not seen.' This link between faith and hope are recalled during the ritual relating to these two Tracing Boards.

The three virtues also appear as the titles of the three 'Theological Orations' in the Installation of a Knight of the Holy Sepulchre. During the third oration on charity, the candidate is informed that the rewards of practising charity are 'to be admitted into the assembly of the just made perfect'. This appears to be a paraphrased version of part of St Paul's letter to the Hebrews, in which he writes to the 'general assembly' and the spirits of 'just men made perfect'. Additionally, the degree makes reference to Masons, after the death of Christ and prior to his resurrection, wandering 'among the woods and mountains in deepest obscurity'. This appears to be taken from Hebrews, where St Paul speaks of people faith wandering 'in deserts, and in mountains'.

Hebrews also contains a reference to the 'throne of grace' which appears in the presentation of the 'working tools' during the First Degree ceremony and in Chapter 9, Jesus is referred to as the 'the mediator of the new testament, that by means of death, for the redemption of the transgressions….'. This is possibly the origin of the section of the Third Degree prayer which refers to the 'tomb of transgression'. A further link to the Third Degree may be contained in the first letter to the Corinthians, where Paul states 'for now we see through a glass, darkly.' This reference to a dim reflection may be the reason the ritual writers used 'I now beg you to observe that the light of a Master Mason is but darkness visible' in the ceremony. The sixth grade of SRIA is also a study of physical death and uses this quotation. The Holy Royal Arch ceremony speaks of the 'last trump, when the graves shall be shaken and loosened and deliver up their dead'. This is also from I Corinthians as is 'Death, where is thy sting?' which is used in the Royal Master degree (See section on Hiram Abif). Both quotations relate to the Christian concept of death and resurrection in heaven.

In Paul's second letter to the Corinthians, he developed the concept of the 'outward man' (the physical body, which decays) and the 'inward man' (the spirit, which can be renewed each day). This 'inward man' is also mentioned in his letter to the church in Rome. The explanation of the First Degree Tracing Board and the Royal Ark Mariner degree contain many similarities and both contain references to the 'inward man'. This is said to represent God's beauty adorning the inner spirit of man. In a similar manner, in his first letter to Corinth, Paul described the human body as a 'temple of God' and punishment will follow for defiling it. This section is quoted during the Knights Templar Priest ceremony. This concept of the body being a building is also part of the First Degree, where the new initiate is described as a foundation stone, which will develop into a superstructure.

The expression 'crown of rejoicing' is used in Paul's first letter to the Thessalonians in Greece when referring to their church. This phrase features in the 'Address to the Master', when he is newly installed, as 'a crown of joy and rejoicing', but here refers to the rewards of good service to the lodge. Perhaps the best example of a Biblical quotation being adapted for Masonic use comes from Paul's account of the Last Supper in I Corinthians. Here he recalls Jesus' words 'For as often as ye eat this bread, and drink this cup, ye do shew the Lord's death till he come.' In the Grand High Priest ritual, the members are reminded that, 'as often as ye eat bread or drink wine, learn therefrom to succour, protect and defend a Companion Anointed High Priest.'

Throughout his letters, Paul encouraged the new Christians to continue to have faith in Jesus and a section of his letter to the Colossians relating to this issue is quoted during the Knights Templar Priest ceremony. This ceremony also contains his warning from II Corinthians about mixing with non-believers. Not only did he influence the early church, his concept of the new religion had a major impact on the theology adopted by the Church as it developed over the next 1000 years. For example, Paul's second letter to the Corinthians ends with a reference to the Holy Trinity, so important in the Christian Masonic Orders: 'The grace of the Lord Jesus Christ, and the love of God, and the communion of the Holy Ghost, be with you all.'

During the Knight of the Holy Sepulchre ceremony, it is related that after the death of Jesus, masons 'no longer built material edifices but contented themselves with spiritual buildings'. This is reference to St Paul's second letter to the church at Corinth, when he states that: 'If our earthly house of this tabernacle were dissolved, we have a building of God, an house not made with hands, eternal in the heavens.'

St Paul Bitten by a Viper on the Island of Malta (1567) by Marten de Vos.

There are references to 'a house not made with hands, eternal to the heavens' in several degrees, including during the explanations of the Tracing Boards in the First Degree and Royal Ark Mariner ceremony. It is also noted in the lecture on the Grand High Priest degree and twice in the Mark ceremony – when the Working Tools are presented during the Advancement of a candidate and the Installation of the Master. Prayers in both the Red Cross of Constantine (Installation of a Knight) and the Super Excellent Master ceremonies, contain references to 'that immortal Temple, eternal in the heavens'.

Paul himself features in a short 'passing degree' in the Knights Templar ceremonies. Here a Priory of the Knights of Malta is opened and the degree of 'Knight of Saint Paul' is conferred on the candidate. Unsurprisingly, the ritual is based on the account of Paul's stay on the island of Malta, which is related in the Book of Acts. Due to his promotion of Christianity, Paul had fallen foul of the Jewish authorities and was imprisoned, but used his citizenship of the empire to demand a trial in Rome. He was placed aboard a prison ship, but during a storm in the Mediterranean he was shipwrecked on the island of Malta. The Latin name for the island, 'Melita' is used in the King James' Version of the Bible and in the Knights Templar ritual.

Whilst making a fire, a viper took hold of his wrist, but Paul was able to shake it off and throw it into the flames. As he came to no harm, the islanders believed that Paul was a god. This incident is an important aspect of the degree. This was one of the many journeys of Paul, who travelled to several of the important cities around the Mediterranean preaching the gospel of Christ. According to Eusebius (see below), Paul was beheaded in Rome during the reign of Emperor Nero.

THE BOOK OF REVELATION

Timeline	100 AD
Biblical reference	Revelation • Chapter 1 v8 (Alpha and Omega)

Biblical reference continued	• Chapter 1 v9 (Written by John on Patmos) • Chapter 2 v7 (Tree of life) • Chapter 2 v10 (Crown of life) • Chapter 2 v11 ('Not be hurt of the second death') • Chapter 2 v17 (Hidden manna) • Chapter 2 v26 ('Power over the nations') • Chapter 3 v5 ('Clothed in white raiment') • Chapter 3 v7–8 ('Key of David') • Chapter 3 v12 ('Pillar in the temple of my God') • Chapter 3 v21 (Sit at the throne of God) • Chapter 4 v1 (Door open in heaven) • Chapter 5 v5 (Jesus opened the seals) • Chapter 5 v6–7 (Description of Lamb of God) • Chapter 7 v9–12 (Great crowd worships God) • Chapter 8 v6 (Seven angels with seven trumpets) • Chapter 11 v19 (Ark in Heaven) • Chapter 13 v9 ('If any man have an ear') • Chapter 16 (Bowls of God's anger) • Chapter 20 v14 (Hell is a lake of fire) • Chapter 21 v1–2 (Beauty of the New Jerusalem) • Chapter 22 v12 (Men rewarded according to work) • Chapter 22 v13 (Alpha and Omega) • Chapter 22 v14 (Blessed do the Commandments) • Chapter 22 v16 (Bright and morning star)
Masonic reference	Craft • First Degree Tracing Board Mark • Ceremony of Advancement Royal and Select Masters • Royal Master Holy Royal Arch • Ceremony of Exaltation Rose Croix • Ceremony of Perfection Holy Royal Arch Knights Templar Priests • Knight of Patmos or Philippi • Installation of a Knights Templar Priest Red Cross of Constantine • Knight of St John the Evangelist • Enthronement of Sovereign Knights Templar

Masonic reference *continued*	Societas Rosicruciana in Anglia • Fifth Grade 'Adeptus Minor'

As Masonic ritual is drawn from the first book of the Bible, Genesis, so it uses parts of the last book, Revelation. The Book of Revelation contains frightful visions of death and destruction in prophetic language. It is, like Freemasonry, very symbolic. Revelation was written at a time when early Christians were being persecuted by the Romans (which started around 64 AD), but for all its prophecy of doom and disaster, it ends with the promise of the return of Christ and a 'New Jerusalem'. The book was written by 'John' on the Mediterranean island of Patmos, where John had been exiled by the Romans because of his Christian preaching. An unworked degree, called the Knight of Patmos, is under the control of the Grand College of Knights Templar Priests.

Whether 'John' was St John the Evangelist or another early Christian has been a matter of great debate that will probably never be resolved. Revelation is written in the form of the letter and was sent to seven churches in modern-day Turkey.

In the first chapter of the book, God describes Himself as the 'Alpha and Omega' – the beginning and end, these words being the first and last letters of the Greek alphabet. This phrase is used in Holy Royal Arch, Rose Croix, Red Cross of Constantine Enthronement ceremony and in the Royal Master degree where Chapter 22 v12–14, which includes the phrase, is quoted.

God announces that seven stars represent the angels of the seven churches being written to. Whilst this does not appear in Masonic ritual, it should be noted that seven stars appear on the First Degree Tracing Board. There follows separate messages for each church with a different reward for each for being part of God's final victory. The churches are promised rewards as follows:

1 Ephesus   To eat from the tree of life in the garden of God.

2 Pergamum   'to eat of the hidden manna, and I will give him a white stone, and in the stone a new name written, which no man knoweth saving he that receiveth it.'

3 Smyrna   A 'crown of life' and not to be hurt by the 'second death' – the 'first death' is physical death and the second is 'spiritual death' – being separated from God and sent to Hell. Later in Revelation the second death is described as being thrown into a lake of fire.

4 Thyatira   Power over the nations.

5 Sardis   To be dressed in 'a white raiment' (white clothes).

6 Philadelphia To become pillars in the church of God and to receive the 'key of David'.

7 Laodicea   To sit at the throne of God

These rewards are all recalled during the Knights Templar Priest ceremony. Some references are easy to understand. The members of the Order wear a white mantle and there are seven pillars in Tabernacle room (this 'white raiment' is also recalled during the SRIA ritual). Others, such as the 'key of David' are harder to comprehend.

The promises are included in several other Masonic ceremonies. The Rose Croix ritual includes the promise of a 'crown of life'. The verse including 'hidden manna' and the white stone are contained in the Knights Templar ceremony and in the Mark Degree. The inclusion in the Mark ceremony is seemingly for no other reason than it contains a reference to a stone. In a similar manner the phrase 'If any man have an ear, let him hear' from later in Revelation is linked to one of the secrets signs in the Mark ritual (as was noted in the section on the Organisation of the Temple Workforce).

The Knights Templar Priest ceremony continues to draw heavily on Revelation and contains at least twelve quotations from it. Chapters 5 to 8 describe the opening of a scroll given by God to Jesus in heaven. The language of Revelation is very symbolic, for example, the 'Lamb of God' (Jesus) is said to have seven horns and seven eyes, representing the seven spirits of God. Seven is said to represent completeness.

The scroll has seven seals and as each is opened by Christ, dramatic events are prophesied as occurring in the future. In the Knights Templar Priest degree, there are seven 'Pillar Officers', who represent each seal being opened. The opening of the first four seals brings forth what are often described as the 'Four Horsemen of the Apocalypse' – Conquest, War, Famine and Death. According to the Bible, the opening of the first six seals will result in the following disasters:

1st   Persecution/Conquest
2nd   War
3rd   Famine
4th   Pestilence/Death
5th   Persecution of saints
6th   Great earthquake, mass destruction and the population flee to the mountains

At this point, a great crowd, gathered from all the nations of the earth, will begin to worship God. The crowd will be dressed in white (a second reference to white clothing) and holding palm branches. This description, and their prayer, are quoted during the first grade of SRIA: 'Blessing and glory, and wisdom, and thanksgiving, and honour, and power, and might, be to our God for ever and ever. Amen.'

When opened, the seventh will result in the appearance of seven angels, who have seven trumpets. When the first six are blown they will produce various types of mass devastation, with a third of the world's population perishing. The blowing of the seventh trumpet will produce a loud voice from heaven, declaring that the earth belongs to God and His son forever. The Ark of the Covenant will then be seen in heaven. To further rid the world of evil, the angels will pour out seven bowls of the 'wrath of God'. These will bring about further disasters.

The book continues with the defeat of Satan (a giant red dragon) and the eventual victory of Christ. In the last chapter of Revelation, the New Jerusalem is described as a crystal clear river, flowing from the throne of God, with the tree of life on each side. This is quoted in the Knights Templar Priest ceremony. Later, Jesus describes Himself as the 'bright and morning star', which appears in the Enthronement Ceremony in the Red Cross of Constantine and is believed to the origin of the 'bright morning star' in the Third Degree ceremony. It has been observed in the section on Solomon that the five-pointed star shown on the Royal Ark Mariner Tracing Board may be an emblematic depiction of the movements of the planet Venus, the morning star, and therefore may allude to Christ.

In the same chapter, Jesus uses the phrase 'Alpha and Omega' again to describe His ever-lasting nature. All men will be rewarded 'according as his work shall be' and this is paraphrased in the Mark Degree, the ritual with the most quotations from Revelation. The Bible ends with a promise of Christ's return or His 'Second Coming' as it is called in the prayer in the Knight of St John the Evangelist ceremony.

NEW TESTAMENT REFERENCES IN DEGREES OPEN TO NON-CHRISTIAN MASONS

Biblical Reference	Quotation/Issue	Ceremony
Matthew Chapter 5 v24	'first be reconciled to thy brother'	Royal Ark Mariner: Ceremony of Elevation
Matthew Chapter 18 v20	'For where two or three are gathered together in my name' (Ritual uses version from the Book of Common Prayer 'in Thy name')	Royal Ark Mariner: Ceremony of Elevation
Matthew Chapter 20 v12	'heat and burden of the day'	Craft: First Degree Tracing Board
Matthew Chapter 22 v12	'how camest thou hither?'	Allied Masonic Degrees: Grand Tilers of Solomon
Matthew Chapter 25 v21	'Well done, thou good and faithful servant'	Mark: Tracing Board
Luke Chapter 2 v14	'Glory to God in the highest, and on earth peace, good will toward men.'	Royal Ark Mariner: Ceremony of Elevation Royal Arch Chapter: Ceremony of Exaltation
Luke Chapter 6 v31	'Do unto others as you would that they should do unto you.'	Royal Ark Mariner: Ceremony of Elevation
Luke Chapter 12 v38	'Third Watch'	Royal and Select Masters: Super Excellent Master
Luke Chapter 14 v11, Chapter 18 v14	he that 'exalted himself shall be abased' but 'he that humbleth himself shall be exalted.'	Allied Masonic Degrees: Knight of Constantinople
Luke Chapter 14 v21	'the maimed and the halt'	Allied Masonic Degrees: St Lawrence the Martyr
John Chapter 9 v4	'the night cometh when no man can work'	Royal Ark Mariner: Tracing Board Royal and Select Masters: Royal Master Allied Masonic Degrees: Knight of Constantinople
John Chapter 20 v16	Jesus called 'Rabboni'	Royal and Select Master: Most Excellent Master
Acts Chapter 2 v11	'wonderful works'	Craft: Second Degree

Acts Chapter 8 v39	'went on his way rejoicing'	Mark: Ceremony of Advancement
Acts Chapter 9 v18	'scales' 'fell from his eyes'	Royal and Select Masters: Royal Master
Acts Chapter 20 v35	'More blessed to give than receive' (This is a later translation than that appearing in the King James' Version.)	Royal Ark Mariner: Ceremony of Elevation
Romans Chapter 2 v7	'by patient continuance in well doing'	Mark: Closing Prayer
Romans Chapter 9 v25–26	'Not my people' = 'Lo-Ammi' 'living God' (In ritual as 'true and living God')	Royal Arch Chapter: Ceremony of Exaltation
Romans Chapter 12 v10	'brotherly love'	Craft: Questions Before Passing
Romans Chapter 13 v1	'the powers that be are ordained by God' (Possible link to The Charge – 'the allegiance due to the Sovereign or Ruler of your native land')	Craft: First Degree
Romans Chapter 13 v10	'love is the fulfilling of the law'	Royal Ark Mariner: Ceremony of Elevation
I Corinthians Chapter 11 v26	'For as often as ye eat this bread, and drink this cup, ye do shew the Lord's death till he come'	Allied Masonic Degrees: Grand High Priest
I Corinthians Chapter 13 v13	'Faith, hope and charity' (Royal Ark Mariner uses older translation 'Faith, hope and love')	Craft: First Degree Tracing Board Royal Ark Mariner: Ceremony of Elevation Mark: Tracing Board Mark: Installation Ceremony (Address to the Overseers)
I Corinthians Chapter 15 v52	'The last trump'	Holy Royal Arch: Symbolical Lecture
I Corinthians Chapter 15 v55	'Death, where is thy sting? O grave where is thy victory?'	Royal and Select Master: Royal Master
II Corinthians Chapter 4 v16 (Also Romans Chapter 7 v22)	'inward man'	Craft: First Degree Tracing Board Royal Ark Mariner: Ceremony of Elevation

II Corinthians Chapter 5 v1	'A house not made with hands eternal in the heavens'	Craft: First Degree Tracing Board Mark: Ceremony of Advancement and Installation Royal Ark Mariner: Tracing Board Royal and Select Masters: Super Excellent Master
Galatians Chapter 6 v16	'as many as walk according to this rule, peace be on them'	Royal Ark Mariner: Ceremony of Elevation
I Thessalonians Chapter 1 v9	'… the living and true God' – in ritual as 'true and living God'	Royal Arch Chapter: Ceremony of Exaltation
I Thessalonians Chapter 4 v9	'brotherly love'	Craft: Questions Before Passing
Hebrews Chapter 4 v16	'Throne of grace'	Craft: First Degree Royal Arch Chapter: Mystical Lecture
Hebrews Chapter 6 v19	'Anchor of hope'	Royal Ark Mariner: Opening Mark: Tracing Board
Hebrews Chapter 9 v4	Contents of Ark of the Covenant	Royal and Select Master: Select Master
Hebrews Chapter 9 v15	'Transgressions' (Possible link to 'tomb of transgression')	Craft: Third Degree
Hebrews Chapter 11 v37	'sawn asunder'	Allied Masonic Degrees: Red Cross of Babylon
Hebrew Chapter 13 v1	'brotherly love'	Craft: Questions Before Passing
I Peter Chapter 2 v4–5	'living stone' and 'spiritual house'	Mark: Ceremony of Advancement
I Peter Chapter 4 v10	'as good stewards of the manifold grace of God' (in ritual as 'manifold gifts')	Royal Ark Mariner: Ceremony of Elevation
I Peter Chapter 5 v4	'Crown of glory that fadeth not away'	Craft: Installation Ceremony (Address to the Master)
II Peter Chapter 3 v10	'Elements shall melt with fervent heat'	Royal Ark Mariner: Ceremony of Elevation
II Peter Chapter 2 v5	Noah is a 'preacher of righteousness' – in ritual as 'teacher of righteousness'	Craft: First Degree Tracing Board

I John Chapter 3 v16–17	'…for whoso seeth his brother have need, and shutteth up his compassion from him, how dwelleth the love of God in him?' (There is a small variation between the Bible and the ritual.)	Royal Ark Mariner: Ceremony of Elevation
Revelation Chapter 1 v8	'I am Alpha and Omega'	Royal Arch Chapter: Ceremony of Exaltation Royal and Select Master: Royal Master
Revelation Chapter 2 v17	'To him that overcometh will I give to eat of the hidden manna, and I will give him a white stone, and in the stone a new name written, which no man knoweth saving he that receiveth it.'	Mark: Ceremony of Advancement
Revelation Chapter 13 v9	'If any man have an ear'	Mark: Ceremony of Advancement
Revelation Chapter 22 v12–14	'I am Alpha and Omega' 'I come quickly; and my reward is with me, to give every man according to his work'	Royal and Select Master: Royal Master Mark: Ceremony of Advancement
Revelation Chapter 22 v16	'Bright and morning star' – in ritual as 'Bright morning star'	Craft: Third Degree

THE DESTRUCTION OF SECOND TEMPLE

Timeline	70 AD – Destruction of the Second Temple 130 AD – Romans rebuild Jerusalem
Biblical reference	II Chronicles • Chapter 5 v12 – (Trumpets used in the temple) Isaiah • Chapter 66 v1 (Earth is God's footstool) Matthew • Chapter 24 v1–2 (Destruction of the temple foreseen)

Biblical reference *continued*	Luke • Chapter 21 v5–6 (Destruction of the temple foreseen) Acts • Chapters 6–7 (Stephen the first Christian martyr)
Masonic reference	Craft • First Degree Tracing Board Holy Royal Arch • Historical Lecture Red Cross of Constantine • Knight of the Holy Sepulchre
Historical context	Roman invasion of Britain in 43 AD Revolt of Boudicca in Britain 60/61 AD Coliseum in Rome constructed between 70 and 80 AD

After the death of Jesus, the status of the temple was a source of dispute between Jewish leaders and the early Christians. The Jews viewed the temple as a house where God resided and this was challenged by Stephen, who quoted Isaiah, to argue that the Lord did not live in buildings made by men. The passage from Isaiah contains the reference to God stating that 'the earth is my footstool.' In Masonic ritual this phrase is used during the explanation of the First Degree Tracing Board to show the vastness of God's creation. Stephen was stoned to death for his claims and became the first Christian martyr (see St Paul). As such, he was honoured by having his saint's day celebrated on 26 December, the day after Christmas.

The Christian view that God does not need a physical building is continued in the Red Cross of Constantine Appendant Orders. In the 'Allegorical Sequel' to the Holy Royal Arch in the Knight of the Holy Sepulchre, it is stated that after the resurrection of Jesus, masons built spiritual buildings rather than material edifices.

In 66 AD, more than three decades after the crucifixion, the Jews rebelled because the Roman Emperor, Vespasian, had demanded that sacrifices had to be made in the Temple in his honour. Four years later the Roman commander Titus attacked Jerusalem. It was captured after a bitter siege, during which, according to the Jewish historian, Josephus, one starving woman roasted and ate her own baby. As the attack drew to its close in August 70 AD, much of the city, including the Temple, was destroyed by fire. Some priests committed suicide by plunging into the flames and those left alive were put to death on the orders of Titus, who declared, 'it is fitting for priests to perish along with their Temple.'

Many of the sacred treasures were seized and taken to Rome, where they were paraded. These included one of the candlesticks and the golden table (described in the Book of Kings and in the Royal Master degree) from the Holy of Holies and the trumpets of Jericho. After his military service, Titus was the Emperor from 79 AD until his death in 81 AD.

It is unclear whether the devastation of the Temple was a deliberate policy of Titus or an accident, caused by attacking soldiers during the 'fog of war'. Its destruction by Titus is mentioned as a simple statement of fact in Chapter ritual, which does not note the enormous impact this event had on world religion. Christians saw the destruction as the fulfilment of Jesus' prophesy of the end of the Temple, which confirmed to them that their new religion had replaced the Law of Moses.

Destruction of the Temple of Jerusalem (1867) by Francesco Hayez. Note the Menorah candlestick being plundered by the Romans.

The Arch of Titus in Rome commemorates his victory and shows treasures taken from the Temple, including the Menorah and the trumpets of Jericho, which were paraded through the Roman capital.

Much of our knowledge of this period comes from the accounts of Josephus. He lived during this period (37–100 AD). He originally commanded Jewish forces in Galilee who fought against the Romans, but when taken prisoner he believed that God had commanded him to assist his captors. He was an eye-witness to the destruction of the Temple and wrote several books on Jewish history.

Jerusalem was rebuilt in 130 AD by the Roman Emperor, Hadrian (in the Red Cross of Constantine he is referred to by his full name – *Publius Aelius Hadrianus*) and following a revolt the Jews were expelled five years later and dispersed throughout the Roman Empire. All that remains of the Temple is the Wailing or Western Wall, which stands on Temple Mount. It is called 'Wailing' as it describes the Jews, who mourn the destruction of the Temple. This is a place of pilgrimage for followers of Judaism.

One of the few artefacts of the Second Temple is a stone excavated from the foot of Temple Mount. The inscription on the stone refers to the use of trumpets in the Temple and the Bible records much use of trumpets and cymbals by priests at the Temple.

10

THE FIRST THOUSAND
YEARS OF CHRISTIANITY

ST LAWRENCE THE MARTYR AND THE
PERSECUTION OF THE CHRISTIANS

Timeline	225 AD–258 AD
Biblical reference	Luke • Chapter 14 v21 ('the maimed and the halt')
Masonic reference	Allied Masonic Degrees • St Lawrence the Martyr Red Cross of Constantine • Installation of a Knight • Knight of St John the Evangelist

Historically, the next Masonic character to appear is St Lawrence the Martyr. He was a Spaniard, but was a deacon in charge of the church treasures in Rome. Whether he was selected for use in Masonic ritual because he was a 'deacon' (an officer of the lodge) is unclear.

In 257, the Emperor Valerian was persecuting Christians and the Prefect of Rome used this opportunity in an attempt to seize the riches of the church. Lawrence requested three days to collate all the treasures, but spent the time busily giving them away, so they would not fall into the Prefect's hands.

On the third day, St Lawrence paraded the blind, crippled and poor in the Great Square. The ritual uses the phrase 'the halt', an old fashioned English to describe the crippled and the same term is used in the Gospel of St Luke. This is taken from Jesus' Parable of the Great Supper, where the master of the household gathered the maimed and blind to eat at his house. Lawrence then said to the Prefect, 'Behold, these are the treasures of the Christian Church.' To punish him, the Prefect had St Lawrence burned alive on a great gridiron. During this torture, the martyr exclaimed 'Let my body be turned, one side is broiled enough.'

This story is the basis of the 'St Lawrence the Martyr' degree, which is one of the five Allied Masonic Degrees. St Lawrence is the first degree taken by candidates for the order and all admin-

Condemnation of St Lawrence by the Emperor Valerian (1447–1449) by Fra Angelico. Note the instruments of torture on the ground.

istrative business of the lodge is conducted in this degree. The secret sign of the degree is based on St Lawrence's bravery during his torture. A small gridiron is placed on the Bible during the ceremony and is the emblem of the Order.

The Emperor Valerian was to suffer for his wickedness. In 259 AD he was defeated by the Persians at the Battle of Edessa (now in southern Turkey). He was captured and the Persian ruler, Shapur, used the former emperor as a human stepping-stool while mounting his horse. Valerian's body was later skinned and stuffed with straw or manure to produce a trophy of Roman submission preserved in a Persian temple.

Like St Lawrence, many Christians were to suffer at the hands of the Romans between the 1st and 4th centuries AD, until the reign of Constantine, whose life is covered in the next section. The sign used in the Red Cross of Constantine ceremony is linked to the martyrdom of these early followers of Jesus and the Knight of St John the Evangelist ceremony recalls 'the persecution of the Christians under the Roman Emperors, and their liberty under Constantine the Great'.

EMPEROR CONSTANTINE

Timeline	272 AD–337 AD
Biblical reference	Psalms • Psalm 15 (Behaviour pleasing to God)
Masonic reference	Allied Masonic Degrees • Knight of Constantinople Red Cross of Constantine • Installation of a Knight • Knight of the Holy Sepulchre • Knight of St John the Evangelist • Enthronement of Sovereign

Constantine the Great was the first Christian ruler of Rome and is of great Masonic importance, having a number of degrees celebrating his life. Born in 272, he served in the Roman Army and was proclaimed 'Augustus' or Emperor whilst in York, England in 306. His mother, Helena, was a Christian and was, no doubt, a great influence in his life (see section on St Helena below).

Despite being proclaimed emperor by his troops, Constantine still had rivals to the throne, including his brother-in-law, Maxentius, the son of a previous emperor, who was favoured in Rome. In the early part of 312, Constantine gathered his forces and reached Rome by October of the same year. He expected Maxentius to defend the city and was therefore ready to employ siege

The statue of Constantine in York, England, where he was proclaimed as Emperor. The author presents the Red Cross of Constantine Division of Surrey banner.

tactics. Maxentius, however, decided to meet Constantine in an open battle, which took place between the River Tiber and Saxa Ruba, to the north west of Rome.

According to the legend recorded by the 'Father of Church History', Eusebius (see below), Constantine, before going into battle, saw a cross in the sky with the words *in hoc signo vinces*, which when translated from Latin mean, 'In this sign you will conquer.' These are significant to the Red Cross of Constantine degree and the initials IHSV are shown on the jewel. Early the next morning, Constantine dreamt that a voice commanded him to have his soldiers draw a special cross, the sign of Christ, on their shields. This cross is called the Labarum and is composed of the first two Greek letters in the word for Christ 'ΧΡΙΣΤΟΣ'. These two letters are called *Chi* and *Rho*. In a Red Cross of Constantine two officers bear standards named 'Constantine' and 'Labarum'.

During the battle, Constantine pushed the superior forces of his rival back towards the River Tiber. The retreating army tried to escape by crossing the Milvian Bridge, but this collapsed and many were drowned, including Maxentius. His head was cut from his dead body and paraded through Rome by Constantine.

The Edict of Milan, signed by Constantine in 313, proclaimed religious toleration throughout the Roman Empire and Constantine's Christian legacy can still be seen today in Jerusalem. In 325 he ordered the building of the Church of the Holy Sepulchre (the Tomb of Christ). This was built on the site where his mother and Macarius, the Bishop of Jerusalem, found the three crosses reputedly used at the crucifixion – this is further discussed in the next section. Constantine is particularly revered in the Orthodox Church, where he has the title *Isapostolos,* meaning the 'Equal of the Apostles'.

The Vision of the Cross (1520–1524), a fresco by the students of Raphael located in the Apostolic Palace of Vatican City.

The Red Cross of Constantine breast jewel. Note cross shape with letters 'IHSV'.

In Freemasonry, the emperor's life is celebrated in the Masonic and Military Order of the Red Cross of Constantine and this includes the degree of Knight of the Holy Sepulchre. According to legend, this Order was established during his reign to guard the tomb and protect pilgrims.

Constantine's quest for humility is a major feature of the Knights of Constantinople degree, where he confers knighthoods on craftsmen and not on the arrogant nobility. At the start of this ceremony, the Bible must be opened at Psalm 15, which explains behaviour pleasing to God (see section on Psalms).

By an edict issued in 321, Constantine declared that Sunday was a day of rest and law courts were to be closed. This resulted in the Christian Sabbath Day being Sunday, rather than Saturday as in Judaism. Masonically, this has resulted in no lodges being permitted to meet on a Sunday, in compliance with the rules of the United Grand Lodge of England. Furthermore, the earliest record of Christmas being celebrated on 25 December is in 336, towards the end of Constantine's reign.

In 325, Constantine called the Council of Nicaea. This agreed the divinity of Christ and the Nicene Creed remains an ecumenical statement of Christian faith. Importantly, this council confirmed the Trinitarian Christian faith of Father, Son and Holy Ghost.

In addition to his religious zeal, Constantine was a shrewd politician, who recognised that Christianity could be used to unite and strengthen his power. He also made Byzantium the capital of the Roman Empire and after his death in 337 the city was renamed Constantinople in his honour. He had considered rebuilding the city of Troy as the new Roman capital, but according to a legend, an eagle swooped down and took a measuring line from one of the Christian workmen employed at the ancient site and flew to Byzantium. This was taken as a sign from heaven. The story is related during the 'enthronement' of the sovereign (Master) of a Red Cross of Constantine conclave.

The walls of Constantinople were extended by Anthemius in 413 AD, almost doubling the size of the city. He is celebrated as the Junior Warden or 'Chief of the Artisans' in the Knights of Constantinople degree. The city is now Istanbul, in modern day Turkey.

Whilst the Red Cross of Constantine celebrates the conversion of the Roman emperor to the new religion, it should be noted that Constantine promoted tolerance of any religious beliefs. It was not until 391, during the reign of Theodosius, that Christianity was declared as the only legitimate imperial religion.

St Helena and the Patriarch Macarius

Timeline	250–330 AD – Life of St Helena
	312–335 AD – Macarius Bishop of Jerusalem
Biblical reference	Isaiah
	Chapter 53 v5 ('He was wounded for our transgressions')
Masonic reference	Red Cross of Constantine
	• Knight of the Holy Sepulchre

A legend from the Middle Ages, which is quoted during the Red Cross of Constantine ceremony, claimed that Helena was the daughter of the King of Britain but she appears to have been born in modern day Turkey. St Helena travelled to Jerusalem, Bethlehem and Sinai to identify locations described in the Bible. She was a very active Christian researcher and discovered many artefacts (including the bones of St Matthias – see The Apostles after the Crucifixion), although many may have been faked or identified as a result of religious zeal rather than thorough research.

The author holding part of the Burning Bush at the foot of Mount Sinai. The bush was 'identified' by St Helena.

Miracle of the Relic of the True Cross (1505–1510) by Benedetto Diana.

Together with the Patriarch Macarius, the Bishop of Jerusalem, she destroyed the Temple of Venus, which stood on top of Mount Calvary and discovered three crosses buried underneath. To establish which had been used to crucify Christ, Macarius suggested that a woman, suffering with leprosy, should touch each one. The first two had no effect, but when she held the third cross, the woman was miraculously cured and quoted from what is taken to be part of Isaiah's prophecy of Christ: 'He was wounded for our transgressions, he was bruised for our iniquities: the chastisement of our peace was upon him; and with his stripes we are healed.'

Macarius advised Constantine on the construction of the church of the Holy Sepulchre and advised on materials, including precious stones, to ornament the building. This was recorded by Eusebius (see next section). The main feature of the church is the actual Sepulchre and this is described in the Appendant Orders of the Red Cross of Constantine.

Macarius's body has now travelled the globe – his skull is held in St Anthony's Chapel, Pittsburgh, Pennsylvania. This is the largest collection of Christian relics outside The Vatican.

Outside the Holy Sepulchre.

The interior of the Holy Sepulchre. This is believed to be the stone where Jesus' body was lain.

BISHOP EUSEBIUS

Timeline	265–340 AD
Biblical reference	Post Biblical
Masonic reference	Allied Masonic Degrees • Knight of Constantinople Red Cross of Constantine • Installation of a Knight

Eusebius is the role played by the 'Viceroy' or second most senior officer in a Red Cross of Constantine Conclave. In the Knight of Constantinople degree, again the second officer is named 'Eusebius', who is also styled as the 'Chief of the Builders'. It is unclear why he should be given this title, as there is no evidence that he was involved in any form of construction work.

Eusebius lived around the time of Constantine and was the Bishop of Caesarea, an ancient city located on the Mediterranean coast near modern-day Tel Aviv in Israel. Little is known of his early life, but he is believed to have been born around 265 AD. He is referred to as the 'Father of Church History' as he recorded the development of the early Christian Church. He is sometimes referred to as Eusebius Pamphili, that is to say Eusebius, friend of St Pamphilus, a renowned Biblical scholar of the time.

During his lifetime, there were continuous disputes regarding the principles of Christian faith. When Constantine called the Council of Nicaea in 325 AD to resolve these matters, Eusebius was prominent amongst the 318 attendees. The statement of Christian faith which he proposed became the foundation of the Nicene Creed (see Constantine).

Eusebius's prominence in the Red Cross of Constantine degree is probably due to the fact that, in addition to his contribution at Nicaea, he wrote the two versions of the emperor's vision of the cross in the sky. In the first, Constantine saw the vision in Gaul, whilst some days march from the battle with Maxentius. In the second version, which is used in the degree, the cross was seen in the sky when the rival armies met near Saxa Ruba. The account of the visions related by Eusebius later resulted in Constantine being canonised as a saint for his contributions to Christianity. Eusebius survived Constantine by only a few years and died around 340 AD.

To confuse matters, there was another man called Eusebius, who lived at the time of Constantine. This Eusebius was from Nicomedia (now the city of Izmit) in Asia Minor. He baptised the emperor and later became Bishop of Constantinople.

In the introduction to the Red Cross of Constantine ritual book it states that both men called Eusebius were supporters of the Arian Heresy, which questioned the doctrine of the Holy Trinity. Support for this theory caused both men to fall out of favour at some point during their lives. Arianism is further discussed in the section on the Development of the Christian Theology.

JULIAN THE APOSTATE

Timeline	331–363 AD
Biblical reference	Post Biblical
Masonic reference	Red Cross of Constantine • Knight of St John the Evangelist

Julian the Apostate (denier of faith), the Roman emperor from 331–363 is vilified in the Red Cross of Constantine degree. He was the last polytheist Roman leader, who attempted to rid the empire of Christianity, especially from the ruling classes. Surprisingly, he was the half-brother of Constantine, who, as we have seen, was a major influence in spreading the new religion. Furthermore, as a young man, Julian was under the guardianship of Eusebius of Nicomedia (see previous section). Despite his links to Constantine and Eusebius and having a Christian wife, Julian was determined to return the empire to paganism. He particularly saw Christian charity as dangerous, as it benefitted Christians and Pagans and put the lives of these Roman citizens outside imperial control.

Julian attempted to rebuild the Third Temple in Jerusalem, but this work was never completed, possibly as a result of an earthquake. Christians believed that it was due to divine intervention – Jesus having prophesied its utter destruction (see section on the Destruction of the Second Temple).

Julian fought campaigns to secure the borders of his vast empire, to the north, on the Rhine and to the east, in Persia, where he met his death at the Battle of Samarra (in modern-day Iran). The Order of the Knights of St John degree states that when dying from the wounds caused by a Persian arrow, he exclaimed, 'Thou hast conquered, O Galilean.' This, of course, refers to Jesus. Julian was succeeded by Jovian, who restored Christianity's privileged position throughout the Roman Empire.

THE DEVELOPMENT OF THE CHRISTIAN THEOLOGY

Timeline	third century – present
Biblical reference	John • Chapter 1 v1–5 (The Word was God) • Chapter 1 v14 ('The Word became flesh') • Chapter 14 v28 ('My Father is greater than I')
Masonic reference	Allied Masonic Degrees • Grand Tilers of Solomon Royal and Select Masters • Select Master • Royal Master • Most Excellent Master Holy Royal Arch • Ceremony of Exaltation • Symbolical Lecture Red Cross of Constantine • Installation of Knight • Knight of the Holy Sepulchre • Knight of St John the Evangelist

As it was noted in the first chapter, it was not until 382 AD that Pope Damascus assembled the first list of the books of the Bible. The inclusion of various books was debated (and still is debated) in the various Christian denominations. Throughout history, Christian leaders have developed the theology of their religion and this has been the cause of much disagreement and even wars. These issues obviously have an impact on the Christian Orders of Freemasonry, particularly the Red Cross of Constantine. We shall see, however, that an early Christian writer invented the vault legend, which features in many degrees open to men of all faiths.

In the section on Constantine, his chairmanship of the Council of Nicaea was recalled and the main area of discussion was the relationship of Jesus to God (the Father) and the Holy Spirit. This is perhaps one of the most debated issues in Christian theology. Perhaps the most important decision made at the Council was that God consisted of three equal parts – Father, Son and Holy Ghost. This is the 'Holy Trinity' or 'Indivisible Three in One' as it is described in the Red Cross of Constantine ceremony. The first verses of the Gospel of St John were seen as proof of Jesus being equal with God: 'In the beginning was the Word, and the Word was with God, and the Word was God. The same was in the beginning with God.'

In the original Greek, 'the Word' is *logos,* which translates as 'word', 'wisdom' or 'reason'. The Gospel of St John adds: 'And the Word was made flesh, and dwelt among us...the only begotten of the Father.' This clearly states the case for Jesus being equal to God, but it does not mention the third part of the Trinity – the Holy Ghost. Furthermore, the phrase 'Holy Trinity' does not appear in the Bible. The first use of the word 'Trinity' in Christian writings to mean three persons in one God was by the Roman author Tertullian, who lived in Carthage around 160–220 AD. It should also be noted that at least one passage in the Bible used to support the Trinitarian concept is of questionable origin. The King James Version of the Bible contains the following reference in the Gospel of St John at Chapter 5 verse 7: 'For there are three that bear record in heaven, the Father, the Word, and the Holy Ghost: and these three are one.'

These words, known as the *Comma Johanneum,* were added into the original text. They do not appear in the earliest versions of the Greek manuscripts and first appeared in translations from the third century. The passage is now omitted from many modern translations of the Bible, including the New International Version (NIV) and the latest Latin translation used by the Roman Catholic Church. Even Jesus said 'My Father is greater than I.'

As a result, the early Christians (and Christians ever since) had divergent beliefs – was Jesus a man, a God, or both? Was he inferior or the same as God, the Father? In the section on Eusebius, the 'Arian Heresy' was noted and this relates to the teaching of Arius of Alexandria in the fourth century. Arianism teaches that God, the Father existed first and He is therefore superior to Jesus, who in turn is superior to the Holy Spirit. This theory may seem perfectly acceptable, but those who admitted such beliefs were condemned as heretics and suffered all manner of awful tortures and death for many centuries. A man named Edward Wightman was burnt at the stake in England in 1612 for a variety of heretical crimes, including expressing such non-Trinitarian ideas.

The Arian Heresy is noted, not in actual Masonic ritual, but in the introduction section to the Appendant Orders of the Red Cross of Constantine. This introduction also mentions, Philostorgius, a supporter of the Arian view of God. Philostorgius was a Greek (from modern-day Turkey), who wrote a book entitled *History of the Church* in the fifth century. This includes a short account of the impact of the Arian controversy on the early Christian church. No copies of the book have survived, but a short summary was written in the ninth century.

Philostorgius, although an obscure Christian historian, has a major impact on Freemasonry as his work contains the first mention of the legend of a vault found under the temple at Jerusalem. His account is that used in the Red Cross of Constantine – a vault under the destroyed Second Temple, where a copy of the Gospel of St John is discovered. The story, however, contains many references used in the Holy Royal Arch ritual – a stone is removed to reveal a cavern, a workman is lowered into the vault with a rope, a book is discovered on a pillar and a signal is given to be drawn up. This idea of a vault under the Temple features in several other degrees – Select Master,

Royal Master, and Grand Tilers of Solomon. Philostrogius also relates accounts of Hadrian's rebuilding of Jerusalem, Constantine's conversion to Christianity and Julian the Apostate's death. These are all used in the various Red Cross of Constantine ceremonies.

ISLAMIC CONQUEST OF THE HOLY LAND

Timeline	614 AD – Persian conquest of Holy Land 715 AD – Al-Aqsa Mosque completed
Biblical reference	Post Biblical period
Masonic reference	Red Cross of Constantine • Knight of the Holy Sepulchre • Knight of St John the Evangelist • Installation of Viceroy Knights Templar

In 614, during the reign of Heraclius, ruler of the Eastern Roman Empire (later known as the Byzantine Empire), the Persians attacked Jerusalem to gain a secure base, which would provide access to the Mediterranean Sea. When their army finally broke into the city after a siege of 21 days, looting on a large scale took place and many churches were burnt. Most importantly, they

On the Mount of Olives. The golden roof of the Dome of the Rock can clearly be seen.

This rock is said to be the one where Isaac was to be sacrificed and David prayed on the threshing floor.

seized the True Cross from the Church of the Holy Sepulchre. Thirteen years later it was recovered and Heraclius carried the cross back to the church barefoot, as a Christian pilgrim. This incident is included in the 'Twelve Grand Points connected with the Cross' related during the installation of the 'Viceroy' of a Conclave of the Red Cross of Constantine.

This period saw the start of warfare between Christians and Islam and by 638 Arab Muslims had seized much of the Persian Empire and after another siege, Jerusalem again changed rulers. Despite an initial slaughter of the Christian defenders of the city, the Arabs practised religious tolerance and appear to have been falsely accused by Pope Urban II in 1095 of all manner of evil deeds towards Christians. The Red Cross of Constantine ritual also claims that Jerusalem 'groaned' under oppressive Muslim rulers.

The consequences of the Muslim invasion live on to the present time, as the site of King Solomon's Temple is now dominated by the Al-Aqsa Mosque (the name means the Farthest or Remotest Mosque), together with the Dome of the Rock. The buildings were completed around 715 AD. Inside the Dome is the rock where it is claimed Isaac was to be sacrificed and the threshing floor, where David prayed to God to stay the pestilence that raged amongst the Israelites. It must be noted that the exact location of King Solomon's Temple is hotly debated and is a constant source of dispute between some Israelis and Palestinians.

THE VENERABLE BEDE AND THE ENGLISH MONASTERY

Timeline	672–735 AD
Biblical reference	Post Biblical

Masonic reference	Craft • Installation Ceremony Royal and Select Masters
Historical context	England composed of several states (it was not unified until the tenth century)

From the Holy Land, we now move to England's green and pleasant land. Christianity spread throughout Britain from two directions, from the missionary work of the Celtic Church based in Ireland and Cornwall and from the south by the Roman Catholic Church, which began with the mission of St Augustine to Kent in 597 AD. In 664 AD, the differences of the two churches were resolved at the Synod of Whitby and the Roman Church attained supremacy.

The earliest Englishman to influence Masonic ritual was Saint (or the Venerable) Bede, known as 'The Father of English History'. He was a monk in the kingdom of Northumbria (in the north east of England), who wrote over 40 books, including translations of scripture, hymns and Psalms. His book, the *Ecclesiastical History of the English People*, is considered to be one of the most important accounts of the Anglo-Saxon period.

He is of interest to Freemasons as his dying words are the only quotation shown as such in some versions of Craft ritual and they appear in the Address to the Brethren, which is the last part of the annual installation of a new Worshipful Master. Bede was taken ill whilst translating the Gospel of St John into English. His young scribe, Wilbert, said to Bede 'Now it is finished' and Bede replied 'It is well finished' – the words used in the Installation ceremony. He then chanted 'Glory be to the Father, and to the Son, and to the Holy Spirit' and died. His body has been moved several times and his shrine was destroyed in 1540 during the Reformation. He is now buried in the Galilee Chapel in Durham Cathedral.

A different monastic link: the office of 'Manciple' is used in the Order of Royal and Select Masters. This officer performs the duties normally performed by the 'Steward' at the lodge meal. A manciple was the person responsible for purchasing and organising food supplies in a monastery.

ATHELSTAN, THE FIRST KING OF ALL THE ENGLISH

Timeline	AD 925–939
Biblical reference	Post Biblical
Masonic reference	Order of Athelstan

By the tenth century, England was still divided into small kingdoms and the Christian religion acted as a unifying force at a time of increasing Viking raids. Athelstan was the grandson of King Alfred the Great and ruled between 925 and 939. He won a number of decisive victories against the Welsh, Scots, Cornish and Vikings, converting one of their rulers to the Christian faith.

His control of mainland Britain enabled him to style himself as 'The First King of all the English'. The Masonic Order of Athelstan is based on the legend of the York Assembly, which was held in 926 AD on the king's orders. At York, the king's half brother, Prince Edwin, laid down the standards for work for masons, which became known as the 'Old Charges'.

Unfortunately, Edwin was far from loyal and was found guilty of plotting against the king. He was cast adrift at sea, without food, but drowned himself rather than slowly starve. This event forms the background of the Inner Workings for the installation of a Master of the order.

When he died, Athelstan left a united kingdom but no children, so the crown passed to his brother, Edmund the Elder. Athelstan had given generously to the church during his life and was buried in his favourite abbey at Malmesbury in Wiltshire, rather than in the family tomb at Winchester. In just over 100 years the Norman Conquest of England occurred, in 1066. This ushered in a new dynasty of French-speaking kings, including Richard the Lionheart (see section on Knights Templars and other military orders).

11

THE SECOND THOUSAND YEARS OF CHRISTIANITY

THE FIRST CRUSADE

Timeline	1099 – Crusaders capture Jerusalem
Biblical reference	Luke • Chapter 24 v13 (Location of Emmaus)
Masonic reference	Red Cross of Constantine • Installation of a Knight • Knight of the Holy Sepulchre • Knight of St John the Evangelist Knights Templar

During the Appendant Orders of the Red Cross of Constantine, the history of Jerusalem at the time of the Crusades is explained in simplistic and romantic terms. According to the ritual, a Frenchman, Peter the Hermit, was prevented from entering the Holy Land by the Muslim Turks and in consequence he encouraged the First Crusade. A French knight, Godfrey de Bouillon, led the Crusade and captured Jerusalem in 1099. In the Order of the Knight of the Holy Sepulchre, the Masonic candidate enters the Conclave with a crescent, a representation of this victory over the Saracens.

In reality, the accusations of Pope Urban II against the Muslims of ill-treating Christians resulted in many western Christians, rich and poor, 'taking the cross' and committing themselves to the Crusade to take the Holy Land. Godfrey de Bouillon (Bouillon is in modern Belgium), and his brother, Baldwin of Boulogne, led one contingent but there were three other main groups of Crusaders; from northern France, Toulouse (southern France) and Taranto in Southern Italy. (An English fleet joined the Crusade in 1098). To their Muslim rivals, all the Crusaders were known as the 'Franks'.

The real Peter the Hermit was a charismatic preacher, who led the 'People's Crusade' of peasants. Much of this group was slaughtered soon after crossing into Asia Minor from Constantinople. After leaving Constantinople in 1097, the Crusaders fought a hard campaign and endured many privations (even Peter the Hermit temporarily deserted at the siege of Antioch in 1098). These hardships are recalled during the installation of the master or 'Eminent Preceptor' of a Conclave of Knights Templar.

In the ceremony it is stated that the war-weary crusaders were at the point of despair as they neared the Holy City, but their (unnamed) leader was determined to complete his quest and on nearing Jerusalem viewed their objective from the hill village of Emmaus (see section on Jesus). The sight of Jerusalem by the first light of dawn inspired the army and they proceeded onwards with renewed zeal. According to Luke, Emmaus is 'threescore furlongs' from Jerusalem – 7½ miles. The location of the village in modern-day Israel is unclear and a matter of some debate.

From leaving their homes, it had taken the crusaders over two years to arrive at the gates of Jerusalem, with the siege commencing in June 1099. In a little over a month, the city was in their hands. Godfrey de Bouillon demonstrated great military skill in capturing Jerusalem, using a siege tower, which was dismantled in the middle of the night and re-built quickly giving an element of surprise. The capture of the city on 15 July of the same year was followed by the brutal slaughter of the inhabitants in true Medieval style. Crusaders covered in their enemies' blood, laden with stolen treasure and driven by religious zeal, then prayed in the Church of the Holy Sepulchre.

As he was the first of the Crusade leaders to enter the city, Godfrey was elected King of Jerusalem, but, according to the ritual, he considered it improper to wear a royal crown where Jesus had worn a crown of thorns. He therefore refused the title and styled himself as the 'Defender and Baron of the Holy Sepulchre'. In truth, Godfrey was aware that if he declared himself king he could lose the support of Alexius I, the Byzantine Emperor, who controlled Constantinople and to whom the area had been promised.

Furthermore, Jerusalem lay in the area controlled by the Greek Orthodox Church and the Crusaders were Roman Catholics. There was also a very practical concern – the capture of Jerusalem had not secured the Holy Land. During the following month, the Crusaders had to march out of the city to defeat an army of Fatimids from Egypt.

Godfrey's personal victory was short-lived and he died the following year in the summer of 1100. The nature of his death is unclear; the Arabs claimed that he was killed by an arrow during the siege of Acre. It is most likely that he died in Jerusalem after a prolonged illness.

Once the Franks' position had been strengthened, Baldwin, brother of Godfrey de Bouillon, had no hesitation in styling himself 'King of Jerusalem' and the Al-Aqsa Mosque became his

The Red Cross of Constantine Appendant Orders jewel. Note the Jerusalem Cross which hangs under the eagle of St John.

royal residence. Around 1119, his son, King Baldwin II, granted part of the building to the Knights Templar (see next section). There is a small Masonic Order named the Rite of Baldwin. Baldwin and Godfrey de Bouillon have tombs in the Church of the Holy Sepulchre. These are noted in the Red Cross of Constantine ritual, but they were destroyed by fire in the eighteenth century. In addition to Jerusalem, several cities had been captured and small Crusader states were established in the area. These were collectively known as the *Outremer* (from the French for 'overseas').

THE KNIGHTS TEMPLAR AND OTHER MILITARY ORDERS

Timeline	1099 – Hospitallers of St John formed 1118 – Knights Templar formed 1147–1149 – Second Crusade 1187 – Saladin takes Jerusalem 1187–1192 – Third Crusade 1191 – Order of St Thomas of Acon formed 1291 – Holy Land lost to Muslims 1312 – Knights Templar disbanded 1530 – Hospitallers establish headquarters on Malta 1538 – Order of St Thomas abolished by Henry VIII 1798 – Malta falls to Napoleon
Biblical reference	John • Chapter 1 v1–5 (The Word was God)
Masonic reference	Craft • Third Degree Tracing Board Red Cross of Constantine • Installation of a Knight • Knight of the Holy Sepulchre • Knight of St John the Evangelist Knights Templar Priest • Knight of the White Cross of Torpichen Knights Templar • Knight of St Paul • Knight of Malta

No military Order has attracted more attention than the Knights Templar. Their connection to Freemasonry, real and imagined, has increased their mystique. They were originally founded around 1118 during the reign of King Baldwin II as 'The Poor Fellow-Soldiers of Christ and the Temple of Solomon'. Their initial role was to protect pilgrims who were travelling via the port at Joppa to worship at the Church of the Holy Sepulchre in Jerusalem. The Order soon became known as the Knights Templar as Baldwin II allowed them to establish their headquarters in part of the Al Aqsa Mosque (The Dome on the Rock), which had been built on the site of King Solomon's Temple.

The Templars were one of the most skilled fighting units of their time and they played a significant part in numerous victories against their Muslim rivals, particularly the defeat of Saladin at the Battle of Montgisard (near Ramla in Israel) in 1177. Such was their influence on history that their distinctive dress of a white mantle with a red cross is often used to depict all Crusaders.

The Templars' military skill could not prevent the loss of Jerusalem in 1187 to Saladin (it would not be ruled by a Western power until the British captured the city from the Ottoman Empire in 1917) and eventually they had to transfer their headquarters to the port of Acre, but this was also lost in 1291. At their peak there were over 15,000 members of the Order, of which one-tenth were knights.

After the loss of the Holy Land, the Templars continued as an independent military order, exempt from local laws and taxes by Papal authority. They became exceedingly rich and operated one of the earliest international banking systems. This attracted the attention of the unscrupulous King of France, Philip the Fair and in 1307 the Order was accused of blasphemy and brutally suppressed. The debts Philip owed to the Order were instantly cleared and many of their assets were turned over to their rivals, the Hospitallers (who are discussed later in this section). The last Grand Master, Jacques de Molay, was burnt at the stake in Paris and the Templars were officially disbanded in 1312.

Many unproven legends exist as to the lost treasures of the Templars, which escaped the king's raids. It would appear that some Templars fled and settled in Scotland. It has been claimed that

Freemasonry is descended from this Order, although there is little, if any, evidence of this. Legends have connected many holy relics with the Order, including the Ark of the Covenant, Holy Grail and Shroud of Turin. The Templars are believed to have excavated under the Temple and may have found various treasures, which may have given rise to the part of the Chapter ritual where a secret vault is found. These treasures are rumoured to have been hidden at Rosslyn Chapel in Scotland and other secret locations. It is unsurprising that the Templars have appeared in all manner of conspiracy theories, novels and Hollywood films, such as *The Da Vinci Code*, which featured the Temple Church in London – once used for Templar initiation ceremonies.

Masonic regalia for a Knight Templar. (By kind permission of Right Excellent Knight Michael Banbury, Provincial Prior of Surrey)

Masonically, the current order is known by the unwieldy title of 'The United Religious, Military and Masonic Orders of the Temple and of St John of Jerusalem, Palestine, Rhodes and Malta'. Unsurprisingly, this is often shortened to 'Knights Templar' or 'KT'. The Masonic Knights Templar degree originated in France in the eighteenth century and does not claim any link to the original military order. The formation of this and other Christian degrees may have been the result of the Craft Freemasonry being de-Christianised and opened to men of all religions. The Masonic Knights Templar must profess the Trinitarian faith and be a member of a Craft lodge and a Holy Royal Arch chapter. The Templar degree is set during the reign of Baldwin II and the candidate undergoes a symbolic period of pilgrimage, before taking his vow as a crusader. The regalia worn in this degree are amongst the most elaborate in Freemasonry.

A separate Military Order at this time was the Hospitallers of St John. It is now linked to the Knights Templar (as can be seen by the title of the Masonic order shown above). According to the Masonic lecture on the history of the Order, it began as the Hospital of St John, which provided medical aid to pilgrims in the Holy Land. This transformed into a military order in 1099 during the First Crusade.

The five headquarters of the Hospitallers are noted in the ceremony with the dates of their establishment:

1099	Palestine
1291	Cyprus (following the loss of the Holy Land)
1310	Rhodes
1523	Candia on Crete (following the loss of Rhodes to the Turks)
1530	Malta (hence the current title of the Order)

Malta was given to the Orders by Emperor Charles V of Spain, who required their assistance in defeating the Moors, or Barbary Pirates, who operated in the Mediterranean. In the King James Version of the Bible and in some parts of the Masonic ritual, the island is referred to as 'Melita', the Roman name for the island. In 1798, Malta was captured by Napoleon and the Order was dispersed throughout Europe, most notably in Czarist Russia. In England it survives most famously as St John Ambulance. The degree of a Knight of the White Cross of Torpichen, which one of the unworked ceremonies in the Order of the Knights Templar Priest, may be named after Torpichen Preceptory. This was a Knights Hospitaller religious house, founded in Scotland in 1140 at the invitation of King David I.

The original Order was divided into eight *Langues* or 'Tongues' situated in Provence (south-east France), Auvergne (south-central France), France (modern northern France), Italy, Aragon (north eastern Spain), England, Germany and Castile (north-central Spain). These are included in the Masonic ritual relating to the Order.

Masonic Knights Templar are eligible to join a small order, entitled 'Thomas of Acon'. 'Acon' is the Anglicised version of Acre and the ceremony celebrates the Order of St Thomas of Acon. The history of this Masonic Order is set around the Third Crusade and the capture of Acre by King Richard I of England ('the Lionheart') in 1191. Richard was a great grandson of Fulk, King of Jerusalem (1131–1143).

A member of King Richard's force, William, the Chaplain to the Dean of St Paul's cathedral in London, established an Order to bury Christian knights who had fallen in battle in the Holy Land. A church was built in honour of St Thomas a Becket, hence the name of the Order. St Thomas had been murdered in 1170 on the orders of Henry II (Richard the Lionheart's father) and he was quickly canonised – only three years after his death. Of the five orders who fought in the Holy Land, including the Templar and Hospitallers, the Order of St Thomas of Acon was the only one with an English origin. As part of the dissolution of the monasteries, the original order was disbanded in 1538 by King Henry VIII.

In Craft ritual, the secrets of the Third Degree are said to be 'at the centre'. This may well be because world maps used at the time of the crusades had Jerusalem in the centre. These are called 'T and O' maps from their circular style and because they are divided into one large section at the top (representing Asia) and two smaller sections at the bottom (the left being Europe and the right Africa).

ST THOMAS AQUINAS

Timeline	1225–1274 AD
Biblical reference	Wisdom of Solomon • Chapter 8 v7 (Cardinal virtues)
Masonic reference	Craft • First Degree • Second Degree Tracing Board Royal Ark Mariner • Ceremony of Elevation Red Cross of Constantine • Knight of the Holy Sepulchre Societas Rosicruciana in Anglia • Third Grade 'Practicus'
Historical context	Reigns of Henry III and Edward I of England 1227 – Death of Genghis Khan 1266 – Marco Polo arrived in China

St Thomas Aquinas (the latter name being the place of his residence in Italy) was a Roman Catholic priest and Dominican friar, who is still acclaimed for his theological work. When considering the creation he named God as the 'Grand Architect of the Universe', a very similar phrase to that used in the First Degree ceremony ('Great Architect of the Universe').

St Thomas Aquinas also outlined the four cardinal virtues, which are included in the First Degree ceremony twice – firstly as part of the 'Charge' (a list of rules for Freemasons) and secondly during the explanation of the Tracing Board. The four virtues – prudence, temperance, fortitude and justice, can be found in some versions of the Bible (see section on the Wisdom of King Solomon) but it was St Thomas Aquinas who designated them as 'cardinal'. 'Cardinal' is derived from the Latin *cardo* for a 'hinge' as the virtues are the hinges on the door of moral life.

During the 'Charge', which is delivered immediately after the initiation ceremony, Freemasons are advised to 'let prudence direct you, temperance chasten you, fortitude support you and justice be the guide in all your

St Thomas Aquinas (1440) by Fra Angelico.

actions.' During the explanation of the First Degree Tracing Board, these cardinal virtues are said to be represented by the tassels, which figuratively mark the four corners of the lodge room. The four virtues are further recalled in the 'Allegorical Sequel' (to the Holy Royal Arch), which forms part of the second part of the ceremony of a Knight of the Holy Sepulchre. In the Royal Ark Mariner, two of the virtues are mentioned in the candidate's obligation – prudence and justice.

In addition to four cardinal virtues, there are three theological virtues – faith, hope and charity (see sections on Jacob and St Paul). These also appear during the explanation of the First Degree Tracing Board. According to Roman Catholic theology, theological virtues differ from cardinal virtues as the former cannot be obtained by human effort. They are received through the Divine grace of God.

St Thomas Aquinas is actually mentioned by name in Masonic ritual, during the third grade of SRIA. During a lecture on the degree, he is noted as one of several men, who were of high rank in the church, who were experts on the ancient science of alchemy. It should be noted that at the time of this saint, education was divided into two courses, the *Trivium* (grammar, rhetoric and logic) and the *Quadrivium* (arithmetic, geometry, music and astronomy). These seven 'liberal arts and sciences' are recalled during the lecture on Second Degree Tracing Board.

THE TRANSLATION OF THE BIBLE INTO ENGLISH

Timeline	1488–1569 (Life of Coverdale)
	1494–1536 (Life of Tyndale)
	1611 (Authorised Version of the Bible published)
Biblical reference	Throughout King James' Authorised Version
Masonic reference	All degrees
Historical context	Reign of Henry VIII of England
	Reign of James I of England (and James VI of Scotland)

Freemasons owe much to the brave men, particularly John Wycliffe, William Tyndale and Myles Coverdale, who took great risks to translate the Bible into English. For this work, Wycliffe was declared a heretic, Tyndale was executed and Coverdale spent time in exile, but their endeavours have had an enormous influence on Masonic ritual.

Wycliffe (1320–1384) can be credited with the first translation of the Bible into English, but copies were limited as the printing press had not been invented. His work resulted in much conflict with the church authorities, but he died a natural death. The church did, however, punish him in the end. He was declared a heretic over 20 years after his death and in 1428 his body was exhumed and burnt. The ashes were then thrown into the River Swift near Lutterworth in Leicestershire. This punishment sounds very much like that in the Third Degree – 'bowels burnt to ashes and those ashes wafted over the face of earth and water by the four cardinal winds of heaven'. Wycliffe is known as the 'morning star of the reformation'.

Tyndale and Coverdale were Protestant reformers, who translated much of the Bible from Greek and Hebrew into English during the reign of Henry VIII. Their work benefited from the recent invention of the printing press, which enabled wide distribution of English translations of sections of the Bible. Both men had to conduct much of their work in Germany, as the Roman Catholic authorities in England did not want the church's power diluted by having the Bible available to the common man.

The execution of Tyndale, depicted in a woodcut from *Foxe's Book of Martyrs* (1563).

In 1526, however, Tyndale's version of the New Testament was printed in the cities of Worms and Antwerp, from where they were smuggled into Britain. The Bishop of London, Cuthbert Tunstall, issued warnings to booksellers and seized copies of the Tyndale's work, which were burnt in public. Furthermore, Cardinal Wolsey, the Papal Legate (Pope's representative) in England accused Tyndale of heresy, which carried the death penalty.

Despite Wolsey's death in 1530 (he had been accused of treason, but died travelling to London) and Henry VIII's break from Rome in 1534 (to establish the Church of England) Tyndale was still considered a heretic and was arrested in Antwerp in 1535. This followed an appeal by the king to the Holy Roman Emperor, Charles V. Tyndale was executed at Vilvoorde Castle near Brussels, by first being strangled and then burnt at the stake.

Tyndale's final words were said to be 'Lord! Open the King of England's eyes.' Less than a century later in 1611, the King James' Version of the Bible was published, using much of Tyndale's work. His poetic phraseology is much admired and as Freemason's look to Ussher for their dating system (see next section), their ritual draws heavily on the work of Tyndale as can be seen throughout this book. In particular, he translated the name of God or Hebrew Tetragrammaton 'YHWH' into 'Jehovah'. He also devised the word 'atonement' from being 'at onement' with God and used the word 'Overseer', which features significantly in the Mark Degree.

It should be noted that Tyndale translated Chapter 13 v13 of St Paul's first letter to the Corinthians as 'faith, hope and love', not 'faith, hope and charity'. The latter appears in the

Authorised Version of the Bible and most Masonic ritual. This use of Tyndale's translation supports the view that the Royal Ark Mariner is one of the earliest Masonic degrees.

The first full English translation of the Bible was completed by Coverdale (later Bishop of Exeter), who used Tyndale's version of the New Testament. Both men had met in Hamburg, whilst in exile. Coverdale's Bible was produced in 1535 and importantly, it is the only English version which uses the name 'Hiram Abif' in the same form as in Masonic ritual. Later editions of the Bible, including the Authorised Version, translate the name in various forms, including 'Hiram', 'Huram my father's' and 'Huram-Abi'.

BIBLICAL AND MASONIC DATING BY ARCHBISHOP USSHER

Timeline	1581–1656 AD
Biblical reference	Throughout King James' Authorised Version
Masonic reference	Craft • Third Degree Tracing Board Royal and Select Masters • Select Master Holy Royal Arch • Historical Lecture
Historical context	English Civil War and rule of Oliver Cromwell

James Ussher (1581–1656) was the Protestant Primate of All Ireland. Using solar and lunar cycles, he calculated the dating system shown in many older versions of the Bible, including the King James authorised edition. His work was first published in 1611 and until the twentieth century his calculations were treated with unquestioned reverence. Now they appear quite bizarre. He calculated that the world was created on Sunday 23 October 4004 BC and that the Ark landed on Mount Ararat on 5 May. Later, Dr John Lightfoot, Vice-Chancellor at Cambridge, investigated the dating further and claimed that the creation started at 9.00am!

For all his flawed calculations, the Biblical dates recorded by Ussher are very relevant to Freemasons, as the Masonic ritual uses *Anno Lucis* or 'Year of Light' as the dating system. Rounding off the odd four years, all Masonic dates are set using 4000 BC as the year of creation. Thus in the Third Degree, King Solomon's Temple is shown on the Tracing Board as being completed in 'AL 3000', not 1000 BC. In the lecture on the Select Master degree, the same *Anno Lucis* date is displayed in Hebrew characters on the side of the replica Ark of the Covenant.

The Holy Royal Arch Historical Lecture is far more 'accurate' giving the dates of events as follows:

AL 2515 Completion of Moses' Tabernacle (described as the First or Holy Lodge) AL 2992 King Solomon's Temple completed (Second or Sacred Lodge)
AL 3469 Temple rebuilt by Zerubbabel (Third or Grand and Royal Lodge)

The Anno Lucis system is also used on certificates issued to Master Masons by the United Grand Lodge of England. For example, the author's certificate is dated AL 5996, not 1996 AD.

Archbishop James Ussher, as painted by William Fletcher.

Ussher died in Surrey in 1656 and was to be buried in Reigate. This was during the rule of Oliver Cromwell, the Lord Protector. At Cromwell's insistence, Ussher was given a state funeral and was buried at Westminster Abbey – such was the reverence Ussher's work commanded.

THE BOOK OF COMMON PRAYER

Timeline	1662
Biblical reference	Psalms • Psalm 44 vi ('We have heard with our ears') • Psalm 50 v14 ('God is the Most High') Matthew • Chapter 18 v20 ('Where two or three are gathered together in my name')

Masonic reference	Craft • First Degree • Third Degree • Installation Royal Ark Mariner • Ceremony of Elevation • Installation of Commander Mark • Ceremony of Advancement Holy Royal Arch • Ceremony of Exaltation • Mystical Lecture • Installation of Haggai Red Cross of Constantine • Knight of Holy Sepulchre • Installation of Viceroy
Historical context	Reign of Charles II of England

The Book of Common Prayer is used by the Church of England and other Anglican Churches throughout the world. The first version was published in 1549 during the reign of Edward VI, son of the founder of the Church of England, Henry VIII. It underwent a major revision in 1662 after the English Civil War, when its use was a made a legal requirement. The 1662 edition is still used in the Church of England, although an alternative book 'Common Worship' (published in 2000) is now generally used for Sunday services.

It contains the format for several services, including Holy Communion, baptism, marriage and funerals. There is also a list of Psalms and set readings from the Old and New Testament. Phrases from the Book of Common Prayer feature in Masonic ritual, most particularly in the Holy Royal Arch ceremony. After the Lord's Prayer, the Holy Communion service begins with The Collect:

> Almighty God, unto whom all hearts are open, all desires known, and from whom no secrets are hid; Cleanse the thoughts of our hearts by the inspiration of thy Holy Spirit, that we may perfectly love thee, and worthily magnify thy holy Name; through Christ our Lord. Amen.

This is paraphrased at the start of the Chapter ritual, with 'Omnipresent God' instead of 'Almighty' and omitting 'through Christ our Lord' as the Holy Royal Arch has been open to men of all faiths since the eighteenth century. During the Chapter ceremony, God is referred to as 'The true and living God Most High'. In the 'Articles of Religion' (the beliefs of the Church of England) listed at the end of the book, Article One refers to the 'one living and true God'. Additionally, Psalm 50 can be quoted during the 'offertory' (when money is collected in the church) and refers to God as 'the Most High'.

The Mystical Lecture in Holy Royal Arch observes that God is 'from all beginning, is now, and ever will remain one and the same for ever'. This is very similar to the declaration of faith in the Trinity used throughout the Christian faith. This appears in the Morning and Evening Prayers services:

Glory be to the Father, and to the Son, and to the Holy Ghost. As it was in the beginning, is now, and ever shall be, world without end. Amen [Gloria Patri, et Filio, et Spiritui Sancto. Sicut erat in principio, et nunc, et semper, et in sæcula sæculorum. Amen.]

The Latin version is used in the Knight of the Holy Sepulchre ceremony (membership of a Holy Royal Arch chapter is a prerequisite of joining this Order). The Chapter ritual ends with the three senior officers stating one after the other, 'Glory to God on high', 'On earth peace' and 'Goodwill towards men'. As we have seen, this is from the Gospel of St Luke (see section on The Apostles after the Crucifixion), but it also appears towards the end of the Holy Communion service and this is likely to be the reason for its inclusion in the ritual. The same words are also used during the Royal Ark Mariner ceremony.

The first verse of Psalm 44, 'We have heard with our ears, and our fathers have declared onto us' (see Psalms) is paraphrased in the Holy Royal Arch ceremony and so it is in the Book of Common Prayer, which uses it to speak of the 'noble works' of God 'in their days, and in the old time before them'. These phrases appear twice during church services – in The Litany (prayers with responses) and during the ceremony of consecrating a deacon. A further link to the Holy Royal Arch is during Installation of 'Haggai', which includes a prayer to 'walk according to Thy Holy Will and Commandments'. This is very similar to part of the Baptism service, where the Godparents promise, on behalf of the child, to obey 'God's holy will and commandments and walk in the same all the days of my life'.

The First Degree also has several references from this book. The Exhortations during the Communion service include the words 'be in perfect charity with all men; so shall ye be meet partakers of those holy mysteries.' This is very similar to part of the explanation of the First Degree Tracing Board, where faith, hope and charity are expounded upon. It should be noted that each of the three Craft ceremonies has an 'Exhortation' section.

One prayer in the book contains the phrase 'to the relief of our necessity' and this may be the basis of the section of The Charge after the First Degree, where Masons are advised to assist their neighbour by 'relieving his necessities'. The Catechism section observes that 'my duty towards my neighbour is to love him as myself, and to do to all men as I would they should do unto me' and to 'keep my body in temperance'. Both instructions feature in The Charge. A further Craft use of the Book of Common Prayer can be heard during the Third Degree prayer, which copies the phrase, 'the continual dew of thy blessing' from a prayer for the clergy. The words 'transitory life', used in the Third Degree also appear in the Holy Communion Service.

The Morning and Evening Prayer services include a prayer of Chrysostom, a fourth-century Greek saint. It is based on Jesus' words in the Gospel of St Matthew: 'when two or three are gathered together in Thy name Thou wilt grant their requests.' Very similar words feature in the prayer in the Royal Ark Mariner degree. In the Installation ceremony in the same degree, the phrase 'unity of spirit, in the bond of peace' is taken from a prayer for the health of people or the 'Conditions of Men'.

Many Biblical phrases used in the ritual appear in the text, including 'the headstone of the corner' and 'Lord of Saboath', but the most influential part of the Book of Common Prayer, however, is in the 'general confession' prayer of the Holy Communion. The last seven words are very similar to those used in many prayers in Masonic ritual: 'to the honour and glory of thy Name'. The same prayer uses the phrase 'thought, word and deed', which are used when investing the Tyler (Outer Guard) during the installation of the Worshipful Master in a Craft lodge. The Book of Common Prayer is arguably the second greatest influence on Masonic ritual, after the Bible.

THE CHURCH AND FREEMASONRY

Timeline	seventeenth century to present
Biblical reference	Post-Biblical
Masonic reference	Craft • First Degree Tracing Board • Second Degree • Installation Ceremony Holy Royal Arch • Installation of Joshua Red Cross of Constantine • Knight of the Holy Sepulchre Societas Rosicruciana in Anglia • Third Grade 'Practicus'

A Masonic Tour of London at the spot where the original Grand Lodge met in 1717 (the blue plaque). It met in the Goose and Gridiron public house in St Paul's Churchyard. Freemasonry and the church could not have been closer!

Speculative (or symbolic) masonry appeared in Scotland and then England during the seventeenth century. At that time it was exclusively Christian. Lodges operated separately, but in 1717, four lodges in London formed the first Grand Lodge. In 1723 Freemasonry was declared open to all those who believed in a 'Supreme Being' and therefore lodges were opened to Jews, Muslims and many other faiths. The first Book of Constitutions for the Grand Lodge was prepared by Reverend James Anderson, a minister of a Scottish Presbyterian Church in London and it contains the first recorded Masonic use of the phrase 'Great Architect of the Universe'. Anderson may have been influenced by the work of the Protestant reformer, John Calvin (1509–1564). In Calvin's influential book, *Institutes of the Christian Religion* God is repeatedly referred to as 'the Architect of the Universe' (see also section on St Thomas Aquinas).

Allowing men of all faiths to join lodges appears to have resulted in Pope Clement XII issuing a Papal order or 'Bull' in 1738 excommunicating any Roman Catholic who refused to renounce their membership of Freemasonry. Seven more Popes have reiterated the ban and the relationship between the Roman Catholic Church and Freemasonry has always been fraught. In 1884 Pope Leo XIII's claimed that the aim of Freemasons was to 'persecute Christianity with untamed hatred' and as recently as 1983, Cardinal Ratzinger (the current Pope, Benedict XVI) stated:

> The Church's negative judgment in regard to Masonic associations remains unchanged since their principles have always been considered irreconcilable with the doctrine of the Church and therefore membership in them remains forbidden. Catholics who enrol in Masonic associations are in a state of grave sin and may not receive Holy Communion. Local Ecclesiastical authorities do not have the faculty to pronounce a judgment on the nature of Masonic associations which may include a diminution of the above-mentioned judgment.

Despite the friction between Freemasonry and the Roman Catholic Church, it should be noted that two Popes are mentioned by name in Masonic ritual – Callistus II and John XXII. In the address on the history of the degree of a 'Knight of the Holy Sepulchre', Callistus is shown as confirming this order in 1122. John XXII is noted in a lecture on alchemy during the third grade of SRIA. He issued a Papal Bull against dishonest alchemists in 1317 (he was, apparently, one of the many honest alchemists).

Freemasons have also used Roman Catholic doctrines in their ritual. The Catechism of Trent from 1566 laid down the beliefs of the Church and Article VI relates to the Ascension and Jesus taking souls into the 'mansions of eternal bliss'. These words are used during the Chapter installation ceremony. Furthermore, the use of the Roman Catholic Corporal Works of Mercy in the Red Cross of Constantine ritual has been explained in the section on the Ministry of Jesus.

In what appears, in this day and age, to be rather obvious, Masonic ritual contains references to the sun being the centre of the universe, in the First Degree (explanation of the Tracing Board), as part of the 'Questions Before Passing' and during the Address to Master at a Craft installation. At the time the ritual was written, however, these views were highly controversial and considered 'false and contrary to Scripture' by the Roman Catholic Church. The famous astronomer, Galileo, was later tried by the Inquisition for promoting Heliocentrism (or sun-centred universe theory). He argued that the Biblical account of the sun standing still in the sky was impossible – a story which features in Masonic ritual (see Joshua and Rahab). Despite his scientific proofs, Galileo was forced to denounce his views and placed under house arrest until his death in 1642. It was not until 1822 that Pope Pius VII allowed books containing the heliocentric theory to be printed in Rome.

In contrast to the issues between Freemasonry and Catholicism, the relationship between Masons and the Church of England was extremely good until the latter half of the twentieth century. Five British kings and therefore, Supreme Governors of the Church of England, have been Freemasons. The Queen's father, King George VI and her uncle, King Edward VIII, were very active masons and the current Grand Master of the United Grand Lodge of England is the Duke of Kent, a cousin of the Queen. Even the titles and ranks used by the United Grand Lodge of England appear to be based on the Church of England hierarchical structure as the table below demonstrates.

Church of England		United Grand Lodge of England	
Title	**Rank**	**Title**	**Rank**
Most Reverend	Archbishop	Most Worshipful	Grand Master
Right Reverend	Bishop	Right Worshipful	Provincial Grand Master
Very Reverend	Dean	Very Worshipful	Deputy Provincial Grand Master
Reverend	Vicar	Worshipful	Master of a Lodge

Perhaps the high point of the relationship was in the 1950s when King George VI was Grand Master of Scotland and Right Reverend Geoffrey Fisher, the Archbishop of Canterbury and most senior clergyman in the worldwide Anglican Church, was the Grand Chaplain of the United Grand Lodge of England.

Since this time the relationship has weakened, to a point where the current Archbishop of Canterbury, Dr Rowan Williams, had to apologise to Freemasons in 2003 after reported comments that he had questioned whether Masonry was compatible with Christianity. He also admitted not promoting clergymen who were Freemasons whilst he was Bishop of Monmouth. He denied, however, allegations that he believed that the ritual was 'Satanically inspired.' It should be noted that Dr Williams' father was a Freemason. Relations with the Methodist and other churches are little better at the current time.

DEVELOPMENT OF MASONIC RITUAL

Timeline	1813 – Formation of United Grand Lodge of England 1823 – Formulation of Emulation Lodge of Instruction
Biblical reference	Isaiah • Chapter 54 v8–10 (God's promises)
Masonic reference	All degrees
Historical context	Industrial Revolution

The development of Masonic ritual is worthy of a book of its own. It would seem that Masonic ritual 'grew on the vine' and developed piece-meal. As we saw in the section on Noah, in the early part of the eighteenth century, the Ark-building patriarch was the central character of Craft Masonry, not Hiram Abif, who is the main subject today. The other Orders and degrees are first formally noted in minutes of lodge meetings around this period. The first record of a candidate becoming a 'Royal Arch Mason' is in 1753 at a lodge in Virginia, USA and in 1769 at a Royal Arch Chapter in Portsmouth, England, several members were made 'Mark Masters'. Whilst familiar sounding degrees may have been conferred, the ceremonies would have been very different to those seen today. For example, the earliest form of Mark ritual contains elements of other ceremonies, as worked today, including the Red Cross of Babylon.

It would seem that prior to the union of the Grand Lodges in England, candidates in the various degrees were taught by the medium of catechism, where the new Mason had to learn answers to set questions. This form of ritual survives in the present in the form of the 'Questions Before Passing' and 'Questions Before Raising', which the candidate has to learn prior to the Second and Third Degrees respectively. The Book of Common Prayer contains catechisms and its size and layout is very similar to ritual books (see section beginning on p.208).

Much of the evidence of early Masonic ritual comes from published exposures by anti-Masons. From this source of evidence, it would appear that the Craft three degree system was being worked by 1724 and by 1766 the Biblical characters Boaz and Jachin (see sections on these subjects) had the prominence in the ritual that they have today. With the move from two degrees to three, came the change to a focus on King Solomon's Temple and Hiram Abif rather than Noah and his Ark. The ceremonies, however, continued to have much Christian content and the present Royal Ark Mariner degree may provide an insight into these early ceremonies (for the level of Christian content in this degree, see section on New Testament references in Degrees open to candidates of all faiths).

The formation of the United Grand Lodge of England (UGLE) in 1813 was a major influence in the standardisation of Masonic ritual and the move to de-Christianise it (see section on The Church and Freemasonry). The Industrial Revolution and the spread of the railways would have played their part in the need to standardise the ritual; just as the same factors forced sports such as football and rugby to play by an agreed set of rules. No longer could each area 'do its own thing'.

Within ten years of the formation of UGLE, the Emulation Lodge of Instruction had been established to ensure that Craft ceremonies conformed to the agreed standard. In 1838, the first Emulation ritual book was published, which included the three degrees and the Installation ceremony. This was followed by other similar, but slightly different, versions of the ritual, amongst them Taylor's, Logic and West End.

When the various Masonic committees sat to agree their version of the ritual, the Bible had such influence (see Chapter 12 for a full account) that only two non-Biblical characters appear in the Craft degrees, Pythagoras and Euclid. (Though in the infinitely more godly Britain of the 19th century, it would be surprising *not* to find Biblical phrases dominant in any formalization of any kind of code or set of rules, whatever the subject.) My research has identified very few non-Biblical quotations. The phrase 'meridian splendour', which appears in the Holy Royal Arch ceremony appears to be from the poem 'The Charms Of Lovely Davies', written by the great Scottish poet (and Freemason), Robbie Burns in 1791. 'Darkness visible' from the Third Degree can be heard in 'Paradise Lost' (a retelling of the Creation story) by Milton. The description of the moon 'borrowing her light' from the sun, which is part of the Working Tools ritual in the Royal Ark Mariner degree, is from the same epic poem.

Christian literature appears to have crept into the ceremonies. Again in the Royal Ark Mariner degree, the candidate is told that God's promise to Isaiah (that His covenant of peace will not be removed) will 'comfort you in trouble, cheer you in the hour of death and make you happy for all eternity'. This may be based on words from the nineteenth-century Scottish churchman, Horatius Bonar, whose books were very popular at the time when the ritual was still being formed. In his book *Follow the Lamb*, Bonar stated that 'Looking to Jesus will give you light in hours of darkness, will strengthen you in weakness, will comfort you in trouble, will cheer you in the day of weariness.'

Likewise, the introduction to 'The Christian's New and Complete Family Bible', published in 1802, states that it will 'guide the reader through the paths of happiness'. This may be the origin of the section in the Installation of a Master when he is advised that the 'Volume of the Sacred

Law is the great light which will … direct your steps in the paths of happiness.' (See also section on Wisdom of Solomon for Biblical influence on this part of the ritual). A further example of the influence of Christian books on the ritual can be heard during the explanation of the First Degree Tracing Board, where God is referred to as 'He who will not be deceived.' This is taken from a work from 1871, the 'Commentary Critical and Explanatory on the Whole Bible' by Jamieson, Fausset and Brown, in which it is noted that God is 'Him who will not be deceived by the mere show of holiness'.

Some very obscure books are utilised by the ritual writers. In the St Lawrence the Martyr degree, the lecture on this saint is taken from 'Sacred and Legendary Art', which was written by Anna Jameson and published in 1857. The ceremonial toast used at the Royal Arch 'Festive Board', given in Latin as *Benedictus benedicat* ('Let him who is blessed, give blessing') was originally used after meals at various colleges at Cambridge University.

The ritual is still evolving and can be driven by outside factors, including public concern or reports on Freemasonry by churches. The blood curdling oaths were removed from English ceremonies in 1986, when Grand Lodge resolved 'that all references to physical penalties be omitted from the obligations taken by Candidates in the three Degrees and by a Master Elect at his Installation but retained elsewhere in the respective ceremonies'. No one seems to have noticed that these oaths were probably based on Biblical text (see sections on David, Psalms and Daniel). In 1989, the controversial word 'Jahbulon', alleged by some to be the name of a separate Masonic god (a claim vehemently denied by Freemasons) was replaced with 'Jehovah' in the Holy Royal Arch ceremony. So unimportant was 'Jahbulon' that it was simply removed from the ritual. The nature of the God used in Masonic ceremonies is further explained in Chapter 12.

The growth in popularity of a Masonic ceremony can also have influence. From 2010, the Scarlet Cord is separate from the Order of the Secret Monitor and becomes a Sovereign Grand Body in its own right. The ritual for the later grades of this Order is still being prepared. The Scarlet Cord, although still based on a variety of Bible characters, particularly Rahab and David, features at least three non-Biblical references – 'Abou Ben Adhem' by Victorian poet James Henry Leigh Hunt, the Siege Perilous (or Perilous Seat) from the Arthurian legends and a hymn, 'Spacious Firmament on High', by the Austrian composer, Haydn.

12

CONCLUSIONS

THE BIBLICAL INFLUENCE ON FREEMASONRY

This book has shown the enormous influence the Bible has had on Masonic ritual. The ceremonies, signs, secret words, lodge officers and jewels worn have clear Biblical links. During lodge ceremonies, over 20 Biblical figures give their names to lodge officers; some famous, such as Noah, Abraham and King Solomon, some very obscure, such as King David's 'Mighty Men'. Old Testament characters appear to be the preferred choice as roles in the lodge (see table below).

Furthermore, of the 39 Old Testament books in the King James' Authorised Version, 35 appear somewhere in Masonic ritual. Indeed of the 929 chapters in the Old Testament, 331 (35 per cent) have some influence on the ritual. Some parts of the Old Testament have an enormous impact, especially Genesis, Exodus, Samuel, Kings, Chronicles, Ezra and Nehemiah, which contain many of the Biblical characters featured in the various degrees – Noah, Abraham, Jacob, Moses and King Solomon. Of the larger books, with 20 or more chapters, Exodus has the greatest percentage used in ritual: 28 out of 40 (70 per cent). Moses does not appear as the main character in any degree, but a re-visit of 'The Time of Moses', shows that parts of his story appear little and often in the ritual. Exodus is closely followed by I Kings with 14 out of 22 chapters (63 per cent), but this is to be expected, given that this book includes King Solomon, possibly the most important Biblical character in Freemasonry.

The Books of the Prophets, notably Isaiah, Jeremiah and Ezekiel, also make a great contribution. The Psalms have always been popular with Christians and so it is unsurprising that the contents have a considerable influence on the ritual of nearly every Order of Freemasonry. With over 30 Psalms appearing in the ritual, it is the biggest contributor (although it is the longest book in the Bible). The Book of Proverbs is also quoted in many different ceremonies.

Some books only have a small influence. For example, the Book of Habakkuk is not mentioned in the ritual, but forms part of the story; in this case, Habakkuk prophesies the fall of Jerusalem and the end of the Babylonian empire. Another prophet, Amos, makes a very small, but significant contribution. It is, perhaps, as a result of his words that Freemasons make symbolic use of the plumb-rule. This appears in various forms – as a model on the Junior Warden's pedestal and as his collar badge, on the First Degree Tracing Board, in the explanation of the Second Degree Working Tools and as a weapon in the Ceremony of Raising. The four Old Testament books which do not appear in the ritual are very short and obscure; few will have heard of Joel, Obadiah, Nahum or Zephaniah.

Whilst the Old Testament stories have a great influence, the most significant section of the Bible for Freemasons is part of the New Testament – St Paul's letter to the Hebrews. This book contains 80 references to the Old Testament and Chapter 11 reads like the index to this book – Abel, Cain, Noah, Abraham, Isaac, Jacob, Esau, Joseph, Rahab, Jephtha, and David are all mentioned (a notable omission is Solomon). In addition, large sections of Hebrews are devoted to comparing Christ to Melchizedek – the 'High Priest Forever'. Nine out of its thirteen chapters appear in ritual and Chapter 11 features in eleven sections of this book.

Freemasons are told that the Volume of the Sacred Law is to 'rule and govern' their faith and Hebrews reads like a sermon reflecting on that very subject. It appears to have greatly influenced the ritual writers when they selected the characters to appear in Masonic ceremonies. Whether he wrote Hebrews or not, St Paul provides the Biblical quotation used in the largest number of ceremonies. Part of his Second Letter to the Corinthians is used in at least six different Orders (including in two ceremonies of the Mark degree): 'A house not made with hands, eternal in the heavens'.

Prior to being stoned to death, the first Christian martyr, Stephen, summarised the Old Testament as part of his defence (Chapter 7 of Acts). This includes references to Abraham, Isaac, Jacob, Moses, Aaron, David, Solomon's temple and the exile in Babylon. Again, this appears to have influenced the ritual writers in their selection of characters and incidents. In a similar phrase to that used by Paul, Stephen stated: 'The most High dwelleth not in temples made with hands.'

Together with Hebrews chapter 11, chapter 7 of Acts is one of the ten chapters of the Bible which feature in five or more sections of this book. The list below shows the most influential chapters of the Bible in relation to Masonic ritual in ranked order:

Book	Chapter	Theme	Appearances in sections of this book
Hebrews	11	Faith and Paul's summary of the Old Testament	11
Acts	7	Stephen's summary of the Old Testament	10
II Chronicles	3	Decoration of King Solomon's Temple	8
Gospel of St Matthew	1	Genealogy of Jesus with Old Testament characters	7
II Chronicles	2	Preparations to build King Solomon's Temple	7
I Kings	5	Preparations to build King Solomon's Temple	6
I Kings	7	Decoration of King Solomon's Temple	6
Gospel of St John	1	Jesus is the Word	6
Ezra	3	Rebuilding the Temple	5

| Hebrews | 9 | St Paul's description of King Solomon's Temple and the laws of Moses and the change to the new faith in Jesus | 5 |

DE-CHRISTIANISED FREEMASONRY?

In the eighteenth century, many Orders of Freemasonry, particularly the Craft and Holy Royal Arch, were supposedly 'de-Christianised' to open them to men of all faiths. As we have seen, this may have caused the subsequent poor relations with the church, particularly the Vatican. Freemasons also seem to have misunderstood the part Christianity plays in their ceremonies. In the introduction to the Allied Masonic Degrees ritual book it notes that the Order of the Grand High Priest 'may be the amalgamation of two distinct degrees' and relates the apparent complex origin of this degree, but it is simply a re-telling of part of the New Testament – Hebrews, Chapter 7. Furthermore, as shown here, over 40 quotations from the New Testament still appear in these sanitised degrees. Such was the level of the hidden influence of Christianity that this book was expanded by two chapters to accommodate it.

From 260 New Testament chapters, 140 are used in the ritual; some extensively, some fleetingly. This is more than half of the New Testament, compared to a third of the Old Testament. The biggest contributing book is Matthew (23 of 28 chapters). The influence of Christianity on all degrees can be demonstrated by the fact that the Royal Ark Mariner ritual contains more New Testament quotations that the Red Cross of Constantine, when only the latter requires potential members to be of the Trinitarian faith. The table below shows the top ten contributors for the Old and New Testaments.

	Old Testament		New Testament	
Rank	**Book**	**Number of chapters featured this book**	**Book**	**Number of chapters featured this book**
1st	Psalms	36	Matthew	23
2nd	Exodus	28	Luke	17
3rd	Genesis	23	Revelation	15
4th	Isaiah	20	John	12
5th	I Chronicles	16	Acts	11
6th	I Samuel	16	Hebrews	9
7th	II Chronicles	16	Romans	8
8th	Jeremiah	15	Ephesians	5
9th	I Kings	14	II Corinthians	5
10th	II Samuel	14	I Corinthians	4

Note – This does not take into account the number of chapters in each book of the Bible (some are much bigger than others), but where the number is tied, this is used in the ranking. For example, I Kings has 14 out of 22 chapters used, whilst II Samuel has 14 out of 24 featured.

The table above reveals another very significant link to the New Testament. The most quoted Old Testament books in the New Testament are Psalms, Exodus, Genesis and Isaiah. Exodus alone is quoted over 250 times. It can be seen in the table above that these same books have the highest number of appearances in Masonic ritual.

In Masonic ritual, the vast majority of characters from the Bible appear to have been selected for the following reasons:

1   Old Testament characters, who are mentioned in various summaries in the New Testament, particularly by Stephen (in Acts) or the letter to the Hebrew or in the genealogies of Jesus.
2   Any person concerned with building or craftsmanship, for example, Tubalcain and Noah.
3   Those involved at King Solomon's Temple, for example Hiram Abif
4   Those concerned with the Second Temple
5   Stories with a particular issue linked to Masonic ritual, e.g. Jephtha and his use of a password (like the secret words in ceremonies) or Zedekiah and his oath.

Some characters fit into at least two categories: Hiram Abif is a craftsman and was involved in the building of King Solomon's Temple. Jephtha is mentioned in Hebrews chapter 11 and he uses a password. Many of the ceremonies stick with one theme, such as the building of the Temple. Some may cover two or three areas of the Bible, such as the Craft Second degree (Joshua, Jephtha and the Temple) or the Royal Ark Mariner Tracing Board (Noah and Moses). The Holy Royal Arch, however, is the most complex and features a large number of Biblical stories from at least 20 books of the Bible, with many quotations. The start and end of the ceremony is also based on the Holy Communion service contained in the Book of Common Prayer.

The degrees based on the New Testament, Rose Croix, Red Cross of Constantine and the Templar orders, rely heavily on the Gospels. Strangely, few of the signs in these orders are based on the Bible, but the jewels are invariably cross-shaped to show their Christian basis.

THE USE OF BIBLICAL TEXT IN THE RITUAL

When the various rituals were being formalised in the eighteenth and nineteenth centuries the Bible was more widely read and even if the writers did not intend to use words and phrases, they crept into the ceremonies. But perhaps some of the words were deliberately used. The first Grand Master of the United Grand Lodge of England, the Duke of Sussex, was a Hebrew scholar and so it is not surprising that Biblical names and words such as 'Machbenah' (meaning 'the builder is smitten') are found in the ceremonies (see section on the Mighty Men of David). It demonstrates the depth of knowledge of these men – a knowledge few modern Freemasons would lay claim to.

As this book has demonstrated, sometimes the ritual writers would use the initial part of a Biblical phrase, but apply it in a completely different context. Consider 'as often as ye eat bread or drink wine' in the Grand High Priest degree, originally referring to the Last Supper, but used masonically to refer how the members should treat each other. Another example is the first verse of Psalm 44, which states 'We have heard with our ears and our fathers have declared unto us' and goes on to recall God's help in securing the Promised Land. In the Holy Royal Arch ceremony, it is used as the prelude to a statement emphasising the rules regarding the pronunciation of God's name.

The Royal Ark Mariner opening prayer includes references to the Wisdom of Solomon, Gospel of John and Paul's letter to Romans; but perhaps one of the best examples of several pieces of scripture being mixed together and amended for Masonic use is the Closing Prayer in the Mark Degree:

> Before the Lodge is closed, let us with all reverence and humility express our gratitude to the Great Overseer of the Universe for favours already received and, as the stone rejected by the builders, possessing merits to them unknown, became the head of the corner, so may we by patient continuance in well-doing be built up as living stones into a spiritual house, meet for His habitation.

This features parts of I Peter, which itself quotes from Psalm 118 ('the stone which the builders rejected') and uses the phrase ('living stone') and Paul's letter to the Romans ('by patient continuance in well doing'). Additionally, the expression 'His habitation' in the prayer may be from Psalm 132. So it can be seen that this short piece of Masonic ritual features four quotations – two from each Testament. The Mark ritual writers appear to have scoured the Bible for references to stones and 'marks' and placed them in the ceremony, whether they are relevant or not. The phrase 'Mark well' in Ezekiel is nothing to do with marking stones, it is God saying to the prophet 'pay attention' or 'take my words seriously.'

In one short passage on how to help a brother in distress, the Royal Ark Mariner degree compresses together four New Testament quotations, taking sections from Luke, Paul's letter to the Ephesians, I John and I Peter (see table on New Testament references). However, the Knights Templar Priest ceremony probably uses the largest amount of scripture, as it is almost entirely composed of Biblical quotations. The lengthy opening prayer ceremony consists of sections of Isaiah, I and II Corinthians, Ephesians, Hebrews, I Peter and Revelation, then when the candidate is admitted the 'First Pillar' officer recites a piece of ritual which consists of unattributed quotations from Job, Psalms, Isaiah, I John and Revelation. In addition to the books already noted, the ceremony also uses passages from II Samuel, Proverbs, Zechariah, the Gospels of Matthew and John, the letters to the Romans, Philippians and Colossians and the penultimate book of the Bible, Jude.

In addition to utilising the Authorised Version of the Bible, the ritual compilers also drew on other sources. This included the Books of Maccabees, which are only treated as scripture by some branches of the Christian Church and the Books of Enoch, which are part of the Apocrypha. Enoch was removed from the Canon of Western Churches many centuries ago, but as we have seen, it is quoted in the explanation of the Royal Ark Mariner Tracing Board.

SATANICALLY INSPIRED?

Is the (alleged) accusation of Dr Rowan Williams, the Archbishop of Canterbury correct? Masonic oaths, with all their blood-curdling punishments have been a point of attack for the detractors of Freemasonry, but as we have seen, a number of these are taken directly from the Bible – for example, the Second Degree punishment of 'having the heart torn from the breast and fed to the ravening birds of the air and wild beasts of the field' is based on Deuteronomy, where the latter part is one of the curses that God will inflict for failing to obey His commandments. The horrible punishment also features in the story of David and Goliath, Psalms and the warnings of Jeremiah. The Bible does not contain the First Degree punishment of 'having the tongue torn out by the root', but the Israelites and their enemies have no problems with cutting off thumbs, impaling people on stakes, putting out eyes and turning homes into 'dunghills'.

It has been claimed that Christian Freemasons cannot be true to their faith as Jesus forbade the use of oaths. The critics neglect to note that Christ was, Himself, willing to be placed on oath when he was arrested and tried before the Jewish High Priest (see section on the crucifixion). It is rather an empty argument, when it is realised that millions of Christians have taken an oath in a court of law, across the world, without feeling that they were betraying their faith.

The issue of Masonic 'secrets' is another area of criticism and the internet is fertile ground for the spreading of such views. Christian detractors of Freemasonry argue that at His trial, Jesus told the High Priest that He had never said anything in secret (John, Chapter 18 v20). It should be recalled, however, that Jesus advised his disciples to say the Lord's Prayer in private, behind a closed door. He also informed them that He taught the masses in parables, as only they were to know the secrets of heaven.

It is important to remember that the Bible is not one book. It is 66 different books, written by many authors over a vast period of time. If 66 books on science, geography or any subject, which had been written over several hundred years, were placed into one volume, there would, no doubt, be many contradictions. It is therefore unsurprising that we find anomalies in the Biblical texts.

It may disappoint some that the devil or other malignant characters are not guiding lights in Freemasonry. The fact is that every candidate has to be initiated and take the First Degree, which is full of Biblical references. When he enters the lodge, the Bible will be open and may be at Psalm 133, if this is the lodge tradition. The Tracing Board, with an image of Jacob's ladder (from Genesis) at its centre, will be prominently displayed. During the ceremony the candidate will hear references from the books of Kings, Chronicles and Ruth. The explanation of the Working Tools contains part of St Paul's letter to the Hebrews and then The Charge includes sections from Romans and the Wisdom of Solomon, as well as recommending 'serious contemplation' of the Volume of the Sacred Law – which is very likely to be an Authorised Version of the Bible. If the Tracing Board is then explained he will hear over 20 Biblical references from the Old and New Testament, together with phrases taken from the Book of Common Prayer. This book has shown, as the Mason progresses through further degrees, he will hear more and more Biblical quotations.

It is true that some characters in Masonic ritual are treated in a romantic manner – Constantine, who used Christianity to gain control of an empire and the brutal (in the typically medieval sense) Crusaders, who slaughtered many of the inhabitants of Jerusalem; but the Bible also champions ruthless politicians and warriors, such as Joshua and King David. The relationship between the Roman Catholic Church and Freemasonry has been fraught for many years, but at least five British kings have been Freemasons. The Archbishop of Canterbury may wish to consider that as these monarchs were also the head of his church, they would be very unlikely to be 'Satanically inspired'.

Detractors of Masonry also point to the existence of 'Masonic Bibles', but these are nothing more than an Authorised Version of the Bible, with a Masonic history and maps or links to the Order as a foreword. There are no secrets or additional books in these versions. Perhaps the most famous Bible used by Masons is owned by St John's Lodge in New York. It was used to swear in George Washington (a Freemason) as the first President of the United States in 1789. It has been used at the inauguration of several presidents since that time.

Some have interpreted Hiram Abif as representing some kind of quasi-Christ figure with particular, hidden significance in the rites, but it should be remembered that in the Third Degree, Hiram Abif (see section) is killed and remains dead. There is no question of him returning from the dead and he is not a replacement resurrection rite.

The ritual writers do embellish the Biblical account to develop the Masonic legend. This is the case with Hiram Abif, who according to Masonic ritual was the 'Chief Architect' at the building of King Solomon's Temple. The Bible does indeed describe such a man, with many skills relating to building and decorating the Temple. It does not, however, contain details of his murder or the flight of the killers. Freemasonry is, according to its own ritual, 'veiled in allegory and illustrated by symbols', so there is no claim that the ritual is Biblically or historically accurate.

Whilst the writers of the ritual may have embellished stories, they were also very diligent in their Biblical research. The description of the pillars outside King Solomon's Temple, so important to Freemasons, contains the information that they were a 'hand's breadth in thickness' – this is hidden away in Jeremiah, far removed from the other details in Kings and Chronicles (see section on these Pillars).

THE GREATEST SECRET

This book's title is *Sacred Secrets* but perhaps the greatest secret of Freemasonry is that there are no secrets. One Christian degree states 'the grand mystery of Christian masonry is a sincere belief in Jesus.' Is this really a secret or a 'mystery'? The vast majority of the 'secret' words can be found in a Bible – if the seeker looks deep enough and knows where to find them. Some Masons seem to think that the 'secret words' belong to them and not the Bible. At a lodge meeting, the author mentioned 'Tubalcain' in an after dinner speech. One Mason tried to intervene, because Tubalcain features in the Third Degree and there were Entered Apprentices (First Degree masons) present. He was, probably like many other Freemasons, completely unaware that the story of Tubalcain is there for all to see in Genesis.

If Masonry is inspired by the Bible, then the lesson for Freemasons to learn is to spend more time contemplating the Volume of the Sacred Law (as they are instructed on their first meeting), instead of learning their ritual book parrot fashion and not understanding its contents. How many Past Masters have pointed out to their successor that the Bible explains the 'whole duty of man', but have never checked to see what exactly this duty is? As we have seen in the section on 'The Wisdom of King Solomon', the answer is clearly shown in the penultimate verse of Ecclesiastes. It is to 'fear God' and 'keep his Commandments'.

The idea of a worldwide Masonic conspiracy seems laughable when the ritual is assessed. The early leaders of Masonry do not seem to have even consulted each other on this simple issue, as some of the ceremonies contradict one another. For example, is King Solomon's Temple the first lodge (according to Craft) or the second (as noted in Chapter)? Additionally, the secret signs vary from country to country and sometimes in the same one. The various versions of the Second Degree signs used in England alone are based on different Biblical stories. These modes of recognition would seem a very essential thing to standardise within any secret society with international 'evil intent'.

Most importantly there is no bizarre Masonic god. As was noted in Chapter 11, the word 'Jahbulon', long used to attack Freemasonry, has simply been erased from the ritual and replaced with 'Jehovah'. I remind the reader of the position of the United Grand Lodge of England, which this book supports: 'Freemasonry is not a religion, it is simply based on religion.' Throughout all the degrees, the God of the Bible is the deity and with 40 per cent (471 out of 1189) of its chapters featuring in the ritual (not including the Apocrypha), this book cannot make clearer the fact that the vast majority of Masonic ceremonies originate from one source – the King James Version of the Bible. The New Testament, despite attempts to de-Christianise much of the ritual, is an enormous influence. This is another Masonic secret, but one that even some Freemasons do not know.

Old Testament Characters used as Titles

Title of Degree (in chronological order)	Main book degree derived from	Officers represent Biblical characters	Secret Signs linked to Bible	Secret Words linked to Bible	Other link
Royal Ark Mariner	Genesis	Noah Shem Japheth	Y	Y	Jewel is rainbow shape
Grand High Priest	Genesis	Mechizedek Abraham	Y	Y	
Second Degree (Craft)	Judges Kings Chronicles	No	Y	Y	
Order of the Secret Monitor	Samuel	David Jonathan Abishai Adino Eleazar Shammah	Y	Y	Jewel has three arrows and Star of David
Mark Master Mason	Kings Chronicles	Adoniram	N	Y	
Select Master	Kings Chronicles	Solomon King Hiram Hiram Abif Zabud Ashihar	N	N	
Grand Tilers of Solomon	Kings Chronicles	Solomon King Hiram Hiram Abif	N	N	
Third Degree (Craft)	Kings Chronicles	Hiram Abif	Y	N	
Royal Master	Kings Chronicles	Solomon King Hiram Hiram Abif Adoniram	Y	N	
Most Excellent Master	Kings Chronicles	Solomon King Hiram	N	N	
Super Excellent Master	Kings Chronicles	Gedaliah	N	N	

Holy Royal Arch	Ezra Nehemiah Haggai	Zerubbabel Haggai Joshua Ezra Nehemiah	Y	Y	
Red Cross of Babylon	Ezra Nehemiah Haggai	Zerubbabel Darius	Y	Y	

BIBLIOGRAPHY

Armstrong K., *The Bible: The Biography* (Atlantic Books 2007)

Ashbridge T.A., *The First Crusade: A New History* (Free Press, 2004)

Baigent M., Leigh R. and Lincoln H., *The Messianic Legacy* (Arrow Books, 2006)

Barker-Cryer N., *The Arch and the Rainbow* (Ian Allan, 1996)

Barraclough, G., (ed.) *Times Concise Atlas of World History* (Times Books, 1982)

Barton J., *The Biblical World* (Routledge, 2002)

Bible, *Youth Bible New Century Version* (Thomas Nelson Publishing, 1993)

Brown D., *The Lost Symbol* (Bantam Press, 2009)

Carr H., *The Freemason at Work* (Ian Allan, 1992)

Goodman M., *Rome and Jerusalem: The Clash of Ancient Civilisations* (Penguin, 2008)

Grand Lodge of New York, *Freemasonry and the Bible from the Masonic Edition of the King James' Bible* (New York Oxford University Press, 1928)

Haag M., *The Templars: History and Myth* (Profile Books, 2008)

Haunch T.O., *Tracing Boards: Their Developments and Their Designers* (Quatuor Coronati Correspondence Circle Ltd, 2004)

Jackson A.C.F., *A Glossary of the Craft and Holy Royal Arch Rituals of Freemasonry* (Lewis Masonic, 1992)

Jackson A.C.F., *The Scripture References to the Rose Croix Ritual* (Lewis Masonic, 1979)

Jackson K.B., *Beyond the Craft* (Lewis Masonic, 2005)

Keats L., 'Semitic and Semantics' (unpublished paper presented to the Grand Council of Surrey, Royal and Select Masters, 2008)

Keller W., *The Bible as History* (BCA, 1983)

Knight C. and Lomas R., *The Book of Hiram* (Century, 2003)

Krosney H., *The Lost Gospel: The Quest for the Gospel of Judas Iscariot* (National Geographic, 2006)

MacCulloch D., *A History of Christianity* (Penguin, 2010)

Mitchell D., *The Mark Degree* (Lewis Masonic, 2003)

National Geographic, *Essential Visual History of the Bible* (National Geographic, 2008)

Ogilvie E.E., *Freemasons Royal Arch Guide* (A. Lewis, 1978)

Oliver M., *The 2005 Collection: Lectures by Freemasons in Hampshire and the IOW* (Harpastum, 2005)

Page N., *The Bible Book: A User's Guide* (HarperCollins, 2008)

Read P.P., *The Templars* (Phoenix Press, 2001)

Roberts M.S., *The Miracles of Jesus* (Lion Hudson, 2006)

Rohl D., *The Lost Testament: From Eden to Exile* (Arrow Books, 2002)

Stayt M.J., *The Rungs of The Ladder* (Flying Dragon, 2000)

Wells R.A., *Some Royal Arch Terms Examined* (Lewis Masonic, 1988)

Wesley J., *John Wesley's Commentary on the Whole Bible* (1754–1765)

Wilkinson R.J.L., *The Cryptic Rite an Historical Treatise* (Mark Masons Hall, 1977)

Index of Bible Chapters

Book of Bible and Chapter	Section of Book	Page
1	Raiders from the East: Biblical Warfare (Part I)	28
3	Raiders from the East: Biblical Warfare (Part I)	28
5	Raiders from the East: Biblical Warfare (Part I)	28
8	Raiders from the East: Biblical Warfare (Part I)	28
18	Raiders from the East: Biblical Warfare (Part I)	28
29	Raiders from the East: Biblical Warfare (Part I)	28
34	Raiders from the East: Biblical Warfare (Part I)	28
Psalms		
11	Book of Psalms	72
15	Book of Psalms Emperor Constantine	72 186
18	Book of Psalms	72
19	Book of Psalms	72
22	Book of Psalms The Crucifixion and Resurrection of Jesus	72 158
23	Book of Psalms	72
24	Book of Psalms	72
25	Book of Psalms	72
33	Book of Psalms	72
40	Book of Psalms St Paul	72 167
44	Book of Psalms The Book of Common Prayer	72 208
50	Book of Psalms The Book of Common Prayer	72 208
55	Book of Psalms	72
57	Book of Psalms	72
65	Book of Psalms	72
68	Moses Book of Psalms	40 72
69	Book of Psalms	72

INDEX